RESURRECTION CITY

Prophetic Christianity

Series Editors

Bruce Ellis Benson
Malinda Elizabeth Berry
Peter Goodwin Heltzel

The Prophetic Christianity series explores the complex relationship between Christian doctrine and contemporary life. Deeply rooted in the Christian tradition yet taking postmodern and postcolonial perspectives seriously, series authors navigate difference and dialogue constructively about divisive and urgent issues of the early twenty-first century. The books in the series are sensitive to historical contexts, marked by philosophical precision, and relevant to contemporary problems. Embracing shalom justice, series authors seek to bear witness to God's gracious activity of building beloved community.

PUBLISHED

Bruce Ellis Benson, Malinda Elizabeth Berry, and Peter Goodwin Heltzel, eds., *Prophetic Evangelicals: Envisioning a Just and Peaceable Kingdom* (2012)

Randy S. Woodley, *Shalom and the Community of Creation: An Indigenous Vision* (2012)

Resurrection City

A Theology of Improvisation

Peter Goodwin Heltzel

William B. Eerdmans Publishing Company
Grand Rapids, Michigan / Cambridge, U.K.

Published 2012 by
Wm. B. Eerdmans Publishing Co.
2140 Oak Industrial Drive N.E., Grand Rapids, Michigan 49505 /
P.O. Box 163, Cambridge CB3 9PU U.K.

Printed in the United States of America

17 16 15 14 13 12 7 6 5 4 3 2 1

Library of Congress Cataloging-in-Publication Data

Heltzel, Peter.
Resurrection City: a theology of improvisation / Peter Goodwin Heltzel.
p. cm.
Includes bibliographical references (p.) and index.
ISBN 978-0-8028-6759-9 (pbk.: alk. paper)
1. Christianity and justice. 2. Justice. I. Title.

BR115.J8H45 2012
261.8 — dc23

2012022085

www.eerdmans.com

To

Samuel and Ann Heltzel
who are building a
Beloved Vicksburg

And I saw the holy city, the new Jerusalem, coming down out of heaven from God, prepared as a bride adorned for her husband.

REVELATION 21:2

Contents

Acknowledgments

My friends, colleagues, and students at New York Theological Seminary are my most generous and critical conversation partners in theology. My vision of prophetic urban theology is shaped by the vision and mission of New York Theological Seminary, from leaders spanning from W. W. White to George "Bill" Webber to Dale T. Irvin. I would like to thank Obery M. Hendricks Jr. for an ongoing dialogue of the relevance of the politics of Jesus for national, state, and city politics today.

I am grateful for the opportunity to discuss chapters 2 and 3 with my colleagues at New York Theological Seminary in a Faculty Development Seminar: Humberto E. Alfaro, Moses Biney, Kirkpatrick G. Cohall, Jin Hee Han, Obery M. Hendricks Jr., Edward L. Hunt, Dale T. Irvin, Wanda M. Lundy, Eleanor Moody Shepherd, Elaine Padillia, Rebecca Radillio, Jerry Reisig, and Keith Russell. I am thankful for my doctoral students at New York Theological Seminary for our stimulating conversations in my Theological Hermeneutics seminar. I am also grateful to my colleagues at the Center for Urban Ministerial Education at Gordon-Conwell Theological Seminary in Boston, especially Eldin Villafañe, Alvin Padilla, and Dean Borgman, who have influenced my thinking in this book.

I would like to thank Bruce Herman for introducing me to John Coltrane's *Love Supreme.* My development of a theology of improvisation has been greatly deepened by an ongoing dialogue with Bruce Ellis Benson, J. Kameron Carter, Catherine Keller, and Shannon Craigo-Snell.

I also am grateful to William "Bill" Eerdmans Jr., who has been a good friend and supporter of my work since I met him at a Science and Religion Conference in San Jose, California, in 2002. I have cherished our conversations, especially our laughing together, during the past decade. I would like to thank Malinda Berry and Bruce Ellis Benson for inaugurating the Prophetic Christianity series at Eerdmans. Theologians in the series who have shaped my thinking in this book include Chris Boesel, Christian T. Collins Winn, and Randy Woodley. Linda Bieze was an elegant editor helping to see this book through to production. My deepest thanks to my literary agent, Giles Anderson.

As I have researched and written the book, several people have read all or parts of it and offered me insightful comments and criticisms. They include Peter Beyer, Edward J. Blum, Paul Borgman, J. Kameron Carter, Catherine Keller, Kendall Cox, Gary Dorrien, Farrell Evans, David P. Gushee, Jason Harris, Mark Heim, Job Henning, Johnny Bernard Hill, Holly Hillgardner, Bruce Herman, Leah Hunt-Hendrix, Serene Jones, Peter Ochs, Vanessa L. Ochs, Philip Luke Sinitiere, Donald and Peggy Shriver, Joe Strife, Richard Sturm, Kathryn Tanner, John Thatamanil, Michelle Thompson, and Eboni K. Marshall Turman. I would like to thank colleagues at Columbia University (Farah Jasmine Griffin, George E. Lewis, and Josef Sorett) and at Princeton University (Wallace Best, Eddie Glaude Jr., Albert J. Raboteau, and Judith Weisenfeld) and at Union Theological Seminary (James Cone, James Forbes, Cornel West) with whom I have discussed African American literature, music, history, and politics. I had the good fortune of hearing George E. Lewis deliver a University Lecture "Improvisation as a Way of Life: Reflections on Human Interaction" at Columbia University, March 7, 2011. Lewis's scholarship has helped me give a more robust account of improvisation. I also want to thank my research assistants, including Gail Davis, Jonathan Knutzon, Larry Perry, Ronell John, Bowie Snodgrass, and, at the final hour, Matthew Lyon.

I have presented portions of this book on different occasions. Chapter 1, "Resurrection City," was presented in Christ Chapel in the Riverside Church in New York City on February 5, 2010, for the Spring Convocation of New York Theological Seminary. I would like to thank Soong-Chan Rah for his invitation to deliver an earlier version of chapter 1 titled "Beyond Evangelical Whiteness: Theology's Jazz-like Future" as the David Nyvall Lecture in Isaacson Chapel at North Park Theological Seminary on April 15, 2010, as part of the "4 Days 4 Justice" Conference. Conversations with Mae Elise Cannon, Mimi Haddad, Terry LeBlanc, Jimmie McGee, Lisa Sharon Harper, Andrea Smith, Richard Twiss, and Randy Woodley deepened this chapter.

I presented parts of chapter 5, "Building the Beloved City: Howard Thurman and Martin Luther King Jr.," in a joint session of the Christian Spirituality Group and the Martin Luther King Jr. Consultation at the Annual Meeting of the American Academy of Religion in Atlanta, Georgia, in 2010. I would like to thank Barbara A. Holmes for her thoughtful response on that occasion. I am grateful to Gareth Higgins for the invitation to present "A Love Supreme" at the Wild Goose Festival in North Carolina in 2011.

Most of all, I would like to thank my wife Sarah for her improvisatory love as I wrote this book. I am deeply grateful to Samuel and Ann Heltzel, my loving parents. They have shown me what it looks like to build a community of resurrection in my hometown — Vicksburg, Mississippi.

Introduction

Resurrection City offers a prophetic Christian vision for justice. In our age of global cities, living out a genuine love of our neighbors becomes Christianity's most pressing task. In the spirit of Martin Luther King Jr.'s vision of the beloved community, I analyze the social forms that love and justice take in our work of building beloved cities.

When Dr. King was assassinated on April 4, 1968, the civil rights movement continued as the Poor People's Campaign. In July of 1968, civil rights activists and poor folks from around the country converged in the capital city. On the National Mall of Washington, D.C., they built a new city. It was called Resurrection City.

Resurrection City has a double meaning. Apart from its symbolizing a new life for the poor, it describes heaven in John's Revelation. "Apocalypse" means a revelatory unveiling of God's gracious activity in the world, and out of this unveiling Resurrection City provides an ethical goal and future destination for world Christianity.

In a season of economic crisis and cultural death, we are witnessing communities of resurrection emerge around the world. In 2010, British students protested tuition fee hikes by occupying universities throughout the United Kingdom. In 2011, Egyptians overthrew President Mubarak during the "Arab Spring." In 2011, Occupy Wall Street erupted and the Living Wage NYC campaign persuaded Speaker Christine Quinn and the City Council of New York to pass the Fair Wages for New Yorkers Act. These are signs of hope that will continue to multiply as we seek to embody the spirit of justice in our communities.

In chapter 1, toward a deeper understanding of prophetic justice, I highlight Christian theology's intriguing resonances with jazz music, specifically the theological potential of an improvisational jazz approach to Christian theology. The improvisation involved in jazz music offers a new way of thinking about the prophetic ministry to which the church is called. I also emphasize a couple of other relevant elements of jazz music, namely, its cultural roots, its moods, but most of all, its improvisational dynamic. If the church rolls like a jazz ensemble, the church is then called to improvise for justice today, creating the conditions that are birthing resurrection cities.

In the next two chapters, I build a biblical theology of shalom justice. What is the prophetic imperative of the Hebrew prophets? If the message of the prophets could be summed up in one word, the word would be "justice." But what does "justice" mean? Throughout the Hebrew Bible, references to righteousness and justice abound, yet often without clarity of meaning, or the references are exclusively to personal morality, personal justification, and personal piety.

Grounded in covenantal theology, I show the voice of the exilic prophets as rooted in a loyalty to a justice that is explicitly described in the foundational writings of Moses and others, an aspiration for the shalom of the entirety of creation. Shalom is God's justice being fully present in all dimensions of life. Through mediating God's vision of Jubilee justice, the prophets move the people of Israel from a hierarchical vision toward a prophetic vision, where they embody an ethic of love and justice, especially toward the weak and most vulnerable.

Prophetic Christianity begins with the person of Jesus of Nazareth, a poor Jew in a marginalized minority group in the Roman Empire. From his position on the edges of the Roman Empire, Jesus gained prophetic traction against the empire's colonial spirit. From this place of suffering and marginalization, Jesus empathized with those in need, reaching out to others who were hurting and offering healing and hope. As Jesus the Jew is contextualized within the broader social struggle against the Roman Empire, new horizons for understanding the political dimensions of Jesus' life and ministry open up. Jesus exercises a prophetic consciousness in contrast to the colonial consciousness of the Roman Empire. While the Torah and the Prophets call Israel to love and justice, Jesus Christ embodies the love and justice of God, and the stories of his life narrate what this love and justice look like in the flesh. Jesus expresses his "being for the other" in three primary ways: proclamation of the kingdom of God, the ministry of healing and exorcism, and his practice of faithful feasting.

In the next two chapters I look at the history of the black freedom struggle by focusing on the contributions of Sojourner Truth, Howard Thurman, and Martin Luther King Jr. toward a prophetic theology of shalom justice in North America today.

In chapter 4 I contrast the freedom dreams of Thomas Jefferson and Sojourner Truth, and also juxtapose their theo-political visions. Jefferson, animated by the revolutionary ideals of the Declaration of Independence, called the American colonies to break from the political power of England, keeping the revolutionary process alive in the Americas. Drawing on biblical and democratic traditions, Jefferson formulated a freedom ideal — all humans are entitled to the inalienable rights of life, liberty, and the pursuit of happiness. However, the freedom ideal proved impossible for him to realize in his own life because he owned slaves. While politically Jefferson thought slaves should be set free, personally he did not have the moral courage to set his own slaves free.

In contrast to the limits of Jefferson's democratic imagination, Sojourner Truth offered a more radical vision of democratic community. As a female slave, she experienced the dark side of the American empire. Upon being freed from slavery, she courageously pursued her children who had been stolen from her. Once she had gathered her family, she traveled the nation to speak about the ravages of slavery. The prophetic Christian vision of Sojourner Truth led her to preach that there was a God, a God who hears, sees, and knows the struggles of the African slaves and women.

In chapter 5, I elucidate the mystical-prophetic theology by placing in conversation Howard Thurman and Martin Luther King Jr. Throughout their ministries Thurman and King searched for a "beloved city." King's dream of a beloved city was driven by an idealism that another world was genuinely possible — a social order based on love and justice, where active citizens worked together to end poverty and war. In today's deep economic crisis, it is time for the church to once again erupt as a movement for love and justice. I describe the deep influence of Howard Thurman on King's theology, arguing for the synthesis between the two: a mystical-prophetic theology. King carried a worn copy of Thurman's classic, *Jesus and the Disinherited* (1949), in his briefcase throughout his civil rights journey. Thurman connects Jesus' outsider status as a Jew within the Roman Empire with the outsider status of African Americans in white America, arguing that Jesus stands in solidarity with all those "whose backs are up against the wall." Thurman further argues that Christians are called to make Jesus' dream of the kingdom a reality today. King actualized this call as he led communities around America to build the beloved community through activism, rather than passively sitting by.

King further emphasizes an active love for our enemies. Jesus called us to love not only our neighbors, but also our enemies. This means channeling our love for God into the way we treat *all* others, that is, into political action. The politics of love opens a new horizon for God's love to be manifest on earth. The "beloved community" exposes racism, sexism, and materialism as unfaithful to God's vision of love, justice, and shalom. In contrast, racial, sexual, gender, economic, and ecological justice symbolize a fully fleshed-out embodiment of God's love for the whole creation.

Chapter 6 argues that we need to imagine the church as a musical theater for love and justice. Christians are called to seek the shalom of the city today in light of the coming city of God. In our age of global cities, where globalization and urbanization have converged, churches must be communities of healing and humanization within the larger community of creation that all beings share. All our "neighbor love" and activism need to embody together the incarnation of the prayer, "Thy kingdom come *on earth* as it is in heaven."

A deep bond of love energizes the mission of the church for the world. My central contention positions the church as a global movement for love and justice. After the civil rights movement, we see the emergence of "theologies from below" that challenged religious communities *and* the U.S. government to stay accountable to the social needs of local communities, especially the poor. Because they seek to embody love and justice, these poor-led people movements continue to help dismantle institutional racism and sexism, reduce domestic poverty, and work to end wars.

Chapter 7 explores the politics of love. By taking a closer look at John Coltrane's *Love Supreme,* I hope to illustrate how this experiment between the spiritual and actual jazz music helps illustrate ways in which prophetic Christianity can cultivate communities of healing, help, and hope, embodying God's concern for the poor, peacemaking, and environmental justice within the urban context of a city. I also hope to relate an earthy jazz song to a song of the heavens, to encourage my readers, that they might feel released in some way to play a little jazz in the city.

Resurrection City calls religious communities to model prophetic politics as rooted in the song of Israel but also to improvise upon the stages of today. In local communities of care and collective action, we can strategically partner with governments to create and uphold social innovations that follow the poor and create a more just society. As religious communities creatively organize for justice, we will see an increasing number of hopeful signs of shared power and shalom justice.

CHAPTER ONE

Resurrection City

The Gates of the city will stand open all day;
they will never be closed,
because there will be no night there.

Revelation 21:25, Good News translation

When Martin Luther King Jr. was assassinated on April 4, 1968, the civil rights movement stopped in shock. Shaken and confused, seeking and searching, its leaders decided to continue King's Poor People's Campaign by building a tent city on the National Mall in Washington, D.C. People from around the country converged on the nation's capital to bear communal witness to the ravages of poverty and homelessness. They called it "Resurrection City," a parable of a loving, equal, and just community.

Resurrection City represented an important moment in the movement for justice in boldly reconfiguring a symbolic American space. Sheltered between the Washington Monument and the Lincoln Memorial, thousands of poor and homeless converged on the National Mall, pitching tents on the grassy knoll and playing in the reflection pool. This was a critical moment when the movement's struggle for racial and economic justice was dramatized for the whole nation to see.

Subjected to slavery and segregation and now the death of King, African Americans took the lead in a full national mobilization to end poverty. As a blues people who had been enslaved and subjugated, they knew what it meant to suffer and could clearly see the ways in which the American empire perpetuated that suffering. Through their prophetic activism and creative music, African Americans transfigured tragedy into triumph, despair into hope, death into resurrection.

Tucked beneath a white evangelical modernity, African American Christians transformed Christianity from within. From slave religion to civil rights, African American Christian communities, at their best, sought to tap into the Hebrew prophetic visions of freedom, justice, and shalom. Prophetic black Christianity unchained a humanitarian hope that another world was possible.

This hope for the future took physical shape in the Resurrection City experiment on the National Mall, testifying to the reality of the injustice that exists and the hope of the justice that can be. Due to torrential rains that necessitated the evacuation of Resurrection City, it is remembered as an unfinished city of hope. Yet, the prophetic power of this collective witness evicted the wielders of institutionalized power and prestige from their perpetual positions. Resurrection City caused the world to take notice of the need to resurrect this city of hope. How can we continue building this city of love and justice today?

* * *

Smalls Jazz Club is a Greenwich Village dive with a mysterious past — it's a late-night hangout with a history of bringing jazz musicians together across generations. Its walls are covered with photos of jazz icons, including one of Louis Armstrong behind the musicians, and jazz lovers of all races and ethnicities pack into every nook and cranny of this basement venue to encounter new songs of the soul.

On May 28, 2010, I found myself also crammed inside (not for the first or last time) with a coterie of good friends: Josef, Larry, Millard, and Sekou. The band featured a virtuoso saxophone player backed by a rhythm section of drums, piano, and bass. They played jazz standards, but improvised, soloing and showing off their chops, riffing on the standards and making that night a space of hope and inspiration. It was a one-of-a-kind experience. Something went down. Something happened. There was an encounter with transcendence.

Jazz is music, multiplicity, and magic all in one. It is a multilayered experience of the musical dimension of our humanity. It touches the blue note in our heart, but offers a new way of experiencing life — *life together.* Making music together gives each musician the chance to sing his or her song. Listening to others' songs propels us to sing our own. May our life song bear witness to the jazzlike Creator, whose Spirit continues to hover over, under, in, and above the creation. Jazz energizes us to move with the Spirit.

Why do I open with the images of jazz and Resurrection City? The struggle to build a Resurrection City in Washington, D.C., provides us with an example of the kind of socially engaged prophetic witness that the world needs today, and jazz music provides us with a metaphor for how contemporary Christians can *improvise* for justice in their specific contexts.

Resurrection City: Eschatological Imagination

The city is an important biblical metaphor for the place of God's presence. From the garden city in Genesis to the heavenly city in Revelation, the city is the home of God. The whole arc of Scripture bends toward this heavenly city of God, a place where God's resurrection power is fully manifest.

Resurrection City narrates a new reality. It tells a story of a place where God's resurrection life is fully present. Jesus of Nazareth was crucified on a Roman cross outside the gates of Jerusalem. On the third day he was resurrected — raised from death to life. Jesus' resurrection is the basis of our future hope. Heaven, or the future hope of the world, is conceived in Scripture as a Resurrection City. Because of the resurrection power of God, heaven makes a difference in our lives today.[1]

We are called to bear witness to God in *this* world through being actively engaged in a coalition of love and life. Peacemaking, faith-rooted organizing, community building, and urban development express our ongoing commitment to building better cities. Remembering the past and leaning into the future, our prophetic ministry seeks to channel God's Spirit now. We as Christians are called to seek the peace of our cities today in light of the coming city of God. What is this coming city?

In the last book of Holy Scripture, Revelation, the apostle John describes heaven as a city in his vision of the apocalypse. Rather than being principally destructive, "apocalypse" means a revelatory unveiling of God's gracious activity in the world. Apocalypse discloses a mystery oft forgotten by the world:

> See, I am coming soon!
> watch and wait

swim in the river, plant trees
Love and be fruitful
Rebuild the beloved city
In light of the City of God
The Alpha and Omega
The First, the Last, the Beginning, the End

Love Supreme

The End, the Beginning, The Last, the First
Omega and Alpha
In the light of God's city
Beloved rebuild
Be fruitful and love
Eat of the Tree, drink of the Water
Wait, watch
See, I am coming soon!

In grace, God comes to bind up a broken creation. The living God comes to earth to dwell with us. God makes earth home, bringing the fires of heaven to the waters of earth. Through Son and Spirit, God leads us into a new future full of endless possibility.

Our heavenly future is portrayed as a "city of God." This heavenly city that will descend from a cloud ignites our prophetic imagination, inspiring us to prepare through disciplines of the Spirit. Like the sunlight at dawn, glimpses of glory break into the cities of our world. Heaven is a city of resurrection, bringing to our global urban landscapes life amidst death, healing amidst destruction, hope amidst despair.

On the lonely isle of Patmos, John, who had journeyed with Jesus, saw a glimpse of the heavenly city. While taken up in a dream, John wrote, "Then I saw a new heaven and a new earth; for the first heaven and the first earth had passed away, and the sea was no more. And I saw the holy city, the new Jerusalem, coming down out of heaven from God" (Rev 21:1-2).[2]

Coming down out of heaven *from* God, the new Jerusalem is not of the form of this world that is passing away (1 Cor 7:31); rather it comes from the realm of the living God, an eternal realm of shalom. The new Jerusalem comes *from* God and leads us back *to* God. The new Jerusalem is the present path and future destination of the people of God.

While Jerusalem is a concrete earthly city, the new Jerusalem is not in one specific geographic location. It is the reality of God's righteous reign. Transcending space and time, light and darkness, the heavenly city is ubiquitous and elusive. It is not here, nor there, but is simultaneously at hand and always coming. Its manifestation is marked by the gracious and merciful love of God. It is Resurrection City.

The new Jerusalem imagery of the book of Revelation presents a city of shalom. Inside the gates of the new Jerusalem is a lush green garden, with a flowing river and a towering tree that grows upward from both sides of the river. The leaves of this tree are for the healing of the nations (Rev 2:7; 22:2). Thus, heaven is a garden-city, full of green places and spaces for healing and renewal. Heaven's green is an echo of Eden.

The lush green of Eden was sprinkled by the red blood of animals slain. Adam and Eve covered their nakedness with animal skins as they walked into the wilderness. These garments of animal skin fashioned by God were symbols of God's gracious provision and protection, as they journeyed east of Eden. These garments of skin show that in God's wrath there is always mercy. The living God is the all-merciful One.[3]

Adam and Eve settled down in the far country and started a family, having two sons, Cain and Abel. In a jealous rage Cain murdered Abel the Just, inaugurating a spiral of violence in the world. The brutal fraternal murder of Abel the Just becomes the founding murder of the first city that Cain builds.

Cities are often built on sacred places. As people gathered to form cities in the ancient world, they would often build temples to appease the gods. Within the temple, sacrifices became transactions with transcendence to seek favor with the gods and symbolically legitimate the political order. For example, Aztecs practiced ceremonial sacrifice in a temple that was the center of the local economy managed by both priest and king. With the temple in the center of the city, there was the possibility of redemption in these cities of sacrifice.

Within the history of the Jews, the temple emerged as a place of sacrifice and remembrance of the mighty deeds of the God of Abraham. On the Day of Atonement during the festival of Passover, the high priest would sacrifice animals to memorialize the way God protected the Jewish families and their firstborn children from the angel of death. God's Spirit protected his people in Egypt and led them through the wilderness into the Promised Land, where one day they would build a temple in Jerusalem as a sacred space to worship the God of Abraham.

Yet, at the center of the new Jerusalem there is no longer a temple in the traditional sense, but a lamb. John writes, "I saw no temple in the city, for its temple is the Lord God the Almighty and the Lamb. And the city has no need of sun or moon to shine on it, for the glory of God is its light, and its lamp is the Lamb" (Rev 21:22-23). Rather than being symbolized as a lion, the king of heaven is a lamb. A symbol of shalom and nonviolent love, the conquering lamb is the focal point of the new Jerusalem.

Cities are places of rule, led by kings in the ancient world and mayors today; the new Jerusalem will be ruled by the Messiah, who is imaged as a lamb (Rev 4:1–5:14). Yet the lamb is not simply a docile servant, but a wounded victor. The victory won over the powers of sin, death, and the devil is a victory through nonviolent love.

> *Vicit agnus noster, eum sequamur*
> [Our Lamb has conquered; him let us follow].

While the Lamb echoes the sacrifice of the Passover lamb described in the Torah, John redirects this imagery toward God's apocalyptic love for the whole cosmos. John refers to the victory of the Lamb as a new exodus. As Moses led the people out of enslavement in Egypt, so too did Jesus of Nazareth lead the new Israel out of the imperial grasp of the Roman Empire. The Lamb of the new Jerusalem unmasks the logic of violence that guides the form of this world that is passing away (1 Cor 7:31).

Babylon is the name John gives to the city that is passing away. Babylon, a city built on violence, will be destroyed with violence (Rev 18:20-24). In antiquity Babylon was a great power. Babylon was a city that boasted it was the richest, the most powerful, the most cosmopolitan. Revelation prophesies that Babylon will be silenced and destroyed, because her hands are stained with the blood of prophets and saints. The musicians are silenced; her art is eviscerated. Instead of the light of a lamp, there is darkness; instead of the joyful voice of bridegrooms and brides, there is an absence of love; her bustling streets of business are empty. Babylon is a wasteland full of smoke and terror.

I entered a wasteland full of smoke and terror in the aftermath of 9/11 in New York City. On September 11, 2001, I was supposed to be working for Fidelity Investments in the World Financial Center. When the World Trade Center Towers fell on that fated day, they hit the World Financial Center; my job was lost, but I was not at work, so my life was saved.

The next Sunday Sarah and I went to Riverside Church to worship. Broken and unemployed, I longed in my spirit to serve in this moment of national crisis. Reverend James Forbes asked if there were any who wanted to volunteer down at Ground Zero. I heard Christ calling in that moment and signed up after church, grateful for the opportunity to serve.

It was a cold, dark morning when we gathered at the church to ride the subway down to the still-smoldering Ground Zero, to work amidst the acrid smoke and the dust of the souls lost that fateful day. Asked to carry some crates of food to a food distribution center on the other side of Ground Zero, I squinted through the air, opaque with ash, gazing into an abyss of soundless nothingness. I walked through the long shadows of darkness cast from piles of debris and wreckage. A policeman who had fought in the Korean War said he had never seen a war zone as bad as this. United in despair and brokenness, rescue workers, policemen, firemen, Red Cross workers, ministers, and all the volunteers entered a collective dark night of the soul. It was there in Gehenna that I felt the call to work for a new future, a more just city and a new world.

Every city is engaged in a struggle between Babylon and the new Jerusalem. Scripture's call to the citizens of the new Jerusalem is to exit Babylon. A voice from heaven told John:

> "Come out of her, my people,
> so that you do not take part in her sins,
> and so that you do not share in her plagues;
> for her sins are heaped high as heaven,
> and God has remembered her iniquities." (Rev 18:4-5)

The call to the people of God is clear — come out of Babylon.

While many American Christians see America as the new Jerusalem, theologian William Stringfellow identified America, a fallen nation, with Babylon in the book of Revelation. Stringfellow called the church to exit the empire and begin to embody more prophetic forms of community in the city.[4]

Exiting the empire is at the heart of the prophetic Christian calling. The way to exit empire is not through a violent departure, but through nonviolent resistance. The Lamb's embodiment of nonviolent love leads the world into the messianic age.

Thinking of Jesus as a lamb changes what we think about his messianic identity and the future of the city. On Golgotha Jesus was slaughtered by a brutal crucifixion on a Roman cross during the reign of Pontius Pilate. His death was not in Jerusalem, but on its margins. He was brutally tortured and murdered at the place of the skull. The sky darkened with storm clouds and an earthquake of unprecedented force tore through the land as Jesus breathed his last.

In his earthly life and ministry Jesus suffered outside the gates of the city, so that all who suffer on the margins of society can gain entrance into the heavenly city. In Hebrews 13:12, we see Jesus standing outside the gate: "Therefore Jesus also suffered outside the city gate in order to sanctify the people by his own blood." Jesus died as an outsider, outside the gates, on the margins of the empire. Being an outsider is Jesus' perpetual identity, an identity that challenges his followers to identify with those outside the gates and to struggle to open up the gates wide for all.[5]

In the new Jerusalem the gates stand ever open. "Its gates will never be shut by day — and there will be no night there" (Rev 21:25). The gates of the heavenly city are open to people of all tongues and tribes to enter and worship the Lamb. All are welcome in the new Jerusalem.

The eschatological image of the new Jerusalem makes it possible to imagine an alternative future for this world now. Martin Luther King Jr. grew up in the segregated South, where African Americans were systematically denied access to money and resources. Thus, King's take on the "many mansions" and "streets of gold" of the new Jerusalem had a this-worldly dimension. He argued that we need to build houses and pave roads here on earth. In his speech "I See the Promised Land," delivered the night before he was murdered in Memphis, King wrote,

> It's all right to talk about "long white robes over yonder." . . . But ultimately people want some suits and dresses and shoes to wear down here. It's all right to talk about "streets flowing with milk and honey," but God has commanded us to be concerned about the slums down here, and his children who can't eat three square meals a day. It's all right to talk about the New Jerusalem, but one day, God's preacher must talk about the New York, the new Atlanta, the new Philadelphia, the new Los Angeles, the new Memphis, Tennessee. This is what we have to do.[6]

Our theology of the new Jerusalem must remain relevant to *this* world — and that means relevant to this world's cities and their concrete social, racial, economic, and ecological problems. King's prophetic theology challenges us to live into the reality of Resurrection City — right here, right now — through doing our part to build communities of resurrection.

Racism: America's Original Sin

To articulate a theology that is relevant to the problems of global cities, we must acknowledge and take seriously their histories of violence. In the Americas, colonial cities were built on Native American land, often by the labor of enslaved Africans. These colonial cities were designed and ruled by white men of European descent. Colonial urbanization was and is shrouded in whiteness.

Racism is America's original sin. Race signifies power relations associated with skin color. Racism is more than personal prejudice. It is prejudice *plus* power. To dismantle systemic racism, a power analysis is necessary to identify its various institutional forms.[7]

In the Americas, racism manifests itself in an ideology of white supremacy, the idea that whites are superior to people of other races and ethnicities and that society should be organized to maintain their hegemony. While Thomas Jefferson penned the first draft of the Declaration of Independence as a manifesto for all Americans, the only folks who were truly independent and free in colonial America were white landowning men. From the Jamestown settlement in 1619 to the Constitution in 1789, every settlement, document, and procedure in the new nation was established to legitimate and perpetuate the power of white landowning men. The Constitution counted enslaved Africans as three-fifths of a person, so that white men who owned slaves would have more political power. White racism took on systemic form in every institution of American life, including government, financial, educational, and religious institutions.

Within the Americas, whiteness was forged through the alchemy of Christian theology.[8] As European colonists began to settle in America, the Christian theological imagination provided a cultural orientation for the construction of their cities. In the Puritan theological imagination, America was seen as a promised land to be subdued as part of God's redemption of the "New World." The colonial encounter with Native Americans created a serious theological problem: How would indigenous people be narrated into this drama of Christian imagination? Indigenous people were seen by Christian missionaries as "heathens" who needed to be converted to Christianity; however, this conversion was not only religious, but also cultural. Native Americans were not only converted to Christianity as a new religious path, but were also converted to a new set of cultural values that were part of the broader Western civilization project. While seeking the conversion of native peoples, colonial missionaries were deeply implicated in the destruction of traditional cultures, the rape of the land, and the deaths of Native Americans.[9] While Christian colonists in the Americas identified with the victorious Jews in the exodus and conquest narratives of the Hebrew Bible, Native Americans identified with the displaced and exterminated Canaanites.[10]

Colonial America understood as a promised land held more promise to some than to others. White colonial Christians lived into the promise of the New World at the expense, labor, and death of black and brown bodies. Enslaved Africans and Native Americans became instruments of colonial production in the emerging New World economy. Christian mission was driven by a theology of conquest that provided a religious rationale for racism and racialized violence in the Americas.[11]

Racialized violence was integral to the process of colonial conquest. Christian theology provided a social imagination that internalized these acts of racialized violence in the drama of "American" redemption. Richard Slotkin writes, "The first colonists saw in America an opportunity to regenerate their fortunes, their spirits, and the power of their church and nation; but the means to that regeneration ultimately became the means of violence, and the myth of regeneration through violence became the structuring metaphor of the American experience."[12] American colonies offered the illusion to Europeans of being able to leave the ancient regime of the Old World behind and begin life anew. One of the greatest tragedies of America is that it offered Europeans the opportunity to regenerate their identity and social power through the violent subjugation of the indigenous population.[13]

Within the context of colonial Christian mission work, racially designating the brown and black bodies as inferior became a theological strategy for justifying and legitimating the white power and privilege of the colonists of European descent. Rooted in classical Greek aesthetics, the white body became the normative standard of beauty in the West, a source of deep travail and alienation for people of color.[14] The racial rendering of the black and brown other was essential to the Christian theological basis of the social formation of white identity in the New World. Its roots lay buried even deeper in the Christian imagination.

The European colonial idea that whites were superior to the indigenous populations of the New World is theologically rooted in the problematic idea that the Christian was superior to the Jew. Racism is rooted in supersessionism, an interpretation of the New Testament that sees God's relationship with Christians as *replacing* God's covenant with the Jews.

Christian "replacement theology" — the idea that Christianity replaces Judaism — is a heresy that must be denied and continually struggled against within the church. Howard Thurman writes in *Jesus and the Disinherited*, "How different might have been the story of the last two thousand years on this planet grown old from suffering if the link between Jesus and Israel had never been severed. . . . [For] the Christian Church has tended to overlook its Judaic origins, . . . the fact that Jesus of Nazareth was a Jew of Palestine."[15] Why did Western Christianity sever the link between Jesus and the religion of Israel that he grew up in? Jesus' Jewish heritage is the key to unraveling the problem of white supremacy in the Americas and reconstituting prophetic Christianity in the twenty-first century.

Since Christianity began as a sect within Judaism, how can Christians dispense of Christianity's Jewish heritage? Christianity is unintelligible without Judaism. Rooted in the religion of Israel, Christianity emerged as a distinctive movement within Second Temple Judaism. To reclaim this Jewish heritage, Christians need to deepen their understanding of the Hebrew Bible and the history of Israel, including the late Second Temple and early rabbinic periods. The faulty idea that Christianity replaces Judaism has led to anti-Judaism within the church and has been the source of tragic and fatal consequences in the history of the West.[16]

Anti-Judaism and racism are intricately related. During the period of colonial expansion, anti-Judaism began to be deployed in new ways in the Christian imagination of Europe. After 1492 and the eviction, forced conversion, or killing of all Jews in Spain, Spanish Christians needed a justification for continuing to be bigoted against their newly converted Christian neighbors. In 1499 the first statute of purity of blood appeared in Toledo, Spain. In trying to consolidate the Iberian Peninsula, the Catholic empire began to promote the idea of the pure blood of old Christians, not tainted by Jewish or Muslim blood. The Catholic Spanish Empire deployed the purity of blood laws to suppress racial minorities at home and in their colonies abroad. The purity of blood laws not only transformed Spanish Catholics' relations to non-Christian others, it also transformed the heart of the Christian religion. As true Spanish Christians were not supposed to be tainted by Jewish blood, so true Christian religion should not be tainted with Jewish religious practice. While there was a virulent stream of anti-Judaism within the Catholic Spanish Empire, it was prevalent throughout Europe.[17]

The purity of blood laws served as seeds that would blossom into large-scale white supremacy in nineteenth- and twentieth-century Europe.

In Germany, anti-Judaism took the form of anti-Semitism, the persecution of all ethnic Jews. Anti-Semitism in Germany unveiled the lengths a European church would go to sever its ties to Judaism. For example, the Institute for the Study and Eradication of Jewish Influence on German Church Life, founded in Germany in 1939, sought to explicitly sever the German church from Judaism as part of an attempt to consolidate German nationalism. Through the corrupting influence of anti-Semitism, modern German theology began to transform Jesus from a Jew into an Aryan. While theologians like Karl Barth and Dietrich Bonhoeffer tried to resist the Nazi regime, most of the Christian leaders in Germany betrayed Christianity's prophetic ideals, standing silently as the Nazi propaganda machine forwarded an Aryan Jesus as a theological justification of German nationalism.[18]

Shorn of his Jewishness, Jesus becomes "white" in much early-twentieth-century German theology. Severing its historic connection to Judaism, Western theology often replaces Jewish identity with "whiteness" as the primary matrix for interpreting and practicing Christian faith. As the primary privileged social marker in the modern world, whiteness refers to the racial identity of people of European descent who are the primary beneficiaries of the power and privileges of the social institutions that continue their power.

Given America's origins in Europe's colonial expansionism, "white" becomes the normative ethnic identity. Whiteness is a fluid category that gradually expanded through the history of immigration in the United States. Different ethnic groups are designated as white at different moments within American history. For example, when Irish Catholics first arrived in droves during the 1840s as a result of the Irish potato famine, they were not considered white; but with time they, too, were assimilated in the "alchemy of whiteness."[19]

The task of prophetic theology today includes dismantling whiteness and following the Jewish Jesus who is leading an intercultural movement of love and justice. While the colonial imagination viewed white Europeans as God's elect in the New World, the Scriptures repudiate this hierarchical racial logic and ground Christian identity in the election of the Jews. Israel, understood as the covenant people of God, offers the proper horizon of Christian self-understanding because it roots identify in the God of Abraham, instead of the modern state apparatus that was forged through the flourishing of the white masculine ideal. God's covenantal history with the Jews offers a robust theological alternative to modernity's narrative of progress.

While Christianity in the Americas was forged in whiteness, there was a prophetic countertradition tucked underneath a white Euro-American evangelical modernity — prophetic black Christianity. Because of their subject position as slaves, African American Christians identified with the Jews who were enslaved in Egypt and with Moses their liberator. Thus, black Christians in the Americas found their primary theological identity marker to be part of the covenant people of Israel, prior to their identity as part of the American nation that enslaved them. Thus, the black freedom struggle pointed to a theological way ahead. Prophetic Christians should dislodge themselves from an oppressive tradition of white supremacy and anti-Semitism, and embrace the Jewish flesh of Jesus of Nazareth, born into the covenant people of Israel with a mission to reconcile all people, black, white, and every shade in between. In chapters 4 and 5, I look at Sojourner Truth, Howard Thurman, and Martin Luther King Jr. as examples of black Christian voices that can help contemporary Christians recover what it means to be prophetically engaged in the tradition of Jesus and the prophets today.

A prophetic eschatological imagination offers an alternative to a white colonial imagination. It provides another way of orienting Christian existence in the Americas that honestly acknowledges its epistemic and ethical wounds. Only through entering the pain of our deepest wounds will humanity heal and become whole once again.[20] I turn now to a brief discussion of improvisation in jazz music. This will help us grasp an essential dynamic at work in this eschatological way of imagining — *improvisation.*

Improvising: A Jazz Approach to Theology

Now is the time for Christianity to live into a jazzlike, improvisational future. Traditionally theology has been most often written in the style of Western classical music. It often sounds like a baritone soloist with a symphony orchestra behind him, reinstating the Western civilization project and its racist and patriarchal underpinnings. In contrast, prophetic intercultural Christian theology today increasingly has the freedom sounds of jazz.

The improvisation involved in jazz music offers a way of thinking about the prophetic ministry to which the church is called. Let me emphasize a few things about jazz music that I find relevant for our discussion: its cultural roots, its mood, and most importantly, its improvisational dynamic.

Jazz emerged from an impressive blending of different musical forms, including slave songs, spirituals, blues, ragtime, European folk music, and opera. It is no coincidence that this new creative concoction originated in Louisiana, where Creole culture was prominent.[21] "Creole" refers to a mixture of races that grew from settlers in colonial French Louisiana who came from France or French colonies in the Caribbean. The French colonizers intermarried with Native Americans, African Americans, and the Spanish, creating an unprecedented zone of intercultural interaction. Through the Louisiana Purchase in 1803, colonial French Louisiana officially became part of the United States, bringing with it a Creole culture that would gradually leaven the nation. The fact of racial and cultural mixing is significant not only for understanding the origins of jazz, but also for understanding what jazz originally was: namely, an essentially intercultural and, therefore, subversive phenomenon.

While the Original Dixieland Jazz Band made the first "jass" recordings in 1917, jazz was being played down in New Orleans for several decades before. Jazz was born when Creoles and blacks were allowed to integrate in the 1890s and began musically influencing each other. While many musical and cultural streams fed into the river of jazz, the deepest waters flowed from the African American musical tradition.

Jazz emerged as a musical form precisely at the time when the North and South were reconstituting whiteness to provide cultural unity for the American nation.[22] While slaves began to be emancipated after the ratification of the Thirteenth Amendment to the Constitution, the journey toward black freedom was slow going because of the powerful specter of white supremacy. During the lynching era (1880-1940), white racist mobs often lynched black bodies to incite fear and maintain social control of the African American community. Taking artistic form during this lynching era, jazz drew on the deep river of the spirituals and the blues that had grown out of the experience of black suffering. Jazz gave voice to the prophetic struggle of resistance and hope.[23]

The spirituals were an indigenous musical form that grew out of the religion of African American slaves. They built on the rhythms and communal chants of African music brought to America through the Middle Passage, that transatlantic slave trade in which enslaved Africans were carried on European ships as part of a triangular system between Europe, Africa, and the Americas. It is estimated that nearly 2 million Africans died at sea during these voyages. The vale of tears of this great tragedy continues to challenge theology and ethics in the Americas. Through these voyages Africans brought with them the pulsating rhythm of the talking drum and heartfelt melodies of their traditional music. In *The Black Atlantic,* Paul Gilroy argues that music was integral to Afro-diasporic identity formation because it could express the horror of the Middle Passage and slavery through its primarily nonrepresentational forms. The heartbeat of love embodied in African music was a mighty river of strength amidst weakness, triumph amidst tragedy, and hope amidst despair.[24]

The rhythm and songs of Africa are heard as echoes in the field songs and ring shouts of the slaves in America. Flowing from African musicality, the spirituals narrated the stories of Holy Scripture that were existentially connected to their struggle for survival. The slaves identified with the people of Israel; this is reflected in their spirituals, sermons, and prayers. They took hope in God bringing Israel out of slavery in Egypt and sang passionately about Moses telling Pharaoh, "Let my people go!" They had deep suspicions of the "white man's religion" and often reimagined Christianity as a movement toward freedom. For the American slaves, those who had their backs up against the wall, the Christian faith was not simply an abstract set of beliefs. Christianity was a song of freedom, offering the promise of resurrection to communities on the brink of death.[25]

Slaves often sang the spirituals down by the riverside in the brush arbors, hidden from the gaze of their master. Because of its often secret and subversive character, slave religion is called an "invisible institute" by historian Albert J. Raboteau.[26] Gathering for fellowship and conspiring for justice down by the riverside simultaneously rendered them invisible from the eyes of their earthly overseer and collectively incarnated communities of resurrection to bear prophetic witness to their heavenly Overseer. These gatherings in hiding were ushering in an alternative form of prophetic Christian witness to the conservative racist regime of the plantation. During these gatherings, for a moment, the slaves experienced authentic freedom in their spirit. Inhabiting a collective subjectivity of freedom helped them reimagine their existence outside of their enslaved state. The slave songs and spirituals often had two levels of meaning, including a veiled political meaning. "Swing Low, Sweet Chariot," "Song of the Free," and "Wade in the Water" passed on wisdom to slaves on how to journey toward freedom as they escaped the plantation.

The spirituals turned to the stories of Scripture to provide archetypes for action in the present. The African American spiritual "Didn't My Lord Deliver Daniel, and Why Not Every Man?" expresses the tragedy of black existence, but also shows the way in which God can show up and save the suffering and oppressed. Having delivered Daniel from the lions' den, the living God can also deliver African Americans from the scourge of slavery. Deliverance was a common theme in the spirituals, having two dimensions of meaning. While final deliverance will happen in the future, God can deliver us here and now. Moreover, we can help others here and now, responding to the call of the spirituals through love and service. The same God that called Jesus from death in the tomb to life in the world, called the slaves from their death-bound subjectivity to a life-affirming movement of freedom.

Like black preaching on the plantation, the spirituals followed a "call-and-response" structure. While much of the white preaching on the plantation was dialectical, black preaching by the riverside was dialogical. The preacher would call, and the people would respond. Then the people would call, and the preacher would respond. Together they would develop a synergistic dynamism that built throughout the sermon, bringing the community to a collective catharsis.

Many of the spirituals were based on a call-and-response structure. "Hush! Somebody's Calling My Name" speaks of a call that demands a response:

> Hush! Hush! Somebody's calling my name
> Hush! Hush! Somebody's calling my name
> Hush! Hush! Somebody's calling my name
> O my Lord, O my Lord, what shall I do?

In Scripture God called Abraham, Moses, Mary, and Jesus, and they had to respond to God's special word to them. The slaves opened their ears and hearts to hear God's Word, discerning what course of action they should take in their lives. Having spoken to the prophets and prophetesses of old, the living God continued to speak to the faithful remnant. When God called out slaves' names, they had to discern their response, "O my Lord, O my Lord, what shall I do?"[27] Through prayer, fasting, and the wise counsel of others, the slaves discerned how they would forge a pathway toward freedom.

While the call-and-response structure of the spirituals shaped jazz, jazz received its deepest spirit and most enduring style from the blues. The blues emerged in the Mississippi Delta as a musical response to African Americans' experiences of suffering during slavery. Growing out of black suffering, the lyrics focused on themes of lost love and surviving in an inhospitable world. The blues were cathartic for African Americans because they affirmed the depth of their existential struggle and provided an outlet for the creative expression of a longing for freedom.[28]

The blues are more than music; they are a state of mind. Responding to the tragicomic existence of African Americans, the blues give voice to the pain and suffering that are part and parcel of black existence in the Americas. While shaped by the tragic feel of the blues, jazz took music in a new direction.

Like the blues, jazz emerged to tell stories from the underside of modernity. But jazz tends to be less melancholic than the blues. While the blues is about the world that was, jazz is often about the world to come. Blues gives voice to the hurt of a painful past, while jazz envisions a way ahead.[29]

Jazz presses forward into a new future, offering an intercultural horizon of hope. The racial and cultural difference and blending typical of jazz culture also point to the possibility of a racially and ethnically reconciled community. This musical "creolization" did not fit the black-white binary that served the interests of the status quo. Jazz was subversive.

With its themes of "religious transcendence and political opposition," jazz music is a countercultural practice for a revolutionary future.[30] John Coltrane, Miles Davis, and Charlie Parker realized that what they were doing was politically subversive. Jazz musicians often saw themselves as doing something that went against standard music and the received tradition. They were sounding off, faking it, creating the conditions for resistance and raising a revolutionary consciousness. Through jazz music a colonized people could tell their story in new, musical, decolonized idiom. Jazz musicians were free to dialogue with the musical motifs of the past, but they were not bound by them. They pressed the limits of freedom, creating new forms of racial and cultural transgression. Jazz creates a counternarrative to the traditional narrative of classical forms, but it does it in musical dialogue with these forms.

Jazz music, then, is not merely an interesting and unique cultural phenomenon; it is a vehicle for giving expression to and empowering a new directionality for life. Improvisation is integral to jazz; it demands and celebrates the opening up of fresh, imaginative possibilities. It opens up new pathways for music, lifestyle, and politics. Improvisation is the heartbeat of jazz music. It is an ever pulsating rhythmic conversation between musicians, riffing on old themes in new ways.

Improvisation is the inner logic of jazz. It involves being open to playing old songs in new ways, and writing new music for a new day.

While driven by spontaneity, freedom, and innovation, improvisation is never so unstructured or so wholly new that it could be considered *creatio ex nihilo,* a creation out of nothing. Rather, it is a *creatio continua,* a continual creation drawing on existing materials to make music in new ways. Improvisation is the creative deployment of traditions and forms that are *at hand;* the dynamic involved in improvisation therefore can be understood as a constant negotiation of constraint and possibility.[31]

We see this improvisational dialectic of constraint and possibility illustrated in John W. Coltrane's (1926-67) song "My Favorite Things." Ever since Julie Andrews sang it in *The Sound of Music,* "My Favorite Things" has been a musical standard in the American cultural imagination. In the movie, Andrews played Maria Rainer, a postulant at a convent who becomes a governess for the children of Captain Georg von Trapp, an officer in the Austrian navy. One evening, during a violent thunderstorm, Maria sings this sunshiny song to the von Trapp children to cheer them up. "When the dog bites, when the bee stings, when I'm feeling sad, I simply remember my favorite things, and then I don't feel so bad," they sing together. Through hearing the festive, funny song and responding by singing along with it, the kids begin to smile, erupting with laughter and a pillow fight.[32]

In a moment of fear of the violent power of nature, this musical meditation on the small things in life that Maria finds joy in becomes a source of hope for her and the children under her care. Yet the darker and more violent storm in the story is the specter of the Nazis, who are occupying Austria, demanding complete loyalty of the Austrian citizenry to the Nazi regime. In the shadow of evil, taking joy in a few favorite things is a form of psychic survival, a gesture toward hope. Resolutely opposed to the Nazis, Captain von Trapp refuses to join the German navy, and leads his new wife Maria and his children to freedom through a journey over the Alps.

Recorded on the album *My Favorite Things* (Atlantic, 1961), Coltrane's improvisation on "My Favorite Things" takes it in a new direction. In a musical dialogue with Rogers and Hammerstein, Coltrane deepens the musical tonality of the piece, propels it with a bebop rhythm, and colors it with a blues sensibility, the heart of jazz. At the start of the revolutionary sixties, Coltrane's interpretation of "My Favorite Things" made it relevant to jazz, giving voice to the deepest longing within the black freedom struggle. As a black man in America, Coltrane had to negotiate two identities, being black and being American. This "double consciousness" that Du Bois described in *The Soul of Black Folks,* Coltrane sought to explore musically. Jazz provided a musical idiom that could explore the two-ness of identity, while moving beyond this binary to a third, a more open-ended space of revolutionary consciousness, where love truly reigns.

In *My Favorite Things* we experience this exploration in the conversation between Coltrane's sax solo and McCoy Tyner's piano solo. Two voices in tension, Coltrane and Tyner depend on each other, searching for a deeper resolution in the movements of the song. Following a call-and-response structure, Coltrane introduces the familiar melody on his soprano saxophone, while Tyner responds with his own interpretation of the melody, in his distinct piano style that includes chords voiced in fourths and his distinctively propulsive, percussive rhythm. As the piece continues, Coltrane's and Tyner's solos dance together with the rhythm of an up-tempo waltz.

Informed by Indian raga tradition and the African polyphonic rhythm of drummer Elvin Jones, *My Favorite Things* is an important watermark in an emerging jazz aesthetic that was more free, modal, international, and improvisational. Coltrane's soprano sax makes the melody his own, deepening the lines, accentuating the phrasing, and playing each note with characteristic color. The higher top of the soprano sax allows Coltrane to take the piece higher, allowing for a more rapid cascade effect through a chordal descent, but it is countered by the rhythmic drone that his quartet learns from classical Indian music. Coltrane took the song and made it his own with the virtuosity of his soprano sax, transforming an old show tune into a jazz classic. Coltrane's "My Favorite Things" is no longer a light, frivolous children's song, but a subterranean song of freedom conveying depth and beauty, bearing witness to the tragicomic existence of Africans in the Americas.

While "My Favorite Things" demonstrates how improvisation can rework a musical standard, *A Love Supreme* (1964) is an original composition that marks the culmination of Coltrane's transformation of the aesthetic of twentieth-century jazz. In *A Love Supreme,* Coltrane offers a fusion jazz of the Spirit, masterfully drawing on all his style and skill for his final meditation on love. Discerning the great spiritual insight in *A Love Supreme,* Cornel West asks, "Is it mere accident that 'A Love Supreme' (1964) — the masterpiece of the greatest musical artist of our time and the grand exemplar of twentieth-century black spirituality, John Coltrane — is cast in the form of prayer?"[33]

A Love Supreme
A Love Supreme
A Love Supreme

Coltrane's song pulsates like a beating heart, a heart surrendered to God in prayer. In this piece Coltrane dialogues with the tradition of preaching and praise he encountered in the black church of his North Carolina youth. As the Psalter is a collection of the prayers, laments, and protests of the people of Israel, the spirituals, blues, and jazz, too, are a collection of prayers, laments, and protests of the people of the African diaspora. A love supreme is a love deep and wide enough to include all God's children.[34]

Whether improvising on a Broadway show tune or the black spirituals, jazz music is ever new. Every live performance is a new improvisation in a new time and space. When the Coltrane quartet played *My Favorite Things* and *A Love Supreme,* the improvisation would continue in the unique setting of each individual live performance. Improvisation is playful, creative, dynamic, innovative, and new. Improvisation is music on the move.

New musical innovations are constrained by traditions of music making, but they are also made possible by those traditions. New riffs are based on old riffs, but because they are reworked in new ways and in new places, they take the musical discourse in novel directions. Improvisation constantly feeds upon itself, reworking and revising the tradition to keep it alive and ever growing. Jazz music is deeply connected to older musical forms, but gives birth to a new genre of music making that will shape new musical forms.

While improvisation is the inner logic of jazz, jazz is an outer constraint on improvisation. Jazz offers a cultural form through which we can better understand how improvisation works. Yet, improvisation is not limited to jazz music, but is witnessed in many forms of music. Music is unique in illustrating it because of its nonrepresentational forms. Music taps into the essence of our human *being.* Beyond the words and ideas, good music expresses our darkest melancholy and most ecstatic joy. Good music connects us to the river of life, where there is laughter underneath tears and tears underneath laughter. Through improvisation, musicians can creatively communicate with other musicians and the audience, at its best, leading them to spiritual transcendence and cultural transformation.

How can the logic of improvisation that energizes the creation and re-creation of jazz music inform the way that we live? In the improvisatory spirit of jazz music, Christians need to discern the way in which they can creatively contribute to the common good, improvising for justice. John Coltrane, Miles Davis, and Charlie Parker understood their jazz music as subversive; it is time for Christian theologians to write theology in an improvisatory, subversive style.

I believe Christian thinking and social witness can be understood analogously with jazz music. Like jazz, Christianity is a dramatic and musical performance.[35] Like jazz, Christian thinking and acting are improvisational, creative, and hopefully forward-looking. Like jazz, they exemplify a dynamic of constraint and possibility. Constrained by the norm of God's Word, Christians seek to creatively engage their world in light of the Word. In their work and witness, Christians use the materials at hand — principally the language and example of the prophets and Jesus in the context of their life — to creatively riff for justice, love, and shalom in the present and thereby open up a new future. That future that we can experience here and now is the one I describe as Resurrection City.

CHAPTER TWO

Shalom Justice: The Prophetic Imperative

Righteousness and justice are the foundation of your throne;
steadfast love and faithfulness go before you.

Psalm 89:14

If Christian theology improvises like jazz, what is the melody it improvises on? Israel's song. The song of Israel echoes throughout Holy Scripture, becoming clearer and deeper with each reiteration throughout the musical theo-drama. God calls Abraham from Ur of the Chaldees to venture forth into the far country. From Hagar and Ishmael's wilderness wandering to the sacrifice of Isaac, God teaches Abraham and his family to be faithful to the promises of God.

God chooses Israel to be a blessing to the nations. Nations that bless Israel and the God of Israel will be blessed. The destiny of the nations is interlaced with the destiny of Israel. When God delivers Israel from the Egyptians, Moses and Miriam lead the people in a song of praise. The song of Israel is a celebration of God being faithful to the covenantal promises that are the heart of the religion of Israel. God is victorious — defeating oppressive powers and leading Israel on toward shalom justice.

Shalom Justice

Shalom justice is rooted in a worshipful acknowledgment that God the Creator is present in all creation and is graciously working for the redemption and reconciliation of the world. The prophet Isaiah presents a picture of God's promise of shalom justice: a wolf and lamb lying down together, peacefully (Isa 11:6; 65:25). Shalom — communal and ecological well-being — is the outcome of the people of God embodying the justice and righteousness of God.[1]

In the Hebrew Scripture, the term *mishpat* is best translated as "justice," even though the King James Version often translates this as "judgment," blunting its radical social dimension.[2] *Mishpat* is a multivalent term, embracing both juridical justice and fair social relations within a community. The self-understanding of the Jewish people was based on the fact that they were the covenant people of God. The Torah frames its narration of God through a series of covenants that God makes with the people of Israel. Israel is covenantally bound to the living God and the moral ideals that were explained in the Torah. When Israel chose not to practice the justice of God *(mishpat),* the wrongdoing was conceptualized as not only against the wronged individual and community, but also against God. Injustice is fundamentally a violation against God.

While Israel's covenant was primarily thought of on a vertical axis — being faithful to the living God — it also had a horizontal axis — being faithful to one another. The social dimension of *mishpat* included many different types of social relations. While always grounded in the covenantal relationship between Yahweh and Israel, it also referred to the relationship among Israelites within their tribe, their relationship with other nations, and their relationship with the community of creation. When nations would deal unjustly with Israel, Israel would cry out through passionate prayers for God's justice to be manifest. It was God and God alone who was the judge of the social dealings among the nations.

Another important horizontal dimension to *mishpat* dealt with the way Israel treated the poor, the widow, and the orphan. When one of the marginalized people was neglected, Israel was guilty of injustice and subject to God's judgment. In love and fairness, the God of Abraham, Isaac, and Jacob was clearly on the side of the poor. Prone to wander, Israel was constantly reminded of their obligation to care for those in need by prophets who preached the justice of God (Amos 5:21-24; Mic 6:6-8; Isa 1:17). Throughout the Hebrew Bible, kings, judges, and ordinary people were judged by how they treated the weakest and most vulnerable in society.

Mishpat is frequently used in a couplet with *sedaqah,* "righteousness"; this is the Bible's most common word pairing (e.g., Jer 22:3-5; Isa 28:17-18). The etymological and semantic proximity of these terms reinforces the social dimension of justice. While *mishpat* is a foundational conception of justice in the Bible, *sedaqah* calls the people of Israel to do what is right. We can think of *sedaqah* as *mishpat* put into practice in the embodied life of the people of God. It is one thing to cognitively understand the importance of the concept of justice; it is another thing to put it into practice in our personal and political life. *Mishpat* acknowledges everyone's basic human rights, and *sedaqah* intentionally works for the establishment of right relations within the community. In summary, the conception of justice in the Hebrew Scripture is not just a matter of personal morality; it also refers to how all people in the community, especially the marginalized, are treated.

Justice is morality in its material form. Social, sexual, physical, relational, institutional, and ecological justice calls for a this-worldly, earthly expression of God's shalom. Justice expresses the various ways that we relate to each other in all realms of life. The prophets continually remind Israel to consider how they are treating fellow humans and the earth. The test of Israel's faith is the quality of their treatment of others.

There is no peace without justice. The struggle for shalom in the community of creation demands a bold and courageous identification and dismantling of injustice in any form. Since shalom is shattered in the community of creation through human injustice, the search for shalom means joining the struggle for justice. The telos of our activism in this world is shalom justice. As long as there is sin and suffering in the community of creation, the ministry of shalom justice is unfinished.

From the Garden to the Tower

Within the Garden of Eden, Adam and Eve lived in a state of shalom, experiencing the presence of love and justice in all aspects of their life together. Shalom in the garden meant that there was complete harmony in the community of creation. Humanity's harmony with God was the basis of the shalom of the community of creation.[3] This order of well-being between humanity and God provides the theological basis for humankind's right relations with all creatures and the community of creation.

The creation accounts say that God created Adam and Eve in the image of God *(imago Dei)*. Humans are to image God. They have a special vocation to care for the community of creation. Humans are called to embody shalom justice, resting in God's presence, walking close to God, listening to God, and following the path of the divine light.[4]

Yet humanity did not always walk in the light. Because God created humans as free, they abused their freedom to shatter the shalom of the garden. Adam and Eve ate the forbidden fruit offered by the seductive serpent. The sky darkened, the temperature dropped, and a mighty wind blew through Eden, as God's presence was manifest in the wind of the storm (Gen 3:8).[5] God was disappointed that the harmonious relationships between God and creation, women and men, humanity and creatures were broken by their rebellion (Gen 3:1-19). When creation harmonies are disrupted, sin, injustice, and oppression grow up to fill the void.

Cain's murder of Abel the Just inaugurates a spiral of violence that emanates throughout human history. As these two brothers sought to please their parents and their God, anger and jealousy grew in Cain's heart. They wondered, whose offering would be most pleasing to God? When God found Abel's offering more pleasing, Cain became distressed. God told Cain he would be blessed if he walked the path of righteousness; "And if you do not do well, sin is lurking at the door; its desire is for you, but you must master it" (Gen 4:7). But Cain could not control his jealous rage; he murdered his brother in cold blood.

After this primordial fratricide, "the earth was corrupt in God's sight, and the earth was filled with violence" (Gen 6:11). The force of violence unto death was unleashed within humanity, creating a dark and dangerous undertow within the community of creation. Lurking in the shadows, the specter of violence always overshadows human attempts to build beloved cities of shalom justice.

In contrast to a city of shalom, humanity too often builds cities of strife. As Adam and Eve's descendants tried to live together in cities, they were unable to overcome the seduction of power. They said, "Let us build ourselves a city, and a tower with its top in the heavens, and let us make a name for ourselves; otherwise we shall be scattered abroad upon the face of the whole earth" (Gen 11:4). This tower was named Babel and became a monument to the human will to power — ultimately a will to be God.

Amidst humanity's will to power, God calls the people of God to have the will to love. Instead of seeking to impose their will on others through violent force, they are called to a path of neighbor love and shalom justice. Delving deep to find the strength to love, Israel is called to be a blessing to the nations, and the nations are called to bless Israel (Gen 12:1-3). The reciprocity of blessing between Israel and the nations is the basis of shalom in the world. Through overcoming the seductive spiral of violence,

Israel is called to live a life of obedient love, embodying God's shalom in its relationship with other nations.

Because of the presence of sin, death, and evil in the world, Israel's pursuit of being a shalom people was an ongoing struggle to be in right relationship with God, humanity, and creation. When Israel wandered, God raised up prophets to proclaim the justice of God to woo Israel back into living a just life. The prophets challenged Israel to care for the orphans, widows, strangers, and poor, those on the margin of the economic order (Zech 7:9-10). Whenever Israel encountered injustice in the world, especially economic injustice, they were called to dismantle this injustice. Working to end oppression was integral to Israel's calling to be a community of blessing for all God's children. Shalom justice is Israel's destination. Shalom justice is the repeated refrain of Israel's song.

Abraham, Sarah, and Hagar: Blessing Bearers to the Nations

Prophetic theology of the late twentieth century often focused on Moses the liberator; however, beginning the biblical script with father Abraham offers a new horizon for revolutionary change. Reading Moses through an Abrahamic lens deepens and expands the liberationist script. Abraham offers a nomadic theology of blessing that is the rich soil through which we witness the growth of Moses' mystical-prophetic theological vision.

God calls Abram to leave Ur of the Chaldees and travel into the far country. "Go," God tells him, "from your country and your kindred and your father's house to the land that I will show you. I will make of you a great nation, and I will bless you, and make your name great, so that you will be a blessing. I will bless those who bless you, and the one who curses you I will curse; and in you all the families of the earth shall be blessed" (Gen 12:1-3). Abram hears the call of God and responds. Called to leave his home and journey to a land he knows not, Abram has faith in the promises of God: divine protection, a great name, progeny that will outnumber the stars in the sky, and the land — a land of blessing and promise. God blesses Abram's family so that they can bless other families who, upon blessing Abram's God, will, too, be blessed.[6]

With faith in the hovering wings of God's provision and protection, Abram ventures forth boldly into the unknown. The only thing he knows with surety is the promise of God. Promise is God's mode of revelation.

When the living God makes a promise to bless people, they can trust that it will come to fruition.[7]

It is through promise that God reveals lasting love. God's promise of many children and a fruitful land is an image of fecundity, expressing the superabundance of divine grace. The divine blessing exceeds Israel. It is a blessing for the nations, a blessing for *all* nations. The destiny of the nations is interlaced with Israel's destiny — to reveal the glory of the Creator to all God's children.

While God gives Abram this initial call and blessing, it will take many decades before we see God's promise fully manifested in the life of Abram and his family. This first visit from God is followed by six more divine visits through which the friendship between God and Abram grows increasingly intimate.[8] In order for Abram to be a blessing to the nations, he has to learn how to be a blessing bearer in the small matters of life. This will entail learning how to embody the way of blessing in his own family, as he cares for Sarah and Hagar, and his children and extended family. Abram encounters many problems, conflicts, and crises throughout his life, but each episode is a learning experience that fosters a deeper trust and intimacy with God and a more discerning wisdom about how to be a blessing bearer in his personal and political life.

God promises Abram that he will be blessed with many children, but his wife Sarai is barren. Sarai asks Abram to take her Egyptian maidservant Hagar as his wife (Gen 16:3). When Hagar conceives, she begins to treat Sarai with contempt (16:4-5). Growing increasingly jealous and angry, Sarai begins to harass Hagar, so Hagar flees into the wilderness to escape Sarai's wrath.

In the wilderness Hagar encounters the living God. God has mercy on her, engaging her in a deep conversation. God asks her where she has come from and where she is going (16:7-8). Seeing the severe suffering at the heart of Hagar's dilemma — harassment at home or death in the wilderness — God exhorts Hagar to return home to Abram's house because she has a promising future of blessing ahead through the son of promise in her womb, a son who shall be named Ishmael (16:11-12).

Because God sees her suffering, Hagar addresses God as El-roi, "the God who sees me" (16:13). Through this personal encounter with God in the wilderness, Hagar emerges as the mystical theologian in the family. Hagar has an ecstatic vision of God. She is the one who both sees and is seen by God. Since God sees her suffering, especially in her wilderness experience as an outcast, Hagar offers the origins of a nomadic hermeneutic from her subject position as an Egyptian slave woman on the margins of Abram's family.[9] God as El-roi, the One who sees Hagar in her pain and suffering as an outcast, demonstrates God's compassionate concern for the stranger, the wanderer, and the outcast. Nomadic hermeneutics privileges the perspective of the poor and the outcast.

When Hagar returns to Abram's house, she surely shares this encounter with him, deepening his family's understanding of God. It is from this place of the suffering and death-bound subjectivity of Hagar that Abram begins to become alive to the pain and suffering of others. Hagar's mystical encounter with God in the wilderness demonstrates the intimacy she shares with the living God and the important role she plays in God's covenant with Abram and his family. Through her naming of God, she has entered a new relationship with God, deepening the covenantal bond between God and the house of Abram.

Through each episode in his life Abram's faith in God grows stronger and his loyalty to his covenant with God becomes stronger. Covenants in Holy Scripture are agreements between two partners that follow the form of the suzerain treaty that was prevalent throughout the ancient Near East.[10] Elements of a covenant included a prologue, stipulations, and promises. We can see this covenantal form in God's covenant with Abram in Genesis 17:1-2:

> I am God Almighty [*covenant prologue*];
> walk before me, and be blameless [*covenant stipulations*].
> And I will make my covenant between me and you,
> and will make you exceedingly numerous [*covenant promises*].

In ancient Near Eastern covenants the prologue would lay out the historical basis for the covenant. Here it is based on the power of God. In this covenant God is named 'El Shaddai, the one of great power. The covenantal blessing is based on the partners fulfilling the covenantal stipulations. Here the stipulation calls Abram to be blameless and walk with God. The Hebrew term for blameless was used earlier in Genesis with Noah (Gen 6:9). Both Noah and Abram are examples of leaders who were obedient and completely surrendered to God, walking prayerfully before God. Noah and Abram were not bastions of moral purity, but they remained passionately in love with and faithful to God through the trials and travails of life. Because of Abram's obedience and God's fidelity, God's covenant promise is to multiply his progeny. Abram is blessed so he can be a blessing to the nations.

When God renews the covenant with Abram in Genesis 17, God gives his covenant partners new names. No longer Abram, but Abraham. No longer Sarai, but Sarah. Later on in Genesis, God, in renewing the covenant with Jacob, tells him his name is no longer Jacob; it's Israel. God elects Israel to be the covenant people of God. Israel, the chosen people of God, comes into existence through the naming of God.

With a renewed covenant and new name, Abraham is increasingly open to the movement of God's Spirit. Under the oaks of Mamre, three strangers visit Abraham (Gen 18). He invites them into his tent, breaking bread with them and serving a choice lamb. Breaking bread in the ancient Near East was the height of hospitality. When tribes were at war, if someone from one tribe walked into the home of someone from the enemy tribe and ate some bread, the host family was bound to care for that person. In showing hospitality to the three strangers, Abraham embodies love supreme.

Hospitality is risky business. Are we willing to invite the stranger into our home, no matter what the outcome or cost? You can invite a stranger into your home, but that person may bring danger. The stranger may rape your wife, murder you, steal your inheritance, or create problems in your neighborhood. When angels visit Abraham's nephew Lot in Sodom, the local men want to rape them, creating a dangerous dilemma for Lot. With the ever-present danger of loving the stranger, God's constant call to Israel is to offer hospitality to the stranger.

God's seventh and final visit with Abraham is the most challenging and dramatic. At every point in Abraham's walk with God, God has challenged him in different ways. At the beginning of his journey, God asks Abraham to relinquish his home and extended family so he can be a blessing to the families of the world (Gen 12:1-3). At the end of his journey, he asks more of Abraham, to relinquish Isaac, his beloved son (22:1-2). God calls him to take a journey with Isaac up the mountain to sacrifice Isaac. When Isaac asks him where the lamb to be sacrificed is, Abraham tells him that God will provide. When they arrive at the top of the mountain, Abraham binds Isaac and unsheathes his knife. When he is about to kill him, an angel of the Lord tells him to stop. God tells Abraham that he will bless him, because he was willing to relinquish his son (22:16-18).[11]

From relinquishing his home to relinquishing his son, becoming a blessing bearer is a process for Abraham. Throughout the rest of his life he embodies what it means to be a blessing bearer. When there is a land dispute between Abraham and Lot, he lets Lot choose which half of the land he wants. Later, when another land dispute arises between shepherds of Abraham and Abimelech, Abraham cuts a covenant of peace with Abimelech, so they can peacefully coexist. Abraham is willing to negotiate to keep the peace, even if it means a financial loss. When his wife Sarah dies and he needs a burial plot for her, the Hittites overcharge him for the cave he wants, asking 400 silver shekels, which Abraham pays as an expression of his being a blessing to the nations. When his son Isaac struggles to find a bride, Abraham sends one of his servants to find a wife for him, culminating in Isaac's marriage to Rebekah. In his encounters with strangers and family members, Abraham models what it means to be a blessing bearer.

From a familiar homeland into the strangeness of a foreign land, from the comforts of family life to the disruption of offering hospitality to strangers, Abraham forges on, making the journey into the unknown on behalf of others. Throughout his journey he becomes closer to God and wiser in the ways of justice and righteousness. Abraham is a leader on the move, a nomad for God's justice and righteousness.

Beginning with his departure from Ur of Chaldees, Abraham embodied a nomadic theology, but Hagar disrupts the journey. Her walk into the wilderness to die is a contrast to Abraham's earlier scrambling to live as he deceives Pharaoh and Abimelech by claiming that Sarah is his sister, so that his life would be preserved and it would go well with him. Hagar's encounter with God in the wilderness shows God's compassionate concern and care of outcasts and the orphans.

Abraham's theology of blessing materially constitutes itself through Israel's call to embody the justice of God. Abraham is charged with forming a new generation of leaders who follow the path of shalom justice: "I have chosen him, that he may charge his children and his household after him to keep the way of the Lord by doing righteousness and justice; so that the Lord may bring about for Abraham what he has promised him" (Gen 18:19). The trope used in this passage, *sedaqah* and *mishpat,* righteousness and justice, will be picked up and amplified by the prophets as they call Israel to manifest divine values in their communal life together.

The way of the Lord is the way of righteousness and justice. Embodying shalom justice is essential to Israel to achieve its mission of being a light to the nations. Israel's spiritual fellowship with the living God becomes the basis of their politics of mission. When Israel strayed away from God or were in a tight spot, God raised prophets to call them back to wholehearted worship and the embodiment of God's love and justice. Prone to wander, Israel was called to stay focused on their primary mission of being a light to the nations.[12]

Moses and Miriam: Singing a Song of Victory

In the book of Exodus, we see the people of Israel enslaved in Egypt after the death of Joseph. As slaves, the children of Israel were forced to build Pharaoh's mighty empire, but this prevented them from fulfilling their destiny of being a light to the nations. Being oppressed by Pharaoh fanned the flames of resentment in their hearts. They longed for liberation and prayed for freedom. As the Israelites grew in number, Pharaoh oppressed them more and more, scared that united, they would become too strong and challenge his authority.[13]

Fearful of losing power, Pharaoh sent a decree throughout the land that every newborn Hebrew boy would be killed. Jochebed, a Hebrew mother, asked her daughter Miriam to hide her baby brother down by the riverside. Miriam watched as one of Pharaoh's daughters saw the baby's basket floating in the reeds and asked her servant to recover him. She embraced the baby Moses and raised him in Pharaoh's court.

Miriam and Jochebed created an underground railroad of sorts as they plotted to keep baby Moses alive. Once Moses was rescued, Miriam improvised until she could find a way of snatching the baby, now rescued, so that he could drink his own mother's milk. Miriam and Jochebed were able to make sure that Moses learned the cultural values, religious rituals, and folkways of the Jewish people.

Miriam and Jochebed provide a model of prophets-in-collaboration. This is a model for all women, working across age and status and nationality, who are working together to save life, to preserve freedom: even when they are, in their societies, beings with limited agency. Together, Miriam and Jochebed mediated the prophetic tradition of Judaism to Moses, which was central to his formation as a prophet in an Egyptian culture. While prophets in Scripture are often portrayed as lonely, *individual men*, Miriam and Jochebed embody an alternative vision of prophecy where *collaborative women* build beloved community through improvisation.[14]

Shaped by the traditions of Israel and Egypt, Moses was a hybrid. Being bicultural, Moses was bilingual, able to move fluidly across traditions. In this sense Moses was a creole, inhabiting a strategic space "in-between" two worlds. In southern Louisiana, Creoles were considered hybrids or mulattos, neither black nor white, but a mixture of two or more cultures. As we learned in chapter 1, jazz music grew up within this Creole culture of New Orleans, shaped by African, Anglo, French, and Spanish cultural traditions. Jazz is a musical language, and improvisation is the conversational creativity that draws from different musical traditions to make new music through deep collaboration. As a prophet in Egypt, Moses had to improvise, speaking both Egyptian and Hebrew, based on the context he found himself in. Throughout his life, Moses' biculturalism, mystical depth, discerning wisdom, collaborative spirit, and prophetic fire would become central features of his prophetic vocation.[15]

Moses the Jew became an Egyptian prince whom God would anoint as a Hebrew prophet. A prophet had to hear the call of God and respond with holy boldness. As Abraham responded to God calling him into the far country to form his descendants into a new nation, Moses responded to God calling him to lead the people of Israel out of Egypt. Against all odds, including a hostile pharaoh and his mighty army chasing the people of Israel, Moses led Israel boldly forward. When he was fearful and faithless, Moses reached down deep and leaned on the power of almighty God. Chased by the chariots of the Egyptian army, he led the people of Israel across the Red Sea. Through Moses' obedience and leadership, God freed the Israelites from the bonds of slavery.

In response to God's victory over Pharaoh's army, Moses and Miriam led the people of Israel in singing. Moses, Miriam, and the Israelites sang:

> I will sing to the Lord,
> for he is highly exalted.
> The horse and its rider
> he has hurled into the sea.
> The Lord is my strength and my song;
> he has become my salvation.
> He is my God, and I will praise him,
> my father's God, and I will exalt him.
> The Lord is a warrior;
> the Lord is his name.
> Pharaoh's chariots and his army
> he has hurled into the sea.
> The best of Pharaoh's officers
> are drowned in the Red Sea.
> The deep waters have covered them;
> they sank to the depths like a stone. (Exod 15:1-5 NIV)

Exuberantly and joyfully Moses proclaims, "The Lord is my strength and my song; / he has become my salvation." While the song has images of violently overthrowing the enemy, it bears witness to God's faithfulness to the covenants that were cut with Abraham, Isaac, and Jacob. When Israel was enslaved and cried out to the Lord, God heard their cry and overcame the death-dealing powers of Pharaoh and the Red Sea to save the people of Israel. The living God is Israel's strength and salvation, and also their song. The people of Israel were a singing community, offering hearty praise and worship to the living God.

Moses is joined by Miriam in celebrating God's faithfulness and strength.[16] She leads worship with a group of spirited women who play the tambourine and dance before the Lord. Miriam leads the women in a liturgical performance of this victory song, expressing the way in which Israel is growing into a musical movement for love and justice. God freed the people of Israel from the bondage of slavery and called them to become freedom fighters on behalf of the poor and oppressed. The Israelites were not chosen to be a culturally isolated and divinely favored tribe; they were set free so that they could be a blessing to the nations. The new songs and new dances of Miriam prophetically and dramatically enacted their recent deliverance from Pharaoh. In an hour of despair, God had mercy on Israel and delivered them.

Moses and Miriam's song is more than a simple praise song; it is a manifesto — Israel's confession of faith. Gerhard von Rad writes, "the deliverance from Egypt and the rescue at the Red Sea are a vast chorale surpassing all the praise she gave for all other divine actions . . . [they] found their way into Israel's confession of faith — indeed, they actually became Israel's earliest confession."[17] Israel confesses her faith through singing. At this critical moment in redemptive history, Israel confesses that God and God alone is her strength and salvation.[18] The song of Israel is a song of the victory of the living God.

Moses on the Mountain: The Origins of Mystical-Prophetic Theology

Throughout Moses' life God called him to ascend a mountain in order to encounter the divine. It was on the mountain that he saw a burning bush. It was on the mountain that he was given the law. It was on the mountain that he entered the thick darkness. It was on the mountain that he encountered YHWH — personally and on his own.

Through these encounters God could mediate the way of the covenant to Moses, who could then share it with the people of Israel. Because of Moses' role as a mediator between God and Israel, he is known to be the father of the prophets. Moses was a shepherd, close to the earth, tending Jethro's flock and caring for the community of creation. He led his flocks beyond the wilderness to Horeb, the mountain of God (Exod 3:1). Moses saw a burning bush and was drawn to it (3:1-12). When he came close to the fire, God called his name, "Moses! Moses!" Moses said, "Here I am." God asked him to take off his shoes because he was standing on holy ground. At that moment of encounter, God reveals Godself as the God of Abraham, Isaac, and Jacob, disclosing God's fidelity to covenantal promises made to Israel. Hearing the name of God, Moses is initiated into an intimate relationship with the living God. In his encounter with the burning bush Moses encountered the "visible voice" of God, which he both saw and heard.[19]

God shares with Moses, "I have observed the misery of my people who are in Egypt; I have heard their cry on account of their taskmasters. Indeed, I know their sufferings, and I have come down to deliver them from the Egyptians" (3:7-8b). God's hearing and responding to the cries of Israel are at the heart of the scriptural vision of salvation. Following Moses' own ascent up the mountain, Israel is called to imitate God through hearing and responding to the cries of the oppressed. The fire of God ignites the flames of compassion, empathy, and care for those who are suffering and in pain. The prophets are those who feel the heart of God when they hear the cries of those who are hurting.[20]

Moses' encounter with God through the burning bush gives birth to a mystical-prophetic vision that is at the heart of the Torah. The mystical dimension comes through in the personal encounter that Moses has with the living God. Through his encounter on the mountain, Moses discovers the deep mystery of God. It is through this personal encounter with the mystery of the living God that we see the mystical stream emerge in the life of Moses.

We can speak about this mystical encounter as an I-Thou relationship described by Jewish theologian Martin Buber. Buber describes God as the Thou who, "whatever else he may be — enters into a direct relation with us men in creative, revealing and redeeming acts, and thus makes it possible for us to enter into a direct relation with him."[21] God is a living, active, personal, vital, communal, transcendent being that we revere and worship, as a Thou. When we are spiritually aligned with God as a Thou, then we are better able to treat other human beings as Thous, offering them the tender love and deep respect they deserve as fellow humans created and loved by God.

The I-Thou encounter Moses has on the mountain in solitude becomes the deep mystical center of his prophetic encounter with Pharaoh. While the *mystical* stream is rooted in a "direct relation" with God, the *prophetic* stream embodies this internal spiritual impulse in the external affairs in the world. It is through the intimate encounter with God in prayer that the work of shalom justice finds and sustains its inspiration.

Moses embodies a holy boldness as he keeps pressing in, further and further into the fire of God. Through the courage of entering the fire of God, he was able to enter into the divine presence. The destination of Moses' journey up the mountain and through the fire is the peaceful presence of God.

After Moses descended from the mountain, he continued to meet with God, but in the tent of meeting (Exod 33:7-11). In this tent outside of the camp, God would meet with Moses, arriving with a storm cloud, inspiring all the people around to worship the living God. Within this tent of meeting, the Lord spoke "to Moses face to face, as one speaks to a friend" (33:11a). This improvisational dialogue between God and Moses is an intimate divine encounter, where the power of the divine presence, the divine energies, is imparted to Moses, who will transmit it to Israel. Moses asks to see the glory of God, but God tells him that anyone who sees God will not live (33:20). God reveals Godself to Moses, but does it in a way that conceals the visible face of God but reveals the invisible divine presence.[22]

As Abraham encountered God on the mountain, so, too, does Moses. Ascending the mountain to encounter God and hear the divine voice is the heart of being a prophet. God calls Moses to cut two tablets of stone and bring them up to Mount Sinai. When he arrives, God descends upon him in a storm cloud, disclosing the divine character. YHWH is

> "a God merciful and gracious,
> slow to anger,
> and abounding in steadfast love and faithfulness,
> keeping steadfast love for the thousandth generation,
> forgiving iniquity and transgression and sin,
> yet by no means clearing the guilty,
> but visiting the iniquity of the parents
> upon the children
> and children's children,
> to the third and the fourth generation." (34:6-7)

God reveals to Moses the heart of his character, *hesed,* "steadfast love for the thousandth generation."[23] God's steadfast love to all and tender mercy toward the suffering are a model for Israel.

Imitating God, Israel is called to respond to the cry of the poor and suffering through fervent prayer and acts of justice. The Word of God shows Israel a vision of the future of shalom. Seeing, hearing, and tasting a better life and land ahead open Israel's heart and senses to the cries of the hungry and hurting.[24]

Through courageously entering the glory cloud of God on the holy mountain and in the tent of meeting, Moses is able to share the radiant light of God with Israel, refracted through Israel as light to the nations. The face-to-face encounter is not completely face-to-face, as we have reached the limits of mystical experience. God remains a mystery. In the still point of silence, Moses enters the presence and mystery of the living God, whose face he can see and not see. Through this encounter Moses' face begins to shine with the light of the radiance of God (34:29-30). Moses' shining face is a sign of restoration of the image of God in Israel and the resurrection of humanity to a glorified state.[25]

Yet, the people of Israel were stubborn and hard-hearted, often shutting their ears to the cry of the other. So God called Moses back to the mountain and gave him two stone tablets with ten commandments that would be a moral guide for the people of Israel. God called Moses to climb Mount Sinai, and there God presented Moses the Ten Commandments, which were the primary laws Israel was called to obey (Exod 19–20:21). The Law presented to Moses on Sinai became the baseline of the song of Israel. The laws of the Torah were the liberating constraints that would provide the musical boundaries of Israel's song of salvation.[26]

The Ten Commandments are the embodiment of God's shalom justice, clearly delineating the ways that we are to relate to God and humanity. The first two commandments discuss how we as humans relate to God, who brought Israel out of enslavement in Egypt. Israel is called to forsake all idols and worship God and God alone (20:1-6).

Being personally connected to Creator is the central thrust of the commandments. Moses himself offers us a model of being in mystical communion with God. After receiving the commandments, Moses descends the mountain through the storm cloud of flashing lightning and thunder clapping like a booming trumpet. As the people cower, Moses exhorts them to not be afraid, but to revere God and stop sinning. He then boldly enters the thick cloud of darkness where God was (20:18-21). Gregory of Nyssa writes of Moses: "the one who is going to associate intimately with God must go beyond all that is visible and (lifting up his own mind, as to a mountain top, to the invisible and incomprehensible) believe that the divine is *there* where the understanding does not reach." Moses the mystic inspires us to enter the thick cloud of darkness, pressing beyond the visible world toward the invisible presence of God that exceeds our imagination.[27]

These first two theocentric commandments are followed by eight more that discuss how we should relate to our fellow humans and the community of creation. These commandments provide moral boundaries for the human community to be able to live in a manner that is stable, fair, and equal.

These commands and the other codes that work them out are better understood as God's household laws. God's whole good creation can be seen as a house that we all live in. These household rules are found in the Covenant Code (Exod 20:22–23:33), the Deuteronomic Code (Deut 12–26), and the Holiness Code (Lev 17–26). The people of God are called to be good stewards of God's house, the whole community of creation. These moral codes are the liberating constraints that we are given by God. Within these constraints the people of God are called to improvise in creative ways so they can see God's shalom justice manifested. Because of sin and human nature, humans were destined to fail, so God built in a regular, ritual element of the economy of grace, the Year of Jubilee.

Jubilee Justice

After Genesis's presentation of Abraham's family history and Exodus's tale of Moses the liberator and lawgiver, in the book of Leviticus we hear the song of Jubilee justice. God's song of shalom is a song of abundance. Jubilee, or *Yobel* in Hebrew, means ram's horn. According to the Torah, every forty-nine years on the Day of Atonement a Hebrew priest would blow a ram's horn announcing the Year of Jubilee.

When this loud horn blew, the poor heard it as good news! Jubilee was a song of freedom (Exod 19:13; Josh 6:4-8, 13). Captives were liberated, poor found riches, and the hurting were healed. Jubilee meant a new world was coming to pass — a world where all God's children were provided for and the community of creation could rest.

Jubilee broadcasts God's coming shalom. The Year of Jubilee refers to the proclamation of liberty to slaves and the restoration of land. The contours of Jubilee justice are presented in Leviticus 25. The Jewish vision of Jubilee justice was truly a vision of proper human freedom and economic equity. According to the Torah, four rules are incorporated into the Jubilee year: (1) the land is to lie fallow, (2) debts are to be canceled, (3) slaves are to be freed, and (4) the land is to be returned or redistributed to its original holder, who had to sell it out of economic necessity (Lev 25:23-24). In the seventh year the vineyards and orchards are to be left untended not only so that the ground may be rejuvenated but also so that the poor may benefit (Exod 23:10-11). The Deuteronomic law extends the law of leaving sheaves and fruit beyond the seventh year to each harvest season (Deut 24:19-22). Creator cares about the whole community of creation, especially the poor and those on the margins.[28]

God's Jubilee justice embodies an economy of life and extreme trust. Holy Scripture offers a vision of economic ordering that benefits all people — *oikonomia tou theou,* the economy of God. The word "economics" is derived from the Greek word *oikonomia,* meaning household management. Thus, an analogy is drawn between the management of a home and the stewardship of the whole "economy" of creation, conceived as a global house. In the creation accounts God gives humans the responsibility to care for the household of God. Caring for the household of God entails ordering human life together in ways that are peaceable, loving, and just for the whole creation.[29]

Jubilee justice is a call to end oppression, especially its economic form. Oppression is the systemic effects of sin that are deeply rooted in human institutions and the human heart. From Cain's establishment of the first city, we see a tendency within the lives of sinful and broken humans to organize institutions that often humiliate, enslave, and kill the poor, who are made in the image of God. Throughout the Hebrew Scriptures, overcoming oppression is central to the sweep of redemptive history (Gen 15; Exod 1–5; Deut 26:5-9; Pss 72; 103; 146; Isa 8–9; 42; 53; 58). Oppressive practices cause unnecessary suffering among the poor people, often unto death. God hears the cries of the oppressed and responds through the spirit of deliverance.[30]

Jubilee justice unveils a new beginning free from the bondage of slavery, especially economic slavery. Jubilee calls the oppressive landowners to repent, relinquishing their power and property for the common good. The poor are given access to God's economy of life through the right to share in the harvest (cf. Deut 24:19-22; Lev 23:22; Ruth 2). Holy Scripture is clear that God calls the people of God to open their lives to offer hospitality to the poor: "Open your hand to the poor and needy neighbor in your land" (Deut 15:11).

The prophetic vision of Jubilee authentically cared about the other, especially the poor, the stranger, and the sojourner: "And if your brother becomes poor, and cannot maintain himself with you, you shall maintain him; as a stranger and a sojourner he shall live with you. Take no interest from him or increase, but fear your God; that your brother may live beside you. . . . For they are my servants, whom I brought forth out of the land of Egypt; they shall not be sold as slaves" (Lev 25:35-42 RSV). Because God had heard the cry of enslaved Israel and led them to freedom, God calls Israel to open up their tribe to extend hospitality to the stranger. Israel is called to imitate God through the practice of hospitality (Deut 15:7-11; Isa 58:6-9; Amos 2:6-7; 5:21-24). Jubilee justice reveals something of the excessive love and grace of God.

In the Hebrew Bible, the primary measure of how Israel was doing ethically was how well they treated widows, orphans, and strangers (Exod 22:21; 23:6; Lev 19:10; Deut 27:19). The lowest in the cultural hierarchy of the ancient Near East, the widow, orphan, and stranger, were economically vulnerable, on the margins of economic and political power. Israel was susceptible to being drawn into the vortex of imperial power, but prophets like Jeremiah called Israel not to "oppress the alien, the orphan, and the widow" (Jer 7:6). Seeking justice for the poor is the heart of Jubilee justice.[31]

Isaiah's Song of Shalom

When Israel strays from the path of shalom justice, God raises up prophets to call Israel back to their missionary vocation of being a light to the nations. Isaiah, son of Amoz, is an embodiment of this tradition of calling Israel to authentic worship and bold social witness. Isaiah is the longest of the prophetic books and the one Jesus quotes from most often. The book covers the period from King Uzziah of Judah, mid–eighth century B.C.E., to Judah's return from Babylonian exile, in the mid–sixth century.[32]

We see the call-and-response structure of prophecy illustrated in Isaiah's prophetic imagination. In search of a prophet for Israel, God asks, "Whom shall I send?" "Here am I," Isaiah responds, "send me!" (Isa 6:8). The divine call always precedes the call of the prophet. The prophet's call to Israel is an echo of the call of God. While God calls the prophet to inspire Israel to be faithful to their covenant with God, the prophet has to constantly improvise in order to deliver a word of awakening.

It's time for the poet to come now! Israel has been seduced by the false promises of idols and other gods. Israel has forsaken the poor and pursued her own riches and wealth. Israel has broken the covenant of love and become a whore. Sad and longing, God raises up Isaiah as a romantic poet to sing a love song to woo Israel back. Singing songs of praise and prophecy is the heart of the worship of Israel.[33]

Creativity is at the heart of the prophetic imagination. Isaiah has to access the boundless depths and subtle emotional tones of the human heart. The prophetic burn melts Israel's hard heart. First Isaiah's prophecy is framed by two songs:

> Shout aloud and sing for joy, O royal Zion,
> for great in your midst is the Holy One of Israel. (Isa 12:6)

> And the ransomed of the Lord shall return,
> and come to Zion with singing;
> everlasting joy shall be upon their heads;
> they shall obtain joy and gladness,
> and sorrow and sighing shall flee away. (Isa 35:10)

In these two love songs we hear the promise of an "everlasting joy." Israel's heart swoons as she journeys to Zion, the space of God's redemptive love. Isaiah sings songs of joy and judgment and paints colorful pictures of the righteous reign of God. God ignites the prophetic imagination and inflames the prophetic heart to inspire Israel to live into her calling.[34]

The prophets call the people to return to the God who is long-suffering and faithful to the covenantal promises. Prophets are conduits of restoration between God and wayward Israel. They repair the breach, bind up broken relationships, and restore the harmonies of creation. Throughout redemptive history we see that Yahweh is faithful to the covenant with Israel. When Israel breaks the covenant, God raises up prophets to call them back.

Isaiah begins his prophecy to Israel with a concise manifesto for justice.

> Wash yourselves; make yourselves clean;
> remove the evil of your doings

> from before my eyes;
> cease to do evil,
> learn to do good;
> seek justice,
> rescue the oppressed,
> defend the orphan,
> plead for the widow. (Isa 1:16-17)

In this opening salvo, Isaiah sees the wickedness of Israel expressed in their giving a multitude of sacrifices (1:11), while their lives are marked with deception, exploitation, and idolatry. In contrast, Isaiah calls Israel to work to end oppression and embody shalom justice.

Isaiah speaks of Israel as a city that has become a whore, forsaking God and the way of justice:

> How the faithful city
> has become a whore!
> She that was full of justice,
> righteousness lodged in her —
> but now murderers! (1:21)

Breaking their covenant with God, Israel gave their loyalty to other gods, leading them into a life of oppression, including murder.

As we saw on the mountain with Moses, there is a deep link between Israel's love and loyalty to God, and Israel's love and loyalty to others. God seeks "blessing for all families" through Israel (Gen 12:3), but Israel is better able to be a blessing to other families if they are blessing the living God. When Israel rejects the way of blessing, there are disastrous consequences for the city and its residents. An ethic of jubilee and life is replaced with an ethic of oppression and death. Given humans' propensity to violence, unto death, the prophets like Isaiah are tireless in calling Israel to remember Creator. Israel is called to build cities of justice, righteousness, and hope.

The book of Isaiah speaks in many voices and on behalf of different communities. Biblical scholars speak of three editors of the book of Isaiah. In First Isaiah we hear Israel's song as a song of victory:

> A shoot shall come out from the stump of Jesse,
> and a branch shall grow out of his roots.

The spirit of the LORD shall rest on him,
the spirit of wisdom and understanding,
the spirit of counsel and might,
the spirit of knowledge and the fear of the LORD.
His delight shall be in the fear of the LORD. . . .
The wolf shall live with the lamb,
the leopard shall lie down with the kid,
the calf and the lion and the fatling together,
and a little child shall lead them. . . .

On that day the Lord will extend his hand yet a second time to recover the remnant that is left of his people, from Assyria, from Egypt, from Pathros, from Ethiopia, from Elam, from Shinar, from Hamath, and from the coastlands of the sea.

He will raise a signal for the nations,
and will assemble the outcasts of Israel,
and gather the dispersed of Judah
from the four corners of the earth. (Isa 11:1-12)

This song proclaims the Jubilee, offering hopeful, redemptive images of the kingdom of the peaceable reign of God. Isaiah describes God recovering the remnant and assembling the outcasts of Israel. Creator as the One who made and sustains the world is the One who resurrects the body and restores the shalom of the community of creation. These images of the restoration of Israel bear witness to the victory of God in resurrection.[35]

Later in First Isaiah there is another victory song that echoes Miriam's song by the sea and the victory song of Deborah. "On that day this song will be sung in the land of Judah," Isaiah sings:

We have a strong city;
he sets up victory
like walls and bulwarks.
Open the gates,
so that the righteous nation that keeps faith
may enter in.
Those of steadfast mind you keep in peace —
in peace because they trust in you.
Trust in the LORD for ever. (Isa 26:1-4)

The composer of this song uses the metaphor of a city to convey the presence of God. The faithful city is an embodiment of Israel living out their mission of being a light to the nations.

Walking the way of Torah and singing the songs of Zion, the faithful city is a city of the open gates. Isaiah is calling Israel to be a community with open gates so that "the righteous nation that keeps faith" may enter the city of shalom. When this happens we will see the reciprocity of the love and blessing among the nations. Instead of a perpetual state of conflict and strife, we will see the emergence of cultures of peace. While the spiral of violence and logic of death are the way of the world, the prophetic imperative calls Israel to embody shalom justice and open their doors to offer lasting hospitality to the nations.

The practice of hospitality is an ambitious task. It entails liberating prisoners, feeding the hungry, finding housing for the homeless, and clothing the naked:

> Is not this the fast that I choose:
>   to loose the bonds of injustice,
>   to undo the thongs of the yoke,
> to let the oppressed go free,
>   and to break every yoke?
> Is it not to share your bread with the hungry,
>   and bring the homeless poor into your house;
> when you see the naked, to cover him,
>   and not to hide yourself from your own kin?
> Then your light shall break forth like the dawn,
>   and your healing shall spring up quickly;
> your vindicator shall go before you,
>   the glory of the LORD shall be your rear guard.
> Then you shall call, and the LORD will answer;
>   you shall cry for help, and he will say, Here I am. (Isa 58:6-9)

In this passage we see that Isaiah challenges Israel not to worship God through empty-hearted fasts and festivals, but to have the moral courage to worship God through acts of justice. The point of the rituals of praying, fasting, resting, and celebrating is to embody the justice of God in the world. When Israel resolutely cares for the poor, who share their "own flesh," God's reign "will break forth like the dawn."

Micah's Challenge

The vision of the eighth century B.C.E. prophet Micah also challenged Israel to embody shalom justice. Micah's prophecy is driven by a dialectic of judgment and restoration. Micah rebuked the people of Israel for their idol worship, dishonest character, and economic exploitation of the poor. Directing his prophetic sights on temple worship in Jerusalem, Micah called Israel to carry the spirit of worship in the temple out into the community through acts of justice and love.

In Micah 6 God states a case against Israel for violating the Sinai covenant. God makes it clear that no amount of ritual sacrifice — thousands of rams and ten thousand rivers of oil — will be found pleasing to him. Then he poses a question that has reverberated through the centuries: "What does the LORD require?" Micah's prophecy makes it clear:

> To do justice, and to love kindness,
> and to walk humbly with your God. (Mic 6:8)

Micah's challenge is a clear distillation of the prophetic imperative. Micah's threefold structure begins with justice and moves to love and humility.

The first feature of Micah's mandate is to do justice *(mishpat)*. The justice of God is the basis of the Law and the Prophets. The prophetic call is always a call back to God, fulfilling a just and right relationship with God. The call to justice must be manifest concretely in the whole of the community of creation. *Mishpat* calls Israel to be in right relations in every dimension of their life together — in relationship with God, in their internal life as a tribe, in their relationship with other nations, and with the whole community of creation.

Like Isaiah, Micah reminds Israel that God desires "obedience, not sacrifice" (Isa 1:10-17; Mic 6:1-8). The Hebrew prophets challenge Israel to internalize the heart of the law, instead of getting distracted by all the fine points of its contours as an external framework (Jer 34:31-34). God is less concerned with *right* sacrifice through the ritual system of Jewish faith, than with the *right* practice of justice in and for the community, especially to service with and for the poor, who are on the economic margins of society. Micah shares with Isaiah a strong opposition to the ways that the ruling class in Jerusalem was exploiting the poor through extensive taxation and seizure of the hereditary land (Mic 2:1-5; Isa 5:8).[36] If the ethic of shalom justice was to materialize in Jerusalem, prophets had to denounce the current system and the people had to work together to embody new alternative forms of egalitarian community.

Micah, "the Morashite," grew up in a small village outside the urban power center of Jerusalem, so he empathized with the plight of the poor and intuitively understood the strategies that the ruling classes used to exploit the peasantry economically (Mic 1:1). Identifying this economic injustice and the oppression it was causing was part of raising the consciousness of the people to end the oppression of the poor in Israel. Through embodying the ideals of economic justice, Jerusalem could achieve its destiny as a city — a city of refuge and shalom (Isa 14:32). To do justice is to act rightly toward your neighbor. Loving the neighbor through concrete acts of justice imitates the love and justice of God. God is calling Israel to a just ethic as a prelude to holy worship. Justice does not replace worship; it embodies it in the life of the community. Justice first, sacrifice second.

The second feature of Micah's challenge is loving-kindness. This notion is known as *hesed* in the Hebrew, which means steadfast love. God is faithful and long-suffering, the One who will never leave us nor forsake us. Israel's destiny depends on being able to be completely open to receiving the steadfast and gracious love of the Lord. No matter how difficult times get or how far Israel has wandered in the wilderness, the living God is there guiding and caring for the people of God.

The steadfast love of the Lord is the font of the never-ending stream of love that flows through God's people into the world. The *hesed* love of God anticipates the double love commandment of Jesus — the call to love God and love neighbor. Micah's challenge "to do justice *(mishpat)* and to love kindness *(hesed)*" brings justice and love into close proximity (Mic 6:8). To love God and our neighbor entails embodying God's shalom justice in our communities. While the people of God join with others in the struggle for justice, all our work must be marked by love.

God expresses love to the people through promises of blessings, providing people with good jobs, loving families, fruitful farms, and peaceful communities. Micah envisions a community where everyone has enough to sustain a family:

> They shall all sit under their own vines and under their own fig trees,
> and no one shall make them afraid. (Mic 4:4)

For each family to have their own fig tree means they each have the means to participate fully in local trade and meet both their needs and the needs of others. Such equitable distribution of the means of production stems directly from a shifting of resources from warfare (which usually only serves the king) to sustainable development for all God's people.

Both Isaiah and Micah call for the transforming of swords and spears (weapons production and arms trade) into the tools of sustainable agriculture (plowshares and pruning hooks) available for all, especially the most vulnerable (Isa 2:4; Mic 4:3). Because God steadfastly loves Israel, Israel is called to love all God's people, especially the most vulnerable. Israel is called to mediate the love of God to the nations, building a culture of shalom justice.

The third feature of Micah's challenge is humility. As Micah challenged Israel to embody love and justice, he exhorted them to walk humbly with the Lord. This was a call to prayer, to a deep mystical union with God embodied by Moses on the mountain. Micah calls Israel to have the spiritual courage to earnestly seek to see the face of God, hidden in thick darkness. This was a call to stay in intimate communion with their God, no matter what the personal cost. Meditating on the law day and night, the people of God are called to daily press in toward a more intimate walk with the living God.

Micah's call to humility is a call to Israel, who became arrogant in thinking that they could live without God. There is not life without God. Our attempts to build empires are futile. The houses under the sea and dancers under the hill stand as a silent testimony to the endless wisdom of humility.

Micah continues:

> The voice of the LORD cries to the city
> (it is sound wisdom to fear your name):
> Hear, O tribe and assembly of the city! (6:9)

The living God's heart is for Jerusalem, the holy city with a temple consecrated for worship. Yet, Israel is not living out the fruitful life of the way of Torah, so God cries out with the heart of a spurned lover, "Return!" "Return!" Come back to the way of the Torah, which is the way of life.

Micah's prophecy offers a clear distillation of the features of the way of the Torah: justice, mercy, and humility. These three virtues are the heart of the prophetic imperative in Hebrew Scripture and can be summed up as shalom justice. The ethic of shalom justice is not for Israel alone, but for the nations, and for the cities of the nations. While Jerusalem is the beloved city of Israel, it becomes a template for God's call to build beloved cities the world round.

Conclusion

To live into Micah's challenge today to act justly, love mercy, and walk humbly with the Lord, the church must be more proactive in entering into places of suffering, working to dismantle the structures of injustice, and modeling an authentic community of hope and healing. We need to boldly enter the places of our deepest darkness, sin, suffering, and struggle. The vulnerability of human flesh is the common ground of our struggle against injustice. The prophetic imperative is a call for the gathering and deployment of a poor-led movement for love and justice working together to build beloved cities.

Listening to God's voice and the cry of the poor is at the heart of what it means to respond to the prophetic Word. Responding to the cry of the poor is the heart of the prophetic imperative. The prophetic imperative is about doing something in response to the Word of God that restores the shalom of the community of creation. Through compassionately caring for those who suffer and seeking to end the conditions that are causing suffering, we join Abraham, Sarah, and Hagar as bearers of God's blessings to the nations.

If we are courageous enough to enter the dark places of our cities, then God's Spirit has the opportunity to show up in a powerful way, transforming places of despair into spaces of hope. We are to restore the shalom of the garden through working for the peace of the nations in our work of building beloved cities. As Isaiah prophesies:

> As the earth brings forth its shoots,
>   and as a garden causes what is sown in it to spring up,
> so the Lord God will cause righteousness and praise
>   to spring up before all the nations. (Isa 61:11)

Isaiah appeals to the garden imagery of Eden here and associates it with the way of shalom justice. As Israel is faithful to the way of the Torah, God will cause "righteousness and praise" to spring up like an eternal spring. We see here clearly that what God longs for more than anything is a vibrant worship that flows into vibrant, collective social witness. The real test of worship is when we leave the temple and hit the streets and encounter suffering with a human face. The face of the widow, the orphan, and the stranger calls us. Will we respond to the cry of the poor? Do we have the moral courage to open the gates of our communities to the God of Abraham, Isaac, and Jacob, so that shalom justice will spring up before all the nations of the world? What are we doing to proclaim and embody the shalom justice of God?

CHAPTER THREE

Jesus the Jewish Improviser

> *And having disarmed the powers and authorities, he made a public spectacle of them, triumphing over them by the cross.*
>
> Colossians 2:15 NIV

Jesus was a Jewish prophet whose message transformed the Judaism of his day. Improvising like a jazz musician, Jesus took the prophetic call to love God and neighbor to a new level. As a jazz musician takes a standard and makes it new, Jesus sang a new song within the framework of another melody, the song of Israel. While his preaching style was familiar to the Jews of his day, Jesus' vision was big, bodacious, and beautiful, pushing Judaism to a renewed and deeper faith in the living God.

Jesus' ministry constantly flowed with the rhythm of call-and-response. Wherever he went, he would always respond to the call of the Holy Spirit. When the Spirit called, Jesus responded, completely surrendering himself to the will of his Father. He marched through the Galilean countryside with his disciples — teaching about the kingdom in the synagogues, exorcising demons, healing the sick, and feasting with the hungry and sinners. When Jewish teachers tried to ensnare him with the rules of Moses, Jesus improvised through reflexive antinomies: "You have heard that it was said," followed by "But I say unto you."[1] Jesus took a standard ("love your neighbor") and deepened it ("love your enemy"). Like John Coltrane took "My Favorite Things" and made it his own, Jesus took Israel's love song and sang a love song to the whole community of creation.

Mary's Protest Songs

God demonstrated the divine love for creation through the incarnation of Jesus of Nazareth. An angel arrived and spoke with a young Jewish woman named Mary. She was to have a child named Jesus, a child who would be "called the Son of the Most High. The Lord God will give him the throne of his father David, and he will reign over the house of Jacob forever; his kingdom will never end" (Luke 1:32-33 NIV). As Mary listened attentively to this angelic song, she may have heard echoes of former kingdoms and messianic prophecies of her Jewish faith; her heart was full of questions. Could she really be the one to bear a child whose "kingdom will never end"?

Although Mary had faith in the divine promise declared by the angel, she was curious about how this conception would take place. The angel explained that she would conceive through the power of the Holy Spirit: "the power of the Most High will overshadow you" (1:35 NIV). Like the *ruach* that blew through the turbulent waters of creation and the shadow of the glory cloud of presence that led Israel through the wilderness to a land of promise, the angelic song expressed that her life would become another beautiful verse in the song of Israel.

After the angel reassured Mary that "nothing is impossible with God" (1:37 NIV), Mary boldly and graciously responded, "I am the Lord's servant. . . . May it be to me as you have said" (1:38 NIV). She responded to God's word as a true disciple, with attentive listening, theological imagination, humble obedience, and prophetic courage. She heard the Word of God and obeyed it in an attitude of prayer and praise, courageously fulfilling her role in the history of redemption. She heard the *call* of God and *responded,* expressing her courageous faith in concrete prophetic action.

During her pregnancy Mary paid a visit to her cousin Elizabeth, who was pregnant with John the Baptist. When Mary greeted Elizabeth, the baby John leaped in Elizabeth's womb and she was filled with the Holy Spirit (1:41). After Elizabeth addressed Mary as "the mother of my Lord" (1:43 NIV), Mary burst forth in song, in one of the most poetic portions of Scripture.[2] Mary sang:

> "My soul magnifies the Lord,
>   and my spirit rejoices in God my Savior,
> for he has looked with favor on the lowliness of his servant.
>   Surely, from now on all generations will call me blessed;

for the Mighty One has done great things for me,
and holy is his name.
His mercy is for those who fear him
from generation to generation.
He has shown strength with his arm;
he has scattered the proud in the thoughts of their hearts.
He has brought down the powerful from their thrones,
and lifted up the lowly;
he has filled the hungry with good things,
and sent the rich away empty.
He has helped his servant Israel,
in remembrance of his mercy,
according to the promise he made to our ancestors,
to Abraham and to his descendants forever." (1:46-55)

While Mary's song has often been heard as a sweet song of praise, in reality it is a passionate prophecy, a song of divine victory that threatens the current social order. Though Mary's song reflects the history of God's mercy and faithfulness to the covenant with Israel, it is also a sharp social critique.

Mary's song is a prophetic rebuke to those who are proud in the "thoughts of their hearts."[3] The rich and powerful have built a way of life that excludes God and the love of neighbor, isolating themselves into lives of nihilism and self-annihilation. Through isolating themselves in corners of comfort, the proud and affluent disrupt the shalom justice of the community of creation. In contrast, Mary holds up the poor and oppressed, including herself, as examples of God's compassionate concern for the weak and the marginalized.[4]

She begins her song with

"My soul magnifies the Lord,
and my spirit rejoices in God my Savior,
for he has looked with favor on the lowliness of his servant.
Surely, from now on all generations will call me blessed."
(1:46-48)

Mary's whole being is taken up in joyful praise unto her God. She is grateful and joyful that God has chosen her from her lowly position as a poor teenage woman and made her the mother of "the Son of God" (1:35). As God chooses her as a servant, her life becomes a metaphor of the kingdom of God, a space of dramatic reversals where God will favor those who are unfavored in society.

Mary's song captures much of her spirit as a young Jewish woman, faithful to the prophetic tradition that she has been raised in and open to the apocalyptic unfolding of God's future. Since Mary grew up as a God-fearing Jewish girl, she is able to place her experience of God's favor within the context of God's covenantal faithfulness to the Jews in the past (1:48c-50). Not only had the "Mighty One" done great things for her, but Yahweh also had extended mercy to generations of people who were reverent (1:50). Since Mary knows of God's loving-kindness to her people in the past, she never questions God's loyalty. By agreeing to be God's servant, she accepts the divine call, allowing her womb to give life to the promised Savior. The angel's news surprises Mary, but she courageously and creatively plays her role in the theo-drama of redemption.

As Miriam sang a new song, echoing the song of Moses, Mary performs her music through improvisational embodied obedience. Her womb will become the site of a new song of salvation. By her prophetic improvisation on the melody of the song of Israel, Mary sets the stage for her son's enacting of redemption in the flesh for all time.

Mary's song is also a song of Jubilee justice. Although her song celebrates God's graciousness and fidelity, it also portrays God's judgment by introducing the theme of the great inversion — the rich will be brought down, while the poor will be lifted up. She praises God for the divine favor upon her, but also announces the elevation of the disinherited everywhere.

Mary's concern for those on the underside of history unveils her identity as a Jewish prophet. Abraham Heschel points out that "The heart of God is on the side of the weaker. God's special concern is not for the mighty and the successful, but for the lowly and the downtrodden."[5] The prophets lift up the care of all God's children, especially the marginalized — widows, orphans, strangers, and the poor — as one of the central practices reflecting our love for God (Zech 7:9-10). In her compassionate care for the poor and her prophetic utterance that the humble will be lifted up, Mary joins prophets like Isaiah and Micah who prepare the way for the Messiah. Mary's song offers a glimpse of how the Messiah would radically alter the systems of world domination through ushering in a new socio-economic order.

The theme of the great inversion is echoed in the song of John the Baptist. After fasting on a diet of locusts and wild honey, John the Baptist came out of the wilderness as a hearty herald, singing an old-time blues classic in a new way. John the Baptist's refrain "Prepare ye the way of the Lord, make his paths straight" was a new riff on the prophecy of Isaiah (Mark 1:3 KJV; Isa 40:3). John describes a leveling of creation, so that all could see God's coming salvation. The mountains would be brought down; the valleys filled up; and crooked roads straightened into laser-like lines shooting toward the horizon of eternity. With God's imminent coming, John calls the people to repent. Those who respond to his fiery call he heartily baptizes. Those who fail to repent, he aggressively rebukes, saying: "Repent! You brood of vipers!" for the kingdom of God is at hand (Matt 3:7).

John the Baptist announces the coming of the Messiah with musical-dramatic verve. Born around the same time, their lives were forever intertwined. Luke juxtaposes these two birth narratives as a way of ordering his Gospel, linking Jesus to the Hebrew prophets through the prophetic ministry of John the Baptist, who embodied the "spirit and power of Elijah" (Luke 1:17).[6] John's father, Zechariah, prophesied that his son would be called a "prophet of the Most High; / for [he] will go before the Lord to prepare his ways" (1:76). John the Baptist proclaimed a "baptism of repentance for the forgiveness of sins. . . . 'The one who is more powerful than I is coming after me; I am not worthy to stoop down and untie the thong of his sandals. I have baptized you with water; but he will baptize you with the Holy Spirit'" (Mark 1:4, 7-8). John the Baptist was in a long line of Hebrew prophets, proclaiming the coming Messiah. Yet, even during John's life, when Jesus proclaims repentance and judgment, you can hear the refrain of repentance from John's song. From playing together in their youth to their own ministerial beginnings, Jesus and John the Baptist were in ongoing improvisational dialogue. Jesus would finish the song, announcing a new age, which they had begun to sing together.[7]

Jesus the Galilean Jew

As jazz music was born of the impoverished sorrow of a blues people in the American South, Jesus' song of shalom was born in a poor Jewish community in Galilee on the outer margins of the Roman Empire (Mark 1:10). Galilean Jews were despised by Jerusalem Jews and were considered culturally inferior because they were from the country, had thick accents, lived in a multicultural area, and did not practice the law by a strict standard.[8] As a Galilean Jew, Jesus grew up experiencing poverty and persecution. Because of their meager income, his parents, Joseph and Mary, took two turtledoves to the temple, the sacrifice allowed for those who could not afford to sacrifice a sheep (Luke 2:24; Lev 12:8). As a result of his family's poverty, Jesus grew up with a deep empathic identification with the plight of other poor people. His prophetic imagination was captured by the prophet's call to Israel to care for widows, orphans, strangers, and the poor (Zech 7:9-10).

Jesus deepened this Jewish tradition of loving the other. While the Torah and the Prophets called Israel to love and justice, Jesus Christ embodied this love and justice of God. Jesus' life narrates what the love and justice of God look like in one singular life dedicated to building a nomadic movement of love and justice. Jesus expressed his prophetic ministry in three primary ways: teaching people about the kingdom of God, healing and exorcising the sick and possessed, and leading the community into faithful feasting. These three charisms (melodies) of Jesus' ministry — teacher, healer, and holy feaster — will be discussed in this chapter with special attention to the Gospel of Luke.

In Luke's Gospel Jesus "jazzes" a new song of shalom, improvising on the song of Israel. Good jazz, transformative jazz, takes old standards and moves them forward into a new place. Coltrane, on *My Favorite Things,* took the popular tune "These are a few of my favorite things" and transformed it into a totally new expression. Listening, one recognizes the song not just from the title. All through his playing, one can discern familiar cadences and echoes of the original Rogers and Hammerstein classic; Coltrane gives us musical metalepsis. It is the musicians' mystical rootedness in the tradition that frees up their creative voice to make something new. Knowing the tradition well gives them an improvisational "gut feeling" of how to move the song forward through the extemporaneous moment. In this creative apex they participate in the creative energies of God; their new song is of the *creatio continua.* Improvisation in the Spirit is releasing the taproot of our creative energies to God's glory.

With the Spirit of improvisation, Jesus, as jazz musician, took the sometimes-uncomfortably familiar shalom-standards of the prophets, of Abraham, Sarah, and Hagar; of Moses and Miriam; of Isaiah and Micah, and played them before Rome and Israel in a bold and unique way. Sure, *mishpat, sedaqah,* and *hesed* were some the prophets' favorite things, but here Jesus "sang" that *justice, righteousness,* and *steadfast love* were central to breaking out of the imperial Roman Empire that Israel was trapped in — this was the *only* way forward.

We feel as if we are listening to a new song, coming from musicians who know deeply and intimately the chords and notes of the original tune. Like Coltrane, who transformed a familiar but different expression, Jesus took the words of Abraham, Moses, and Isaiah and improvised them so that we hear echoes of ancient music, but in the form of a new song.

Shalom Justice: The Song of the Kingdom of God

Jesus, the Jewish prophet, proclaims and embodies the message of shalom justice. He understands his identity and mission as a continuation of the prophets of Israel (Mark 8:27-28; Luke 24:19; 13:33-34). While the song of Israel anticipated God's coming reign of righteousness, Jesus announces that God's reign is here and now.[9]

"The *basileia* of God has come near to you," proclaims Jesus of Nazareth (Luke 10:9, 11). In the Greek, *basileia* was the word for kingdom. In empire-critical studies of the New Testament there is a growing consensus that the term *basileia tou theou,* "kingdom of God," was intentionally deployed as a critique of the imperial pretensions of the Roman monarchical kingdom. Because "kingdom of God" has monarchical and patriarchal connotations in modern English, some theologians suggest replacing this language with "reign of God" or "kin-dom." I maintain the translation "kingdom of God" because of its explicit critique of any earthly empire's claims to absolute power; however, I repudiate the language of the "kingdom of God" being used in patriarchal and monarchical ways to oppress women, people of color, and the poor.[10]

The kingdom of God is the righteous reign of God, on earth as it is in heaven, unveiled in the presence of Jesus Christ. This reign is God-centered, rooted in the Hebrew notion of *malkut shamayim,* which literally means the "sole sovereignty of the heavens," expressing the sovereignty of God.[11] Throughout his ministry, Jesus improvises on *malkut shamayim* through his teaching of the kingdom, arguing that God's "sole sovereignty of the heavens" has claimed "sole sovereignty on earth."

Jesus' proclamation of the kingdom unveils that what is coming to pass from heaven is overtaking what is passing away on earth (1 Cor 7:31). In the life span of Jesus of Nazareth a new socioeconomic order is born. Jesus' earthly life offers a promissory presence for the coming of a fundamentally just and compassionate future.

Jesus' song of salvation hearkens back to the prophets' songs of Jubilee. Jesus sang the song of Israel for his solo in the synagogue:

> "The Spirit of the Lord is upon me,
> because he has anointed me
> to bring good news to the poor.
> He has sent me to proclaim release to the captives
> and recovery of sight to the blind,
> to let the oppressed go free,
> to proclaim the year of the Lord's favor." (Luke 4:18-19)

After he reads the scroll of Isaiah, he rolls it up and sits down. All eyes are fixed on him. The Jews gathered want commentary, they want an explanation, and they want a sermon. But after a pregnant pause, Jesus tells them, "Today this scripture has been fulfilled in your hearing" (4:21).

This first "sermon" demonstrates many things. First, we see Jesus unveil his messianic identity through arguing that Isaiah's prophecy has been fulfilled in that very moment of its reading. Jesus proclaims and embodies the year of God's favor to the poor, the oppressed, the sick, and the imprisoned. With echoes of the trumpet of Jubilee justice of old, Jesus blows the horn of justice inaugurating a new socioeconomic order. Through enacting this Isaiah vision Jesus' prophetic song echoes Mary's Magnificat and John the Baptist's song of repentance. His proclamation is heard as good news by the poor who have been longing for release from their captivity. Jesus' ministry of release entails forgiveness of sins and economic debts, as well as freeing the afflicted from the demonic and social chains that bind them.[12]

When Jesus reads this scroll he is not merely reading words, but is performing a personal reception of the Spirit of the Lord that is anointing him in that moment. In hearing Jesus sing his first public solo, the Jews gathered in the synagogue that day experience the first messianic performance. The difference between Jesus and the Hebrew prophets is that Jesus is the fulfillment of Hebrew prophecy in his very person. Jesus Christ "is the Prophet who knows and proclaims the will of God which is done in His existence."[13] Jesus fulfills Hebrew prophecy not simply because he says he does, but because he concretely acts out the prophecy in an improvisational performance of the shalom justice of God.

Jesus proclaimed the year of the Lord's favor, choosing the Isaiah scroll as his first sermon to announce the apocalyptic realization of Jubilee justice (Lev 25:8-10). I follow André Pascal Trocmé's notion that Jesus' proclaiming the Year of Jubilee in his first Nazareth sermon should be taken seriously as characterizing his message as socioeconomic "good news."

Trocmé described Jesus' teaching of the kingdom as a "nonviolent revolution" that was a particular kind of eschatology in realization. The kingdom of God was no longer seen as a theocracy "out there" in the future, but as a socioeconomic order that was coming into being "here and now." Jesus was calling the people of God to follow him in establishing love and justice "on earth as it is in heaven." Jesus' teaching of the kingdom had concrete political and economic consequences.[14]

Within Jesus' historic context, his teaching of the kingdom was heard as good news to the poor but bad news to the Romans. Given the history of the Davidic kingdom within Judaism, Jesus' kingdom teaching was heard as politically subversive — the kingdom of God was greater than the kingdom of Rome. Jesus announced that God's reign was becoming manifest amidst the Roman claims of complete imperial control.[15] In contrast to the Roman Empire's focus on the wealth and power of the elite, Jesus' teaching of the kingdom advocated an egalitarian vision of economic justice for all people.[16] Throughout his ministry Jesus continually identified with those on the underside of the Roman Empire — the hungry, the thirsty, the stranger, and the naked (Matt 25:40). His teaching of the kingdom tells a story of an economic order where all people's basic human needs will be cared for.

The politics of Jesus challenged the politics of Rome.[17] Jesus commandeered the language of the Roman Empire and redirected it to the divine Son of God, the source of true, ultimate authority. Titles used of Jesus like "Son of God," "Lord," and "Savior of the World" were used of Caesar Augustus within the Roman Empire. Jesus' taking on the titles of the emperor would have been seen as a political threat to the Roman Empire. In our contemporary American context, it would be like saying Jesus is president.[18]

Jesus' messianic identity placed him in conflict with the ruling authorities of Rome and the Jewish temple in Jerusalem. Through encounter with Jesus' interpretation of the kingdom, as the *basileia tou theou,* Jesus' early disciples were forced into an identity crisis. They had to discern how to live their lives completely aligned to the vision and values of Jesus, while also fulfilling their responsibilities to both traditional Judaism and the Roman government, which increasingly colluded with each other. One of the ways the Roman government and the Jewish temple colluded was through demanding excessive taxes that forced most of the Galilean Jews into severe debt.[19] When asked if the Jews should pay their taxes to Rome, Jesus retorted, "Give to the emperor the things that are the emperor's, and to God the things that are God's" (Mark 12:17a). While encouraging the Jews to pay their taxes, Jesus was clear that it was the living God, not *mammon,* who should be given ultimate and ongoing allegiance. While Rome sought to possess the Jews' money, Jesus exhorted the Jews to guard against Rome possessing their soul. That so many of Israel had been possessed by the power and authority of Rome, be it with seduction or violence, shows why Jesus would begin to disclose his messianic identity with such a strong emphasis on exorcisms and healings. Believing that he was dealing with authentic supernatural powers, Jesus saw them as active not merely in the individual lives but also deeply nested in the politico-economic and religious structures of his day.

Jesus as Exorcist and Healer

Jesus' healings and exorcisms are enactments of his teaching of the kingdom. Given the power of the demonic world, Jesus spiritually prepares himself for his ministry of release (Luke 4:18-19). After Jesus is baptized by John the Baptist, he goes into the wilderness for forty days of preparation for his ministry. In the wilderness Jesus commits himself to fasting, roots himself deeply in prayer, and surrenders his heart to his *Abba,* praying for the fiery passion of the prophets. When Satan comes to try and seduce Jesus to turn a rock into a roll, he is met with jazzlike agility; Jesus returns with the well-known "It is written, 'One does not live by bread alone'" (Luke 4:4).

Satan is a cunning adversary; using bread much like the forbidden fruit, Satan attempts to get Jesus to discover how easy it is to empower the self without recourse to the divine. Yet the risk that Jesus shrewdly sees is that human-oriented empowerment is only a death, a self-binding in the sleepy nap of a full belly. In relying on "every word that comes from the mouth of the Lord" (Deut 8:3) instead of his own ability to transform stones, Jesus avoids recapitulating injustice and unrighteousness. Instead we see one of his first expressions of creativity in the Spirit, *creatio continua:* jazz.

While Jesus travels throughout Galilee teaching the "sole sovereignty of heaven," the inauguration of YHWH's socioeconomic order, he also dramatically embodies and performs the *basileia* song through several powerful exorcisms and healings. The new order will become manifest only through a direct confrontation with the powers. As Ched Myers argues, Jesus' exorcisms and healings, in addition to bringing physical restoration to the afflicted, also function as symbolic critiques of the ruling powers of Jewish life.[20] Luke gracefully interweaves "authority" with "teaching" into a colorful and provocative tapestry in order to separate Jesus' teaching from the teachings of the Jewish scribes and scholars of his day. Within the scribal culture of the day, the notion of teaching, especially when coupled with authority, could rightly be construed as power, particularly political power. Jesus engages in direct encounters with all pretenders to the throne, whether their power plays are political, physical, or spiritual.

Having overcome forty days in the wilderness and thus taken the authority to proclaim release, Jesus enters the arena of village life in Galilee, where the pretenders play, and begins not only to speak out but also to physically enact his kingdom reign. The first action he performs after his announcement of *releasing captives* (Luke 4:18-19) is exorcising a man with an "unclean demon" in the synagogue at Capernaum (4:31-37). Luke sets up the encounter with a clear focus upon power. This exorcism takes place in a synagogue, the seat of religio-political power in the village. In this scene Jesus is brought face-to-face with an evil spirit. The spirit seems shocked and expresses visceral fear at Jesus' presence, saying, "Let us alone! What have you to do with us, Jesus of Nazareth? Have you come to destroy us? I know who you are, the Holy One of God." The encounter is a showdown; the demon recognizes divine power in Jesus and is threatened by his new, commanding authority. Jesus does not even allow a fight; he silences the demon and orders him out. Jesus demonstrates his authority through both his teaching (4:31-32) and his exorcising the unclean demon (4:36). Jesus' ministry of *releasing captives* is a ministry of resurrection; he brings liberation and resurrection life to places of captivity and death. Jesus is bringing the life-giving waters of renewal back to the Jewish faith.

After this exorcism, Jesus heals Simon's mother-in-law and then eats a meal at the house (4:38-39). At sunset, everyone who is sick in the village comes to Jesus and he heals them (4:40-41). At daybreak the next day Jesus travels to a deserted place for prayerful retreat (4:42). To summarize, in Jesus' first day of ministry in Capernaum, there is an exorcism in the synagogue in the morning, feasting in the afternoon, and the healing of the sick into the dark of night. We see this rhythm of teaching, feasting, and healing throughout Jesus' prophetic ministry. These three forms of ministry embody Jesus' ministry of *releasing the captives* — a ministry of resurrection.

What we have here are the three main expressions of the authority of Jesus, authority over spiritual powers and principalities, authority over physical ailments, and authority to gather people for meals, all three subversive practices aimed at the political powers that have failed time and time again to demonstrate the *dynamos* of the *malkut shamayin*.

Jesus' exorcisms and healings are a dramatic embodiment of a new form of prophetic action, offering the promise of a new socioeconomic order. The oppressive socioreligious system of the day had turned the song of Israel into a heavy, concussive symphony, blasting forth across the countryside as if no one were really listening. Jesus' prophetic intervention at this musical moment is disruptive. It is as if Jesus walks onto the stage, breaks the conductor's baton, and silences the symphony orchestra. Then Jesus pulls out his saxophone and plays a new song, with echoes of the motifs of the orchestra, but played in a jazzlike idiom. Some of the musicians in the orchestra recognize Jesus' musical brilliance and begin to play with him, while others pack up their instruments and go home.

Jesus' song is a call to Israel. With echoes of the prophets of old, Jesus sings a new song. He calls disciples to join his messianic movement of love and justice. Instead of calling scribes and teachers, he calls disciples from the margins of Galilee — fisherfolk and tax collectors (Luke 5:1-11, 27-32; 6:12-16). After calling his disciples, Jesus heals a man with leprosy (5:12-16). According to Jewish law, the lepers were unclean and unapproachable. They were destined to a life outside of the community, completely alone (Lev 13:46). Those who touched them would also be unclean until nightfall (Num 19:22). By touching the leper, Jesus fully embraces the sick person, even at the risk of becoming a leper himself.

Jesus also heals a man born blind (John 9:1-3). Yet, Jesus not only gives him physical sight, he also gives him spiritual sight to see his messianic identity. Jesus wants to heal bodies *and* souls, our whole humanity. Through these healings and exorcisms Jesus dismantles the barriers that have kept the afflicted from offering their full gifts to the cultivation of their communities. Healings and exorcisms are metaphors of the reality of the *basileia tou theou.* In a world where humans are bent and broken, Jesus says "Come unto me; I will heal you and give you rest." The healing that Jesus brings to individuals is part of a broader ministry of establishing shalom in the cities across Galilee.

Galilee was under Roman occupation, with a strong and constant presence of Roman soldiers stationed throughout the region. When Jesus arrived in the country of the Gerasenes, he met a demon-possessed man who was homeless, living in the tombs on the outskirts of town (Luke 8:26-39). The man was wild and could not be bound by chains. He even injured himself, cutting himself up with rocks. The community was scared of this man on the outer margins of their community.

Jesus has compassion on the Gerasene demoniac. Jesus asks him his name and he responds, "Legion," for many demons had entered him. Jesus casts the demon Legion from the Gerasene demoniac, sending it into pigs, who drown in the sea. During that time the name Legion would have immediately called to mind the legions of the Roman army, like the infamous Tenth Legion. By calling this demon by name, Jesus is not only saving a demon-possessed man but also critiquing the Roman political occupation and the oppression that had developed in its wake. The exorcism becomes a parable that unveils the brutal violence of the Roman army that traumatized the Jews of Galilee. During a colonial occupation, the colonized people often internalize self-hatred and begin to act out in self-destructive ways. In this exorcism Jesus clearly identifies the Roman legions as the oppressors, and offers a parable of restoration of the oppressed. After being healed, the man from Gerasa becomes an evangelist, "proclaiming throughout the city how much Jesus had done for him" (8:39).[21] Every person that Jesus heals becomes a new leader in the messianic movement for love and justice.

As Jesus heals and exorcises, he also is forming a new generation of Spirit-filled leaders who can continue his prophetic ministry when he is gone. Jesus passes on to his disciples the power he has over the demonic world. When the seventy disciples joyfully return to Jesus after being sent on their first mission, Jesus says to them, "I watched Satan fall from heaven like a flash of lightning" (Luke 10:18). Jesus has received a prophetic vision concerning the descent of Satan. Writes René Girard, "Evidently he falls to earth, and he will not remain inactive. Jesus does not announce the immediate end of Satan, not yet at least. It is rather the end of his false transcendence, his power to restore order through his false accusations, the end of scapegoating."[22]

After affirming his spiritual authority over Satan, Jesus imparts his disciples with the power of the Spirit to energize their ministries: "See, I have given you authority to tread on snakes and scorpions, and over all the power of the enemy; and nothing will hurt you. Nevertheless, do not rejoice at this, that the spirits submit to you, but rejoice that your names are written in heaven" (10:19-20). The disciples are not to be arrogant about their spiritual power, but are to use it wisely as they proclaim and embody the kingdom of God. There is a spiritual struggle at large in society between Jesus' kingdom and the kingdom of the prince of the air. Being heralds of the just and peaceable kingdom means being prepared to exorcise demons from possessed bodies and sinful institutions.

Jesus encounters a crippled woman while teaching in the synagogue on the Sabbath (13:10-17). He lays his hands on this woman, who was bent over, and prays for her, and she immediately stands up straight. The leader of the synagogue rebukes Jesus since the law forbade healing on the Sabbath (Exod 20:9-10; Deut 5:13-14). While Jesus knows the rhythm and rules of the Sabbath, he improvises in this situation in order to restore this woman to full health. Jesus' ministry of release includes direct confrontation with Satan: "Ought not this woman, a daughter of Abraham whom Satan bound for eighteen long years, be set free from this bondage on the sabbath day?" (Luke 13:16).

This healing of the crippled woman on the Sabbath echoes Jesus' earlier healing of a man whose right hand was withered, even though the scribes and the Pharisees were dismayed (Luke 6:6-11). The Psalms say,

> If I forget you, O Jerusalem,
> let my right hand wither! (Ps 137:5)

Jesus' healing of this man with a withered hand becomes a metaphor for the restoration of Israel. As Israel is restored, we will see restoration of the shalom in the community of creation. Jesus is restoring blessing to the house of Israel so that Israel can fulfill its destiny promised to Abraham that his family would be a blessing to the families of the world (Gen 12:1-3). Through healing on the Sabbath, Jesus claims his authority as the Messiah, revealing the true intent of the Sabbath — rest, renewal, and restoration of shalom within the community of creation.

Exorcisms are songs of victory over the devil and his mission of destruction. As Jesus sings songs of victory, he demonstrates the power of the Spirit of God against the satanic forces of darkness.[23] The struggle for righteousness is against the very cosmic powers of darkness and spiritual forces of evil (Eph 6:12). From Hendrikus Berkhof to Walter Wink, a growing group of biblical interpreters argue that these "powers and principalities" are also manifest in the institutional structures of society.[24] The struggle against the powers and principalities is both a spiritual and an earthly struggle; Jesus seeks not only to redeem individuals, but also to redeem the structures of institutional power like the synagogue. The ministry of healing entails a healing of the socioeconomic order.[25]

Throughout his ministry, his healings and exorcisms are signs of the new creation. Jesus' healing miracles demonstrate his compassionate concern for the physical body, while his exorcisms are warnings to all spirits of the air and powerful institutions that Jesus, and Jesus alone, is the Lord of

Creation. Jesus' healings and exorcisms are integral to the formation of a new community — a new social body of disciples who live together in a prophetic community as a critique of the politics of power, be they from far-off Rome, or closer to home.

Luke is clear; Jesus' jazz is a song of power — the power of love to overcome any obstacle. Jesus' song is not meant only for the virtuoso; Jesus is not merely playing jazz, but teaching it to others. The disciples, too, have authority to teach, to heal, to exorcise, to empower and invite others to create their own jazz music, and in so doing, to be bound together in a community, a community that listens deeply and closely to the needs of the people and not merely to the desires of the ruling class. One of the ways the wisdom of love is passed on is through faithful feasting.

Faithful Feasting: "Jesus Welcomes Sinners and Eats with Them"

Luke demonstrated with meticulous detail how Jesus Christ welcomed sinners, healed the sick, fed the hungry, and preached good news to the poor.[26] In Luke's Gospel of the good news to the poor, salvation has both a spiritual and a social dimension.[27] One of the ways that Jesus demonstrates that social dimension of the good news is through the practice of faithful feasting.[28]

Luke's Gospel follows a ritual rhythm based on Jesus' breaking bread with others. "In Luke's Gospel Jesus is either going to a meal, at a meal, or coming from a meal," writes Robert J. Karris.[29] What do we make of this? If Jesus is interested in interventions that facilitate power shifts, the in-breaking of the kingdom, then why is he so often caught between feasts? Ought Jesus be attending more fully to the face-to-face showdowns of power, teaching, and authority, as with the exorcisms and healings? Why is breaking bread with the other so integral to his prophetic ministry?

The act of feasting, for Jesus, is a transformational improvisation upon both the act of exorcism and the act of healing, taking the old song of division and jazzing it up to inspire the embodiment of a prophetic egalitarian community. Jesus' meals with sinners and tax collectors subvert the cultural hierarchies of his day (Mark 2:16). In this way, Jesus wields a more radical power and authority than other religious teachers, and can not only critique the seemingly staid places of power and oppression in society but also effect real change in them.

Throughout his ministry, Jesus often invites those rejected by the world to join him for a meal. Since Jesus sees value in people whom the world sees as without value, he improvises and crosses the established boundaries of Jewish ritual meals. The people whom the Jewish laws deem unclean and sinful are precisely the people Jesus came to save.

Jesus' parable of the great dinner illustrates his commitment to eating with those on the margins of society (Luke 14:15-24; Matt 22:1-14). In this parable a rich man invites many guests to come to a dinner party, but they all make excuses for not being able to attend. So the rich man asks his slave to go out on the streets and invite "the poor, the crippled, the blind, and the lame" (Luke 14:21). Through this parable, Jesus is calling his followers to feed the poor with generosity and respect: "When you give a luncheon or a dinner, do not invite your friends or your brothers or your relatives or rich neighbors, in case they may invite you in return, and you would be repaid. But when you give a banquet, invite the poor, the crippled, the lame, and the blind" (14:12-13). These people of low status in the society are the ones Jesus is encouraging his followers to focus their ministry on. Eating with the least of these is a radical act of hospitality.

Jesus' feasts are subversive encounters. He intentionally eats with people of all walks of life, especially the poor, marginalized, and disinherited. His encounter eating with those on the margins turns the cultural hierarchy on its head. When Jesus encounters impure people on the margins of society, instead of segregating himself from them, he breaks bread with them. Jesus' improvisational ethic allows him to constantly insinuate himself into the preexisting political, religious, even psychic structures of the poor, transforming those structures to be more fundamentally loving and just. Through exchanging his heart with the rabble of society, Jesus creates the conditions for the great inversion his mother sang about to materialize.

Jesus does not avoid meals with Pharisees, though they wish to entrap him. Instead, he turns the trap they set for him back onto them. He does not deny eating with tax collectors and sinners, but uses the table as a place to imagine what the *basileia tou theou* looks like from their perspective. When the poor and the sick are gathered in the countryside, he does not disperse them to go and find food, but multiplies the food for them, a jazzlike riff on the manna that kept Israel alive during their wilderness wandering.

Along the highways and byways of Galilee, Jesus' subversive feasts with sinners and tax collectors facilitate an intimacy with those on the underside. These subversive feasts inspire small, underground communities that are akin to jazz clubs like Smalls in New York City, a small basement performance space with no stage that facilitates an intimacy between the musicians and the audience. In a like manner, Jesus' feasts with the least of these foster subversive intimacy that is the basis of revolutionary friendship. By breaking social conformities and eating with people we are not supposed to, we are faithful to the true inclusive intention of faithful feasting — transgression for shalom justice. Faithful feasts are places of creativity and celebration — spaces of hope! What jazz club is staid, dispassionate, repressive, or empty? Are they not fonts of musical subversion, intimate fellowship, and liberating places of festival?

Jesus eats with both mysterious strangers and dear friends. After Jesus had entered Jerusalem, he gathered his disciples for a final meal. The Twelve gathered, including the one who would betray him. They broke bread together, drank wine, reminisced, laughed, and cried. However, there comes a time when coercion loses its strategic value and direct action is required. In this last feast, Jesus lifts up the inverted logic of divine power — *kenosis* — self-emptying on behalf of the other. Revolutionary power in life is found only in living for something worth dying for, or as Jesus exampled, dying for something worth living for. N. T. Wright writes, "The Last Supper was Jesus' own alternative symbol, the kingdom-feast, the new exodus. . . . Jesus would defeat evil by letting it do its worst to him."[30]

Jesus lived his life with vigilance, embodying the kingdom and inaugurating a kingdom of God movement. But this kingdom was not like kingdoms of this world built on gaining more financial power, more military force, and more colonial expansion. Christ's kingdom was based on emptying oneself into shalom justice, emptying oneself into practical pacifism, and emptying oneself into neighbor love. During the Last Supper, as Jesus shares bread and wine with his disciples, he says, "This is my body, which is given for you. Do this in remembrance of me. . . . This cup that is poured out for you is the new covenant in my blood" (Luke 22:19-20). At this moment of intimacy with his disciples in the Last Supper, we see that at its heart the feast is a ritual where we share our hearts with each other. Through the physical and emotional sustenance of the feast we are prepared for the costly walk of discipleship.

The Jesus Way: Costly Discipleship

"When Christ calls a man, He bids him come and die. It may be a death like that of the first disciples who had to leave home and work to follow

Him, or it may be a death like Luther's, who had to leave the monastery and go out into the world. But it is the same death every time — death in Jesus Christ, the death of the old man at his call," writes Dietrich Bonhoeffer.[31] Being a disciple of Jesus demands a complete surrender of your life. This may be giving up what you think your dreams and aspirations are, but it also may mean holy martyrdom.

After Peter confessed that Jesus was "the Messiah of God" (Luke 9:20), Jesus told his disciples, "The Son of Man must undergo great suffering, and be rejected by the elders, chief priests, and scribes, and be killed, and on the third day be raised. . . . If any want to become my followers, let them deny themselves and take up their cross daily and follow me" (9:22-23). While the disciples and the Jewish people expected the Messiah to be an earthly warrior, Jesus reminded them of the blue note of Hebrew prophecy where the promised one would be a suffering servant (Isa 53:3). Jesus took up his cross on a torturous trek to Golgotha to give his life for the salvation of the world. Jesus' way of the cross beckons his disciples to take up their cross and follow him unto the path of suffering and strife (Luke 14:27-33).

"When the days drew near for him to be taken up, he set his face to go to Jerusalem" (Luke 9:51), for within the walls of that city the destiny of Jesus and the world would be unveiled. After preaching throughout the villages, hamlets, and towns of Galilee, he turned his focus to the city with the temple. From growing up in marginal Jewish existence in Galilee to journeying to Jerusalem, Jesus moved from the periphery to the center with revolutionary verve and prophetic punch.

Jesus entered Jerusalem upon a donkey, fulfilling the prophecy of Zechariah:

> Rejoice greatly, O daughter Zion!
>   Shout aloud, O daughter Jerusalem!
> Lo, your king comes to you;
>   triumphant and victorious is he,
> humble and riding on a donkey,
>   on a colt, the foal of a donkey. (Zech 9:9)

While a king in the ancient Near East would ride a warhorse into town during a period of protracted war, during periods of peace it was common for him to ride into town on a colt.[32] This royal symbolism was not lost on the Jews of Jerusalem, as Jesus' disciples loudly proclaimed,

"Blessed is the king
who comes in the name of the Lord!" (Luke 19:38)

These shouts of "Hosanna" would have been heard in the Jerusalem of that period as "Long live the king" or "God save the king."[33] Furthermore, Jesus' entry into Jerusalem is a parody of the victorious entry that Pilate made into Jerusalem every Passover from Caesarea Maritima. Jesus rides into Jerusalem claiming his authority as Messiah — not as warlord, but rather as a Prince of Peace (Isa 9:6).

Jesus' entrance during the Passover festival is immediately perceived as a threat by both the Jewish religious establishment and the Roman military. Popular insurgents often surfaced during the Passover feast, which was an electric time in Jerusalem, as thousands of Jews pilgrimaged to the city and Roman soldiers were out in full strength.[34] Some Pharisees ask Jesus to stop his disciples, but Jesus quotes the prophet Habakkuk:

The very stones will cry out from the wall,
and the plaster will respond from the woodwork. (Hab 2:11)

This prophetic phrase caught both the festive fervency in the air around Jesus' messianic procession and the prophetic critique of the way in which even the very architecture of the city ("the very stones" and "the plaster") was weary of being a place of oppression and yearned for something new.

In this mobile, musical street drama, Jesus and his followers occupy Jerusalem. They place their bodies in public places, converting the public space into a celebratory festival. Street theater presents opportunities to make public declarations to the powers that the spirit of Jubilee justice is being resurrected in Jerusalem's streets. Stanley P. Saunders and Charles L. Campbell write of Jesus' royal entry: "We should probably imagine the event accompanied not by a drum roll and a precision marching band, but by a group of raucous New Orleans jazz musicians."[35] This passionate procession simultaneously subverts both the pretensions of the Roman Empire and the expectations of Jewish messianism. The royal entry makes an undeniable jest at the empire before the watchful eyes of Pontius Pilate and his legions, yet it also rebuffs the high priests and scribes through its distinct lack of pomp and circumstance.

The Hebrew prophets had sung the song of Israel for centuries, calling Jerusalem to return to right worship of the living God. Yet Jerusalem did not always heed their prophetic word, often casting them out and sometimes killing them. Jesus seems to see martyrdom as an inevitable outcome for himself when he laments, "'I must be on my way, because it is impossible for a prophet to be killed outside of Jerusalem.' Jerusalem, Jerusalem, the city that kills the prophets and stones those who are sent to it!" (Luke 13:33-34). Jesus expresses deep lament over the hard heart of Jerusalem because of his deep love for her. Jesus sees Jerusalem's destiny as a city of shalom, but is disheartened because she will not surrender herself completely to the way of *mishpat* and *hesed.*

Jesus also laments over Jerusalem when he prays on the Mount of Olives (22:39-46). That night he struggles in deep and anguished prayer. With the company of his disciples he tries to press into the heart of the Father, but is abandoned in a dark abyss of terrifying loneliness. He prays, "Father, if you are willing, remove this cup from me; yet, not my will but yours be done" (22:42). He tells his disciples to stand watch, but they fall asleep. Abandoned and lonely, Jesus forges on through that dark night of the soul because of his allegiance to God and abiding love for humanity.

In the dark of the night a mob come for him (22:47-53). Judas runs up to Jesus, betraying him with a kiss. As the officers of the temple police apprehends Jesus, Peter the Zealot lashes out in violence. With the swing of his sword he chops off the right ear of a slave of the high priest. Peter's resort to violence gives Jesus the opportunity to teach Peter that the kingdom of God is a *nonviolent* revolution. Jesus tells Peter, "Put your sword back into its place; for all who take the sword will perish by the sword" (Matt 26:52). At this moment, Jesus chastens the hot-blooded zealot who is ready to roll for a strong-armed insurrection. The Jesus Way is not the way of violence, but the way of shalom justice. Jesus embodies God's shalom by touching the ear of the slave and healing him (Luke 22:51).

The powers of the Roman Empire and the Jewish religious establishment colluded in Jesus Christ's death-bound destiny. Jesus' execution and death *sub Pontio Pilato* name the historic moment that he was killed in the Roman Empire. Pilate eventually delivered Jesus up to be crucified as the assembly accused Jesus of "perverting [their] nation, forbidding [them] to pay taxes to the emperor, and saying that he himself is the Messiah" (Luke 23:2). Jesus was sentenced to a death by crucifixion.

On the road to Calvary, Jesus was spit upon, insulted, mocked, and beaten. The tortured One marched from Jerusalem to Golgotha, the place of the skull. When Jesus' strength failed, Simon of Cyrene picked up his cross and carried it, embodying Christ's call to his disciples to carry their own crosses (14:27-33). When they reached the top of the place of the skull, the Roman soldiers crucified Jesus on a cross between two insurgents (23:26-43).

At the height of his pain and suffering, Jesus showed mercy on the Roman soldiers who crucified him, praying, "Father, forgive them" (23:34). In this prayer of forgiveness we see a subversion of the violent logic of Roman colonial hegemony. For Jesus to offer not merely direct forgiveness, but earnest intercession, was a demonstration that even at the threshold of death, Jesus had the ability to demonstrate loving service. In this act of forgiveness, the cycle of violence, fear, and malediction was radically broken. The powers of hate could not maintain a grasp on him.

The demonic forces at work in the grim social solidarity produced by such public sacrifices were confounded by Jesus' merciful response; not only was he breaking the cycle of violence begetting violence, he also was courageously proclaiming a new reality of grace and shalom to those who would bloody his Jewish flesh for the sake of the Roman state. Jesus' forgiving his murderers was an act of improvisation in the Spirit. In a word, this was jazz: on the cross we see a man who loves his enemies, forgives his murderers, gives his cloak to the naked, comforts a thief, cares for his mother, prays for those who despitefully use him, and dies with a stout heart — unveiling a Love Supreme.

The iron logic of the cross stood in opposition to Jesus' loving improvisation. The cross was a form of torture and execution in the Roman Empire. To maintain the *pax Romana,* the Romans used crucifixion as a form of large-scale social control.[36] Crucifixions were public spectacles that instilled fear in the hearts of the Jews and others who were subjects under Roman occupation. Through the power of spectacle, Roman leaders could satiate their subjects with violence. The brutal torture of bloody bodies found guilty of sedition transformed the dangerous crowd into sedated spectators. Rome's political theater formed docile subjects, while the *pax Romana* continued unbroken.

Roman crucifixions were theaters of oppression that Jesus turned into a theater *of* and *for* the oppressed. On the cross that Jesus died on, God made a spectacle of the spectacle of Roman imperial ambition. By God becoming a Jewish peasant prophet and dying on a Roman cross, God "disarmed the principalities and powers and made a public example of them, triumphing over them" (Col 2:15 RSV). According to Luke's Gospel, the "principalities and powers" of Jesus day were crystallized in human rulers and regimes (Luke 23:13, 35; 24:20; cf. Acts 4:8-10, 26; 13:27-28). These "principalities and powers" are spiritual forces that take social form in the institutions of society (Col 2:15; Eph 1:20-22).

The fallen angel Satan is the origin of these "principalities and powers." The devil *(diabolos)* is the Greek title for Satan, the Hebrew name of the angel who rebelled against God and fled God's presence. Satan was the seducer in the Garden of Eden and throughout Jesus' earthly ministry. From the start of his ministry to the end, Jesus was in conflict with Satan. According to Luke's Gospel, Jesus spent forty days in the wilderness where he was tempted by Satan (Luke 4:1-13), saw a vision of Satan fall from heaven like a flash of lightning (10:18-20), and proclaimed Satan's hour of dark power shortly before his arrest (22:53). In all four Gospels, Jesus acknowledged Satan as a hostile adversary.

"Prince of This World" was the title that Jesus gave to Satan in the Gospel of John (John 12:31; 14:30; 16:11). Satan's chief purpose is to thwart the purposes of God — Satan is always seeking to seduce people to forget about the living God and God's purposes. One of Satan's most effective strategies was to seduce the leaders of larger institutions, including the Roman *imperium* of Jesus' day. Satan's strategy of institutional takeover proved to be an effective way to aggregate power directed away from worshipful obedience of the living God.

But Satan wanted Jesus. He waited and watched. When Jesus went to the wilderness — alone and in the beginning of his ministry — Satan planned his attack. He would attack Jesus in his most vulnerable places and at the most vulnerable time of his ministry. If Satan could take him out at the start of his ministry, he thought Jesus could never recover. Satan had become a master at testing the faithfulness of the children of God (Gen 3:1-19; 22:1-19; Exod 15:25-26; Job).

In the wilderness, Satan used Scripture to try to persuade Jesus to be unfaithful to his heavenly Father. Satan promised Jesus independence (Luke 4:1-4), adopted sonship (4:5-8), and freedom to deny God's purpose (4:9-12). Satan improvised when seducing the Son of God, thus unveiling the problem with improvisation — sometimes wicked people are the most gifted improvisers; however, Jesus proved to be a more agile interpreter of Scripture and improvisational prophet because he listened and responded to the voice of God.

When Jesus entered Jerusalem at Passover on the back of a colt, Satan saw another ideal opportunity to seduce him to rebel against his Father. During the Passover in Jerusalem, the chief priests and scribes were looking for a way to kill Jesus. When Satan heard this rumbling, he sensed it was time to move and he entered Judas called Iscariot. Then Satan was able to play his role in a plot to kill Jesus that would include Judas's betrayal (Luke 22:1-6). With Jesus dead, Satan, as the "Prince of This World," could continue his reign of terror. The plan worked — Jesus was arrested, convicted, and crucified.

Satan celebrated during Christ's crucifixion. But the suffering, mortal human flesh of Jesus concealed his deity. According to Gregory of Nyssa, God concealed himself in the humanity of Jesus Christ in order to be an attractive lure to capture Satan. Gregory describes this divine lure as a *fishhook:* "through the covering of the flesh the divine power is made accessible, so that the enemy will not take fright at God's appearing and so thwart his plan for us. . . . Hence it was that God, in order to make himself easily accessible to him who sought the ransom for us, veiled himself in our nature. In that way, as it is with greedy fish, he might swallow the Godhead like a fishhook along with the flesh which was the bait."[37] Thus, the human flesh of Jesus Christ is the bait and the divinity is the fishhook that God uses to catch Satan by surprise. In the case of Satan, God conceals naked deity in order to capture him.[38] Thus we see the concealing of the divine nature in the flesh of Christ for a redemptive purpose.

The devil's claim of victory on the cross in the death of Jesus is shown to be a lie on the third day after his death. Mary Magdalene, Joanna, Mary the mother of James, and other women return to the tomb, expecting to find the body of Jesus, but instead encounter a stone that has been rolled away and two men who ask, "Why do you look for the living among the dead? He is not here, but has risen" (Luke 24:5). That risen one would appear to his disciples and proclaim, "Thus it is written, that the Messiah is to suffer and to rise from the dead on the third day, and that repentance and forgiveness of sins is to be proclaimed in his name to all nations, beginning from Jerusalem" (24:46-47).

Jesus Is Victor

Jesus' bodily resurrection demonstrates his power over life and death. Not even the power of death can bind the Son of God. The resurrection decisively demonstrates Jesus' defeat of sin, death, and the devil. By God becoming a Jewish peasant and dying on a Roman cross, God "disarmed the principalities and powers and made a public example of them, triumphing over them" (Col 2:15 RSV). Early Christian theology interpreted the death and resurrection of Jesus as a victory over sin, death, and the devil, a theological vision that Gustaf Aulén refers to as *Christus Victor*.[39]

Irenaeus was one of the first patristic thinkers to develop this theological vision. For him the resurrection is, according to Aulén, "the manifestation of the decisive victory over the powers of evil, which was won on the cross; it is also the starting-point for the new dispensation, for the gift of the Spirit, for the continuance of the work of God in the souls of men 'for the unity and communion of God and man.'"[40] Elsewhere Aulén asks, "For what purpose did Christ come down from heaven?" Irenaeus's answer: "that He might destroy sin, overcome death, and *give life* to man."[41] In Irenaeus's description of Christ's life-giving purpose, we see that *Christus Victor* is not just a *negative* triumph over the powers of sin and death, but a *positive* affirmation of Christ's vivifying victory, a witness to a conquering Savior whose victory opens up streams of living water, who heals our wounds and binds up our broken hearts, who gives us life as a catalyzing, energizing, improvisational force that invigorates and transforms the world. It empowers our spiritual warfare against the political powers. In Jesus' victory through his death and resurrection, those living in darkness can now see a light that truly triumphs over the despair, nihilism, and existential angst that plagues the human soul.

The resurrection of Easter morning expresses that Jesus Christ is a *living* Lord not just for individuals, but for the whole community of creation. The resurrection of Jesus is the "proleptic fulfillment of Israel's great hope."[42] Through the death and resurrection of Jesus Christ, a decisive war was won by Christ over sin, death, and the devil. Those powers were broken *in* time, but for *all* time.

The day of Jesus' resurrection is the first day of the "new creation" (Gal 5:24; 6:14; Rom 6:6). While a new order has arrived, and the unholy principalities and powers have been eschatologically broken, the struggle for life, freedom, and justice continues until its fulfillment in the heavenly city. Between Jesus' rising on the third day and the promise of the new Jerusalem, we live into this Resurrection City here and *now*. Marked by faith, hope, and love in Christ, but also covered in mud, troubled by uncertain leadership, and constantly threatened by the demonic "powers," the struggle for resurrection continues.

CHAPTER FOUR

Freedom Dreams: Thomas Jefferson, Sojourner Truth, and the Promise of Freedom

When the oppressor is no more,
and destruction has ceased,
and marauders have vanished from the land,
then a throne shall be established in steadfast love
in the tent of David,
and on it shall sit in faithfulness
a ruler who seeks justice
and is swift to do what is right.

Isaiah 16:4-5

The greatest analogue of crucifixion in the United States is the lynching tree. "Anyone hung on a tree is under God's curse" (Deut 21:23). James Cone writes, "Theologically speaking, Jesus was the 'first lynchee,' who foreshowed all the lynched black bodies on American soil. He was crucified by the same principalities and powers that lynched black people in America."[1] In *The Cross and the Lynching Tree,* Cone reimagines Christian theology from the underside of history — prophetic black Christianity. From this vantage, the lynching tree, a place of brutal violence, also opens up the possibility of transformation. By affirming that the same "principalities and powers" that lynched Jesus also lynched black people in America, Cone deepens a *Christus Victor* vision.

On the cross, Jesus defeats the powers of evil — sin, death, and the devil. Cone expands this *Christus Victor* vision by connecting Jesus' cross with other crosses in history. Within Jim Crow America, Cone writes, "Every time a white mob lynched a black person, they lynched Jesus."[2] According to this black liberationist perspective, Jesus' crucifixion continues in the crucified people of history.[3]

This prophetic vision stands as a challenge to Christian theology in the Americas; our witness to Christ's resurrection must be subject to the truth of the suffering and struggle of those crucified in the name of Christian colonial expansionism. We need to decolonize Christian theology, resurrecting the spirits of the crucified ones who have been buried in the past, reconstituting the struggle for justice in the present, so we can usher in a prophetic promise of the future.[4]

Historians often speak of the European "discovery" of the New World, but the New World was far from new. It was an existing world for the indigenous people of the Americas, who had long-standing religions and cultures. When the colonists showed up, they stole the land from native people and began a process of colonization that would eventually destroy indigenous people and their folkways. While Christian missionaries from Europe preached Jesus, they were also exporting Western civilization, bringing in its wake capitalism, patriarchy, and white supremacy.

The transatlantic slave trade became a case in point. The origins of the modern world in the Americas are tied to the advent of the slave trade in the transatlantic context. In 1441, Portuguese crusaders captured Africans off the coast of Mauritania, beginning the Atlantic slave trade. In 1502, African slaves were brought to Hispaniola, the first to arrive in the Western Hemisphere. In 1619, about twenty Africans arrived in Jamestown, Virginia, the start of a quickly accelerating slave trade. The flow of ideas and bodies from Europe to Africa to the Americas created the conditions for the emergence of what Paul Gilroy calls "the Black Atlantic."[5]

While Africans came to the Americas as slaves, with time they would rise up to be the prophets of a new age of prophetic Christianity and democracy. Beginning with the first and second Great Awakenings (1740-1820), we see massive conversions to Christianity among African American slaves. Albert Raboteau argues that out of this evangelical revivalism emerged "slave religion," an "invisible institution" on the underside of American history. In time, slave religion would transform American Christianity from within.[6]

Slavery was not only an ethical problem, but also a *theological* one. Christian theology has often been deployed as a white, Western, male enterprise. From the "Pilgrim Fathers" to the Puritan Divines, it was primarily the white male missionaries and ministers of European descent who brought Christianity to the Americas. However, since they also mediated Western cultural values, Christian theology was always embedded within the Western civilization project. What accounting can Christian theology give of its complicity in the genocide of indigenous populations and the enslavement of Africans? How could Native Americans and enslaved Africans accept the "white man's religion"? Given the evils that they suffered, how could a just God allow them to suffer so terribly?

Prophetic Christian theology must unmask the ways that Christian theology and colonization were cobelligerents in furthering the project of Western civilization. Since the transatlantic slave trade exposes the moral contradiction of Christianity in the United States, we need a new historiography of North American Christian movements that begins with the encounter between African Americans and European Americans.

The "black-white encounter" model of American religious history provides a framework that can actively deconstruct Christian theology's whiteness and Western-ness. On the underside of a white Euro-American modernity there emerged a robust tradition of justice-focused Christianity in which racial justice was a central commitment — prophetic black Christianity. Prophetic black Christians transform the Christianity that they received from white missionaries and ministers, redirecting it toward a fuller embodiment of Christianity's prophetic ideals.[7]

The biblical story of Moses bringing the enslaved Jews out of Egypt became central in the theological imagination of African American Christians. While the Declaration of Independence articulated a vision of freedom for the white landowning men of the United States, prophetic Christians sought to push this vision of freedom even further, to include freeing slaves and empowering women to lead and shape the growing nation. The black freedom tradition would facilitate the embodiment of the democratic ideals of the founding fathers. The quest for freedom looks different from the underside of history.

In this chapter I contrast the theo-political visions of Thomas Jefferson (1743-1826) and Sojourner Truth (ca. 1797-1883). Jefferson was animated by the revolutionary ideals of the Declaration of Independence, including "life, liberty, and the pursuit of happiness." He called the American colonies to break from the political power of England, keeping the revolutionary process alive in the Americas. He believed in the power of human rationality and saw religion as a source of social cohesion for the republic. Jefferson found Jesus of Nazareth to be a compelling moral figure who inspired ethical behavior, yet he rejected Jesus' divinity, prophecies, and miracles. Drawing on biblical and democratic traditions, Jefferson formulated a freedom ideal — all humans are entitled to the inalienable rights of life, liberty, and the pursuit of happiness; however, the freedom ideal was difficult for him to realize in his own life because he was a slave owner and depended on their labor to keep his two plantations running. While politically Jefferson thought slaves should be set free, personally he did not have the moral courage to free his own slaves. Jefferson's dilemma is emblematic of a moral contradiction at the heart of the American experience — white male supremacy. The couplet of racism and patriarchy was a perpetual problem that the American empire would have to face throughout its journey, and even faces today.

In contrast to the limits of Jefferson's democratic imagination, Sojourner Truth offered a more radical vision of democratic community. From the subject position of a female slave, she experienced the shadow side of the American empire. Even when she was set free from the dark night of her enslaved state, she continued to struggle internally with the "the burden of acquired and transmitted habits incidental to her past condition of servitude."[8] Upon being freed from slavery, she courageously sought to rescue her children who had been stolen from her. Once she had gathered her family, she set out across the nation to speak about the ravages of slavery. Truth took Christianity to heart and understood that there was a God, a living God who hears, sees, and knows the struggles of African slaves. Jesus was not merely a teacher of ethical wisdom, but was a true friend and ever-present help in a time of need. It was the living God that gave her strength on her nomadic journey toward Resurrection City.

While Jefferson builds a neoclassical city in Charlottesville, Virginia, Truth is in search of Resurrection City wherever she goes. Truth's courageous struggle for freedom unveils the improvisational movement of love and justice. Her attempts to build postslavery communities throughout her journeys offer fragmentary glimpses of what communities of resurrection look like. Sojourner Truth represents the start of a decolonization of Christian theology from its white male "slave owner" image of God. Here theological vision offers the possibility of a prophetic womanist intercultural future.

Thomas Jefferson's Dreams of Freedom

A farmer and statesman from Virginia who was inspired by the French Revolution, Jefferson dreamed of democracy. Jefferson was a visionary leader of the revolutionary freedom movement within the British colonies in America. Through his writing and political leadership, Jefferson advocated a philosophy of freedom for the fledging colonies. In *A Summary View of the Rights of British America,* a tract he wrote in 1774, he laid out a rationale and resolutions for the American colonies to break ties with the British crown, arguing that the colonists were a free people whose inalienable rights derived from the laws of nature and were not established by the chief magistrate. The next year, in March 1775, during the Richmond Convention, Patrick Henry said, "Give me liberty or give me death!" The colonial revolt had begun, and was based on a theological conviction — people's freedom was based on an equality that all humans shared since they were made by one Creator God.

Because of his clear mind and eloquent prose, Jefferson was asked to draft the Declaration of Independence, which held out the promise of universal freedom for the people of this new nation.[9] The Declaration was formally adopted on July 4, 1776, inaugurating a new moment in the American search for democracy. Through his patient and prodding penning of the Declaration, Jefferson sought to inaugurate a new political embodiment of freedom in the Americas. In the editorial process, one of Jefferson's sentences renouncing the institution of slavery as a "cruel war against human nature itself" was removed because of opposition from the colonies of Georgia and South Carolina. Jefferson's democratic imagination saw the moral contradiction in the institution of slavery; however, colonial America, including Jefferson himself, was not ready to dispense with the immoral practice that was quickly building its economy.

One aspect of Jefferson's democratic vision was a fierce commitment to religious freedom. Earlier in the nation's history, Baptist thinker Roger Williams had challenged the Puritan establishment of Massachusetts by arguing that civil authority had no right to rule over the religious beliefs and practices of individuals. Banished from the colony on October 9, 1635, Williams journeyed south to found Rhode Island, where all people, whether Christian or not, whites of European descent or Native Americans, had complete freedom of religious expression without the fear of being coerced by the state. Jefferson continued this tradition, authoring the Virginia Act for Establishing Religious Freedom. His rhetoric of religious freedom was well received by Baptists, pietists, and evangelicals who shared his independent spirit. Yet, while Williams remained moored to the Christian tradition, Jefferson's theology drifted seriously into Deism. Jefferson carried on the Puritan project of establishing a "City on the Hill," but parallel to his secular Christology the biblical vision of the kingdom of God was transposed onto the symbol of a secular city, Charlottesville, Virginia.[10] While Jefferson continued the tradition of Roger Williams, arguing for a clear separation of church and state, in Jefferson's case the break reflected a more severe, modernist perspective.

In Jefferson's Unitarianist Deism we see the seeds of a profound secularization that will cast a dark shadow over the young republic. While Jefferson helped forge a break with Britain, the colonial freedom that was forged still bore the imperial logics of European colonization and a colonial Christology. While the Puritans sought to maintain the vibrancy of a sovereign, living God, Jefferson's Christology marked a significant shift from the Christian Trinitarian idiom toward a more Deistic Unitarian idiom. The secular turn toward Deism was already taking place in seventeenth- and eighteenth-century Europe, at precisely the moment when the thirteen American colonies were being forged into a nation-state.[11]

Jefferson's christological doctrine was forged in the fires of Deism. For Jefferson, Jesus was a historic man who provided an ethical example for humanity to follow; however, Jefferson did not believe that Jesus was the divine Son of God. We see this demonstrated most clearly in the Jefferson Bible, in which he removed all the miracles, healings, exorcisms, and supernatural occurrences. For Jefferson, Jesus becomes a Socratic teacher who shares universal truth with the world. Jefferson's christological vision is problematic because it completely exorcises the supernatural dimension of the Jesus narratives of the Bible, and at the same time is concealing core logics of colonialism. Jefferson replaces the biblical story of the redemption of the people of Israel with the narrative of Continental modernity. Christianity is helpful as Jesus offers good ethical wisdom to live by, but the true well of inspiration lies in the revolutionary movements of Europe.

Jefferson's christological vision is problematic because it completely erases many of the signs of Jesus' "beloved community." The Holy Spirit, working in the world in ways that are not ordinary, inspires prophetic work that a secularized religion cannot. Thus, in Jefferson, we have an ethical religion without the Holy Spirit–breathed power for fueling the prophetic imperative to justice. Without the prophetic imperative of *mishpat* and *hesed,* religion can be ignored or even used to legitimate the racist and patriarchal politics of the American nation and the violence that sustains it.

While Jefferson was inspired by a universal freedom, on the ground in the American colonies the revolution delivered freedom primarily to white, male landowners. Furthermore, the logics of colonization played themselves out on Jefferson's two plantations, Monticello and Poplar Hill, where Jefferson would maintain his own agricultural production based on slave labor.

Monticello, Jefferson's primary residence in Charlottesville, was a "panoptical plantation." Jefferson was inspired by Jeremy Bentham's Panopticon, an architectural design for homes and prisons that allowed for an unseen central point of surveillance. As Michel Foucault points out, the panopticon is a "political technology" in capitalist society. Monticello was built so the surrounding gardens, farmland, and communities could be observed by a single individual, who was not seen by anyone else. Jefferson reinforced the culture of surveillance with his morning horseback ride around the plantation to check up on everything, especially the work of the slaves. There was no question who was the center of power, both in the built architecture and in the daily rituals of the plantation.[12]

The architecture of Monticello also resembled a slave ship. During the transatlantic slave trade, Willie Jennings points out, the slave ship was emblematic of the white colonizers' reconfiguration of space and the commodification of Africans as bodies profitable as labor.[13] The captain of the slave ship, as the absolute authority figure, was analogous to the owner of a plantation in the antebellum South. Like Thomas Jefferson on Monticello, the white man was the absolute authority figure, while enslaved Africans had to improvise to survive. Like a slave ship, Monticello had an observation tower that was analogous to the captain's vantage point on the ship. Some of Jefferson's slaves slept in the basement of Monticello, which was the equivalent of the hold on a ship below the main deck. This same basement collected the refuse from the first indoor toilet installed in America in Jefferson's bedroom. These configurations of space, all of which Jefferson designed, embody the social dominance of white, Western coloniality.

As a plantation owner, Jefferson had the power of life and death over black bodies and lives. However, Jefferson understood the shadow side of this inordinate power. His correspondence with John Adams in 1821 provides a window into Jefferson's fears of a slave revolt, where he writes, "The real question, as seen in the states afflicted with this unfortunate population, is are our slaves to be presented with freedom and a dagger?"[14] Jefferson lived in fear of a slave revolt that could end up killing many white folks, including himself — the slaves had him outnumbered. He recognized the immorality and precariousness of chattel slavery, but was entrenched in the system, unable to free his slaves because of the benefits he was receiving.

Jefferson's benefits were both economic and sexual, as Jefferson's dreams of colonial freedom were entangled with colonial desire.[15] Upon the death of his wife, Martha Wayles Skelton, on September 6, 1782, Jefferson became sexually involved with one of his slaves, Sally Hemings. Jefferson vowed to Martha that he would not remarry; however, he took up a practice that was common in his family in Virginia: white male masters taking on one of their female black slaves as a mistress. The covert deployment of sexuality was one of the ways that the white power establishment in the antebellum South conducted the administration of black bodies and the calculated management of black life. Colonial desire was deployed not just for erotic pleasure, but to increase the population of slaves, to increase the production of slave economies. Colonial desire propelled colonial production, all shrouded in whiteness.

In addition to Jefferson's ethical struggles with slavery, his colonial consciousness played itself out in his acquisition of the Louisiana Territory and its aftermath. Rumors had begun to percolate that Spain was about to cede Louisiana, in Spanish hands since 1762, back to France, its original owner. As president of the United States (1801-9), Jefferson understood the strategic importance of this territory, as three-eighths of the produce of the country had to pass through New Orleans. Through Jefferson's focus and persuasion, Napoleon sold the Louisiana Territory to the United States on April 30, 1803, for fifteen million dollars. While it was a massive acquisition of land for the growing nation, Jefferson's securing the Louisiana Purchase with a racist "Indian policy" in place led to the displacement and death of many of the indigenous tribes of the Americas.[16]

While Jefferson was governor of Virginia (1779-81), he ordered that the Shawnee Indians be removed from their lands. Virginia and Kentucky militia overran villages of Shawnee Indians, displacing them from their ancestral lands to make room for the white male landowners of European descent. Indian removal forced thousands of southeast Indians — the Chickasaw, Choctaw, Creek, Seminole, and Cherokee — west of the Mississippi. More fragmented, less powerful peoples in the northeast — Shawnees, Ottawas, Potawatomis, Sauks, and Foxes — were also removed. Of these other tribes, approximately half would die of disease, starvation, and exposure. Jefferson's "Indian policy" was an expression of a colonial expansionist logic that would eventually lead to the destruction of Native American tribes culminating in the Great Sioux Wars.[17]

While colonial freedom produced a revolutionary break with Britain, its development in the United States was at the expense and death of the bodies of enslaved Africans and Native Americas. Thus, Jefferson enacted the colonial consciousness, through his expansionistic trajectory of the nation. Jefferson's Deistic Christianity offered theological legitimation for this colonial project, including the secularized kingdom of manifest destiny and the deradicalization of Christian ethics. Thus, Jefferson's Christ is reflected in an American image, an image that legitimates patriarchy and white supremacy.

Jefferson's freedom ideal remained a dream for African Americans who were trapped in systems of slavery and segregation. Jeffersonian democracy was built on the broken backs and shed blood of African Americans and Native Americans, peoples that Jefferson saw as inferior. In his *Notes on the State of Virginia,* Jefferson writes, "To our reproach it must be said, that though for a century and a half we have had under our eyes the races of black and of red men, they have never yet been viewed by us as subjects of natural history. Advance it therefore as a suspicion only, that the blacks, whether originally a distinct race, or made distinct by time and circumstances, are inferior to the whites in the endowments both of body and mind."[18]

Critiquing *Notes on the State of Virginia,* David Walker's *Appeal to the Coloured Citizens of the World* (1829) offered a direct assault against Jefferson's racism and the scourge of American slavery.[19] Walker argues that slaves in the Roman Empire were treated better than slaves in the nineteenth-century antebellum South. Walker unveils the hypocrisy in Jefferson's claim that "all men are created equal." If this were the case, Walker contends, then enslaved Africans should be liberated immediately.

David Walker challenges Jefferson's view of history. Walker places black Americans in the larger view of slavery and world history.[20] Walker challenges Jefferson's logic of oppression by calling for black writers themselves to counter Jefferson's claims. "We, and the world wish to see the charges of Mr. Jefferson refuted by the blacks *themselves,* according to their chance. . . . I know well, that there are some talents and learning among the coloured people of this country, which we have not a chance to develope, in consequence of oppression; but our oppression ought not to hinder us from acquiring all we can. For we will have a chance to develope them by and by. God will not suffer us, always to be oppressed. Our sufferings will come to an *end,* in spite of all the Americans this side of *eternity.*" Walker understands that justice can speak to the reality of the new Jerusalem and ponders the possibility that through the oppressed and the marginalized in American society God will bring about justice and righteousness. "It is my solemn belief, that if ever the world becomes Christianized," Walker writes,

> it will be through the means, under God of the *Blacks,* who are now held in wretchedness, and degradation, by the white *Christians* of the world, who before they learn to do justice to us before our Maker — and be reconciled to us, and reconcile us to them, and by that means have clear consciences before God and man. — Send out Missionaries to convert the Heathens, many of whom after they cease to worship gods, which neither see nor hear, become ten times more the children of Hell, then ever they were, why what is the reason? Why the reason is obvious, they must learn to do justice at home, before they go into distant lands, to display their charity, Christianity, and benevolence; when they learn to do justice, God will accept their offering, (no man may think that I am against Missionaries for I am not, my object is to see justice done at home, before we go to convert the Heathens).[21]

Like a Hebrew prophet of old, Walker called out the moral contradiction in Jefferson's vision of democracy, and argued that the "God of the *Blacks*" would be the source of the political and social renewal of America. In the context of the tragic history of the Americas, it was black Christians who most inhabited the Christian theological imagination, seeking to embody it in prophetic and creative ways.

While Walker called out Jefferson's personal hypocrisy, Jefferson planted an important seed for the future of American democracy. Americans sought to put their rights on a firmer basis than the British constitution. When Jefferson and the Continental Congress asserted in the Declaration of Independence that God had created "all men equal," they established the ultimate grounds of appeal for fundamental human rights. While the older European Christian theological paradigm had focused on inherent hierarchy and difference, this emerging American theological paradigm highlighted human equality by common creation. Jefferson, a slave owner, ironically gave critics of slavery one of their most effective arguments against slavery in the doctrine of equality by creation. The doctrine of equality by creation would be taken up by abolitionists like Sojourner Truth.[22]

Sojourner Truth

On the underside of a white Euro-American evangelical modernity, a prophetic black Christian vision was birthed that conceived of the church as a freedom movement for love and justice. The prophetic church in America is rooted in radical movements of resistance that unveil a more just social order. In contrast to Jefferson, Sojourner Truth, through her abolitionist activism, embodied a notion of freedom for all, starting with those who most acutely experienced unfreedom, enslaved Africans. Sojourner Truth provides a counterethic to Jefferson's secular ethic of modernity: prophetic instead of colonial, opening up a trajectory toward freedom for all people.

Born a slave to James and Elizabeth Baumfree in 1797 in Ulster County, New York, Truth was originally named Isabella Baumfree. Isabella was moved among slave masters throughout her youth and witnessed the severe cruelty of the system of chattel slavery. She witnessed her mother grieve the loss of her children who were ripped out of their family. Every time her mother would remember the separation, it would "crucify her heart afresh." When Sojourner and the other children were discouraged by their dire estate, their mother, "Mau-Mau," would tell them in Low Dutch, the only language she knew, about a God "in the sky" who listened to their cries and prayers. Mau-Mau encouraged Isabella, "when you are beaten, or cruelly treated, or fall into any trouble, you must ask help of him, and he will always hear and help you."[23]

Isabella learned of the power of the living God through the faith and prayers of her mother. It was through her personal experience with the living God that she would encounter Jesus. Sojourner prayed fervently for her release, and her prayers were answered. A Quaker couple, Isaac and Maria Van Wagener, bought and freed her. Isabella had a dramatic encounter with Jesus around the time she was set free from slavery.

The image of Jesus mediated to her through her white male owners was Jesus as a white male, "an eminent man, like a Washington or Lafayette." But after her personal encounter with Jesus, "he appeared to her delighted mental vision as so mild, so good, and so every way lovely, and he loved her so much! And, how strange that he had always loved her, and she had never known it! . . . I saw him as friend, standing between me and God, through whom, love flowed as from a fountain."[24] Jesus was Savior and intercessor, pleading to God on her behalf. Isabella formed a relationship with this Jesus. Many of her speeches around the country centered on Jesus and emphasized the relevance of Jesus' teaching of the kingdom for the abolition of slavery. Even on her deathbed, her last words were recorded as "Be a follower of the Lord Jesus."[25]

Her being set free from slavery was a type of conversion experience. As a result of her being set free from slavery, she conceived of salvation as *release for the captives,* the heart of Jesus' own ministry (Luke 4:18-19). Throughout her life she conceived of God as her "ever present help in time of need" and the "great deliverer" who had the power to help her in her struggle to overcome evil. From that point on, she felt God's presence throughout the world and knew that Jesus loved her. In spite of the comfort and assurance granted by her faith, however, Isabella longed for a home, a place to belong, a community of love and hope outside of the slave master's quarters. This deep feeling of longing for home coupled with the desire to be treated as a woman and a human being caused Isabella to be vulnerable and trusting of those she met.

Although she impressed others with her steely strength, in the 1830s another vulnerable and diminished part of her seems to have felt at home when being treated badly. When Robert Matthews, calling himself "the Prophet Matthias," appeared at Isabella's doorstep in 1832, a vision caused her to ask, "Art thou the Christ?" He answered, "I am," and she kissed his feet and burst into tears of joy.[26] This charismatic "prophet" built a community of faith, with himself as leader; at this place Isabella felt included yet treated as an outsider. She gave all her money to the community, served as Matthias's housekeeper, and followed him wherever she could. In New York City she was yearning for a family and faith community, and in the Kingdom of Matthias she found both. The synthetic family around Matthias resembled the one she had grown up in over sixteen years with the Dumonts: abusive but familiar.[27]

Because of her deep longing for home, she was often vulnerable to exploitation and abuse. Although free, Sojourner encountered betrayal and lost her life savings — ripped off by white men during the Matthias movement days in the city of New York. Burned by her experience in the Kingdom of Matthias and tired from trying to earn a living through cleaning houses for white folks, she was ready for a change, ready to preach and teach, ready for a new name.

On June 1, 1843, Isabella left New York and changed her name. She wrote, "My name was Isabella; but when I left the house of bondage, I left everything behind. I wasn't going to keep anything of Egypt on me, and so I went to the Lord and asked him to give me a new name. Oh God, give me a name with a handle to it, oh that I had a name with a handle. And it came to me at that moment, like a voice as true as God is true, 'Sojourner Truth,' and my heart did leap for joy. Sojourner Truth, why, I said, thank you God, that is a good name. Thou art my last Master and thy name is Truth. So shall Truth be my abiding name until I die."[28] Isabella's new name, Sojourner Truth, had theological import — Sojourner because she was embarking on a prophetic journey, and Truth because she was going to speak the truth about the evil of chattel slavery. The Hebrew prophet Isaiah describes leadership, shaped by the Spirit of God, as a throne shaped by steadfast love *(hesed),* and on it shall sit in truthfulness *(emet)* a ruler who seeks justice *(mishpat)* and is swift to do what is right *(sedaqah)* (Isa 16:5). Of the prophetic virtues of steadfast love, truthfulness, justice, and righteousness, Sojourner Truth focuses on truthfulness. Slavery and sexism were based on lies that whites were better than blacks, and men superior to women. Sojourner Truth deconstructed both of these lies and made a constant, courageous stand for love, justice, and truth.

Naming herself was a transformational moment in claiming her authority as faith-rooted feminist abolitionist activist. Helen LaKelly Hunt writes, "Naming herself was an act of taking authority. By claiming her freedom and renaming herself, Sojourner came into full voice . . . the claiming of her whole voice transformed her from a slave called Isabella into a spiritual pilgrim who helped bring America into alignment by proclaiming God's vision of the world."[29] God called Sojourner to claim her voice for the voiceless, the enslaved Africans and women who were marginalized by a white supremacist and patriarchal society. Boldly entering her own places of deepest pain from the shadow of slavery, Sojourner Truth was empowered by God's Spirit to creatively use her strong voice to lift up the disinherited, in a lifelong fight to end slavery and sexism.

After 1840 the abolition movement offered new opportunities for women to lecture around the country. Truth was inspired by other independent women lecturers like Maria Stewart (1803-79), who developed an apocalyptic biblical vision to frame her antislavery lecturing, summarized in her *Religion and the Pure Principles of Morality, the Sure Foundation on Which We must Build* (1831). Stewart was one of the first women in the United States to give public political speeches; she deployed biblical language as a political discourse on behalf of the black freedom movement. Stewart saw America as a Babylon that enslaved Africans must exit in order to achieve authentic freedom. Valerie Cooper persuasively argues that Scripture in Stewart's vision is not constructed as an arbitrator of orthodoxy, but rather as a playbook for revolutionary political activism.[30] Stewart interprets Scripture politically, drawing out strategies and tactics from Jesus' teaching of the kingdom that were vital for the black freedom movement. Maria Stewart predicted an age of African ascension, where the "daughters of Africa" would rise up and take their rightful places of leadership. Sojourner Truth was one of those women who stood up and spoke prophetically on behalf of oppressed women at the Ohio Women's Rights Convention, convened in the Stone Church in Akron, Ohio, in 1851.

Truth traveled around the country lecturing against slavery in the 1840s and 1850s. A tall, lanky person, Sojourner Truth was a towering speaker, and her prophetic message rang out across a nation, North and South, that was dominated by white supremacy. Truth's reputation grew as she delivered passionate sermons in the camp meetings across the northeastern seaboard, unveiling the sin of chattel slavery.

Sojourner Truth's theology was grounded in the story of Israel seeking release from captivity. Like many slaves, she learned the Bible and theology aurally, improvising on what she heard. Allen Callahan states: "Slaves were rarely introduced to the Bible through the medium of the printed page. For many slaves biblical literacy began with spontaneous aural memorization and oral recall. Slaves mimicked what they heard in sermons from white preachers and readers, and in repeating what they heard they often improvised on it."[31] Throughout her journeys to find her lost children and to liberate slaves, Sojourner Truth would improvise on Scripture, speaking Scripture against the white resistance that would come her way.

Sojourner felt a strong leading of the Holy Spirit in her life. She wished to compare the teachings of the Bible with the witness to the Spirit within her, and she came to the conclusion that the Spirit of Truth spoke in those records, but that the recorders of those truths had intermingled with them their own ideas.[32] Discerning the spirits became a critical practice of discerning Scripture. As Sojourner journeyed on and people asked why, she simply responded, "the Spirit calls me, and I must go." Led by the Spirit, Sojourner improvised along her nomadic journey for justice.

Sojourner Truth was in search of Resurrection City — a space and place where all people were loved and respected regardless of their gender or skin color. Always on the go, she never had a place to lay her head. While Jefferson had Charlottesville, Virginia, as a home city, Truth was in a real sense homeless. She was a wanderer who was always in search of home. Jefferson was a settled subject, while Sojourner Truth was a nomadic subject.[33]

Throughout her life she was involved in a wide variety of Christianities in different communities (e.g., Dutch Reformed, Methodist, pietist, utopian, millennialist), many of which had majority white membership. Her religious experience was eclectic, but through these experiences she boldly forged a mystical-prophetic vision committed to liberating the oppressed.

Truth had to stand up as a strong woman, often among hostile opponents. When she spoke in Silver Lake, Indiana, in 1858, some men questioned that she was a woman because she was tall and had a deep voice. Determined and undaunted, she courageously challenged the white men to the point that she had to reveal her breasts in a public meeting to prove that she was a woman.[34] Whatever obstacles she faced, she overcame them as she searched for Resurrection City.

Because Jefferson owned land and slaves, and had political influence through serving as governor of Virginia and president of the United States, he had the resources to build a city. The pinnacle of this effort was the University of Virginia. In contrast, throughout Truth's journey she sowed seeds of hope through inspiring and empowering people to embrace themselves as people of dignity made in God's image. She never found the city she was searching for, but helped form communities of resurrection in several places, small cities of hope with jagged edges that remained unfinished urban landscapes.

She rose up and transformed the communities where she lived into postslavery communities of resurrection. Through boldly entering the revolutionary crossroads of religion and racial formation, Truth played an important role in pointing American Christianity toward a more prophetic, womanist, intercultural embodiment. She was an "American Lazarus" whose resurrection brought hope to many, creating small but growing cities of resurrection wherever she went.[35]

Unlike Jefferson's project, lodged in the narrative of modernity, Truth lodged hers in the narrative of Israel. In contrast to Jefferson's Deistic rationalism, Truth opened up a new *episteme* of prophetic biblical politics. Instead of performing the rituals of the European Enlightenment, Truth performed a dialogical, jazzlike, improvisational journey for justice that is animated by a future hope. Because of the prophetic activism of abolitionists like Sojourner Truth, slavery was overturned with the passing of the Emancipation Proclamation in 1863. However, the struggle against racism and colonization would continue. In the wake of the Civil War, a more resilient form of internal colonization would metastasize within the American body politic.

Conclusion

Sojourner Truth traveled into the places of suffering in order to liberate the suffering slaves, guiding them on a pathway toward true and lasting freedom. She heard Jesus' call and responded by dedicating her life to a nomadic ministry of release (Luke 4:18-19). The renewal of theology today will take place only when it begins in these places of suffering. African American women have been particularly affected by suffering from slavery and sexism. Interpreting Sojourner Truth as not only a historical agent but also a theological subject opens up a new horizon for theology from the perspective of African American women.[36] Sojourner Truth was a "proto-womanist" theologian who interpreted Scripture from an experience of being disinherited, circumscribed by both race and gender, while seeking to cultivate communities of resurrection.

In Truth's navigation of Christian faith in and out of hostile religious institutions we see an improvisational theology that funded her prophetic abolitionism. This same creative, often subversive appropriation of Christian tradition in service of a movement of Christian freedom is something we must continue to riff on today, a blue note that speaks the truth of hope and freedom in a world of sin and slavery.

While the abolition struggle successfully overturned slavery with the Emancipation Proclamation of 1863, much of the South was to descend into decades of violence and terror, marked by the modern crucifixion of the lynching tree. Prophetic Christian theology today must ponder this in its heart, a postcolonial account of American history that recognizes the ways in which a Christianity-inspired project of Western civilization birthed this violence. As long as black, brown, and female bodies are being crucified, prophetic Christology must continue to build on Cone's Christology of the oppressed, especially his concern with Jesus' identification with the oppressed that energizes the struggle for justice in the here and now.

While Jefferson left a legacy of false freedom through colonialism that remains institutionalized in white male privilege, Sojourner left a legacy of struggle, a song of freedom that has been picked up by others, albeit often in a new key. We see this song, this spirit, in the Underground Railroad movement, an underground movement of the oppressed for freedom. Sojourner Truth went into the heartland of America to find those in captivity and bring them back to the North where a new, truer freedom awaited. Her leadership inspired others to risk, to move, to proclaim and embody the spirit of truth.

We see this spirit of resurrection and moral courage continued in the struggle against segregation and Jim Crow. Martin Luther King Jr. carried forth this abolitionist spirit as he sought to free the captives of racial and economic oppression through their struggle for the transformation of their cities. While Sojourner Truth helped enslaved Africans escape oppressive cities, King helped them transform their cities to reflect the justice of God. King deployed concrete faith-rooted organizing strategies in the urban struggle for more fair laws, more just social programs, living wage jobs, and nonviolent peace. From Montgomery, Alabama, to Memphis, Tennessee, King sought to bring the light of Christ to cities around the world.

The power of the prophetic ministries of Sojourner Truth and Martin Luther King Jr. was that faith in Jesus was the energetic epicenter of the movement. It was this theology of Christ-centered prophetic resistance that would provide the heart of the struggle to abolish slavery, end lynching, and end segregation. Out of these abolitionist roots, the mystical-prophetic theology of Howard Thurman and Martin Luther King Jr. continued the faith-rooted freedom struggle, redirecting it toward an active political struggle for civil rights and human rights and a nationwide antipoverty campaign.

CHAPTER FIVE

Building the Beloved City: Howard Thurman and Martin Luther King Jr.

For he [Abraham] looked forward to the city that has foundations, whose architect and builder is God.

Hebrews 11:10

When Howard Thurman was visiting India in 1935, he was challenged by a Hindu man who was part of Gandhi's circle: "You have lived in a Christian nation in which you are segregated, lynched, and burned. Even in the church, I understand, there is segregation. . . . I am a Hindu. I do not understand. Here you are in my country, standing deep within the Christian faith and tradition. I do not wish to seem rude to you. But, sir, I think you are a traitor to all the darker peoples of the earth. I am wondering what you, an intelligent man, can say in defense of your position."

This Hindu man identified the moral contradiction at the heart of Christianity in the United States. He talked about how white Christians would go to a lynching of an African American on a Sunday morning and then immediately go and worship "the Christian God" in church. The moral conscience of America had been seared. Since Thurman was a Christian minister, the Hindu man accused him of being "a traitor to all the darker peoples of the earth" because the Christian church was not doing enough to fight against racial injustice.[1]

Thurman would deeply ponder this question for over a decade and answer with one of the most important interpretations of Jesus Christ in the twentieth century. In *Jesus and the Disinherited* Thurman explains "what the teachings and the life of Jesus have to say to those who stand, at a moment in human history, with their backs against the wall."[2] Thurman seeks to reimagine Christianity from the perspective of those who are struggling for survival. If Jesus stands on the side of the oppressed, how does the church reflect that commitment in its public witness today?

Thurman draws an analogy between poor Jews in the ancient Near East and poor African Americans in Jim Crow America. He connects Jesus' outsider status as a poor Jewish man in a minority community within the Roman Empire with the outsider status of African Americans in white America, arguing that Jesus stands in solidarity with all those whose backs are up against the wall.

King carried a worn copy of Thurman's classic, *Jesus and the Disinherited,* in his briefcase throughout his civil rights journey. In this work Thurman interprets Jesus as a poor, marginalized Jew within the Roman Empire. Thurman writes, "How different might have been the story of the last two thousand years on this planet grown old from suffering if the link between Jesus and Israel had never been severed. . . . [For] the Christian Church has tended to overlook its Judaic origins . . . the fact that Jesus of Nazareth was a Jew of Palestine."[3] Thurman calls Christian theology to reclaim its Jewish heritage as integral to it fulfilling its prophetic destiny. In 1949, the year Thurman's manifesto was released, King was attending Crozer Theological Seminary, writing outlines and papers on Jesus. In one of his outlines for class, "Who Was Jesus of Nazareth?" King writes, "Jesus was a Jew. It is impossible to understand Jesus outside of the race in which he was born. The Christian Church has tended to overlook its Judaic origins, but the fact is that Jesus of Nazareth was a Jew of Palestine. He shared the experiences of fellow-country men. So as we study Jesus we are wholly in a Jewish atmosphere."[4] This quote is an explicit recapitulation of Thurman's Christology, as Thurman wrote, "the Christian Church has tended to overlook its Judaic origins. . . . Jesus of Nazareth was a Jew of Palestine." Since Thurman was a family friend and King's statements so closely resemble Thurman's, it is highly likely that King received a copy of the book the year it was published. Thurman's Christology provided a template for King's conception of Jesus and the earthly struggle for justice. Thurman understood Jesus chiefly as a poor, disinherited Jew, a conception that would become central to King's vision of the beloved community.[5]

In *Jesus and the Disinherited,* Thurman goes on to argue that Christians are called to make Jesus' dream of the kingdom a reality today. This is precisely what King did through leading communities around America to work toward building the beloved community. Jesus' dream provided both the vision and the motivation for the church's prophetic mission in the world. Thus, a prophetic Christology was foundational to the theology that undergirded King's leadership of the civil rights movement. By a prophetic Christology I mean a Christology that emphasizes the continuity between Christ's life and teaching and the theological vision of the Hebrew prophets that emphasizes God's shalom justice.

Mystical-Prophetic Theology

The black freedom struggle that produced Thurman and King was animated by a mystical-prophetic theology. While Thurman emphasized the mystical and King the prophetic, both poles were operative in their theologies. Furthermore, the collective force of their lives worked toward a fuller expression of the mystical-prophetic theological vision.[6]

But what is the mystical-prophetic vision? Theologian David Tracy sees Christian theology's future in its ability to offer a robust synthesis of two of its primary orientations: the mystical and the prophetic. Discussing the synthesis of these two streams, Tracy writes,

> The prophetic and apocalyptic trajectories of the tradition will always develop the central Christian insight that "God is love" into more explicitly cross-centered understandings of that very God as revealed *in* hiddenness. The mystical trajectories of the tradition will always develop that same central Christian insight into deeper and often radically apophatic understandings of God's very incomprehensibility in and through comprehensibility. . . . A future mystical-prophetic theology of God, moreover, will prove daring in its very fidelity to the central Christian meaning of the holy mystery: God *is* love. That classic Christian metaphor will inform every new naming of the hidden-revealed, the comprehensible-incomprehensible God of Jesus Christ.

For Tracy the claim that God *is* love is the heart of the mystical-prophetic synthesis.[7]

What does Tracy mean by "*is*" in the statement "God *is* love"? 1 John states, "Beloved, let us love one another, because love is from God; everyone who loves is born of God and knows God. Whoever does not love does not know God, for God is love" (1 John 4:7-8). The Johannine theology of Holy Scripture emphasizes love as the primary window into who God is.

Love is more than an attribute of God; it describes God's essence. Christians believe that God is a Trinity, three persons united in one essence. The Godhead itself is a communion of love. Love describes the dynamic interrelationality that is part of the Godhead and is poured out in grace to the community of creation. Within the early Christian movement on into the medieval era there is a strong emphasis on mystical union with God through the cultivating of love.

By mystical, I mean personal union with God in communal context.[8] While mystical union with God is often constructed as an individual union with God in Christ, it is better understood as mediated through covenantal participation in God through being an active member of the church, the people of God. The mystical spirituality of the African diaspora was always conceived communally, with individual experience being interpreted in and through the lens of the community.[9] Mystical experience is based on a personal relationship with the living God, but one that is always mediated through the community. Mystical experience with God is in and for the community.

By prophetic, I mean seeking to restore the shattered shalom of creation through justice making with an all-embracing love. The prophetic imperative in the Hebrew Bible is based on God's justice and righteousness, *mishpat* and *sedaqah.* Justice and righteousness are brought together in prophetic discourse as a reminder to Israel of their mission to restore creation's shalom as a concrete way of worshiping their Creator.[10]

Central to living shalom was the practice of justice, especially as expressed in caring for the marginalized — widows, orphans, strangers, and the poor (Zech 7:9-10). Shalom justice is the destination of the path of the prophets. This prophetic call to justice converges in the person of Jesus Christ. Jesus of Nazareth in his person embodies God's love and justice for the world. His teaching of the kingdom of God unveils the pretense of imperial power, and offers the contours of a new order of love and justice. As a Jewish improvisor on Torah, Jesus presses the tradition to a radically inclusive love.

Jesus' mystical-prophetic identity is unveiled through Jesus' mysterious incarnation into human flesh. The *logos* becomes *sarx,* so that the prophetic message of Jewish teaching might find a radical example enfleshed in a singular human life. Throughout his ministry Jesus listens to the Spirit to lead him in the right direction, as he teaches parables, heals the sick, exorcises demons, confronts the authorities, and steals away in prayer. Jesus' entire life span is a mystical-prophetic witness to the mysterious and loving triune God. Following in the footsteps of a Jew from Palestine, prophetic Christianity seeks to imitate Christ through prophetic, parabolic action.

They Looked for a City

While many have interpreted Martin Luther King Jr. as a prophetic theologian, interpreting King as a mystical-prophetic theologian influenced by Howard Thurman deepens the transformative possibilities of this theological trajectory for twenty-first-century theology.[11] The lives of Howard Thurman and Martin Luther King Jr. were themselves a search for community. Walter Fluker has insightfully pointed out that Thurman and King use the metaphor of the city as one of the central designations and destinations of their work of community building and social transformation.[12] The beloved city in their writing stands as an ideal of community, but it also poses an open question of how we actualize deep urban community today.

Thurman and King both grew up in the segregated South and had to go deep into the Christian heritage to find the theological resources to sustain their social struggle. King rendered Jesus' teaching of the kingdom through the metaphor of the "beloved community."[13] Beloved community is the "creation of a society where all men can live together as brothers, where every man will respect the dignity and the worth of human personality."[14] Creating a society built on dignity, reconciliation, justice, and love is a daunting task. This universal ideal must seek local embodiment. Since the city is the primary place that people gather in community, we can deepen Thurman and King's call to beloved community and see it more aptly named as a search for the beloved city.

Howard Thurman: The Mystic as Prophet

Thurman's commitment to the oppressed and marginalized was not new. Growing up without his biological father amid racial discrimination in Florida, Thurman had a special sensitivity to other people's suffering. As a high school student, he was inspired by a speech given by Mordecai Wyatt

Johnson at the annual YMCA student conference at Lincoln Academy in King's Mountain, North Carolina. Thurman wrote Johnson a letter that expressed his call to the ministry:

> I want to be a minister of the Gospel. I feel the needs of my people. I see their distressing condition, and have offered myself upon the altar as a living sacrifice, in order that I may help the "skinned and flung down" as you interpret. God wants me and His precious love urges me to take up the cross and follow Him.
>
> I want advice from you as to how to direct my efforts. I am scheduled to finish here next year. As you know, the war is on and young men are being snatched daily. I am patriotic; I am willing to fight for democracy, but my friend Rev. Johnson, my people need me.[15]

In this letter it is clear that Thurman is called into the ministry in part because of his broken heart for his people, especially those "skinned and flung down." This experience helped Thurman connect his call to ministry with the pain of his people. Johnson heard Thurman's cry and encouraged him to stay connected to his people as he pursued his studies. While at Morehouse College, Thurman would hone his poetic sensibility, deepen his theological vision, and fall in love.

Mysticism was a way of life for Thurman. From long walks on Daytona Beach as a child, to meditation under his "special oak tree," to ecstatic worship at Fellowship Church, to standing in silence before a theology class, Thurman sought union with God in his daily practice of the disciplines of the Spirit. While Thurman mastered the art of turning loneliness into solitude, he would share the power of these experiences with the community. Thurman would share his heart journey with others through sermons, lectures, and pastoral conversations, always punctuated with seasons of silence, creating the space for the other to be in deeper communion with God and neighbor.

While Thurman was a mystic by spirit, he was also a student of the mystical tradition. He studied Quaker mysticism with Rufus Jones at Haverford College.[16] Here Thurman would deepen his understanding of the Quaker tradition interpreted in conversation with the broader mystical tradition of Saint Teresa, Julian of Norwich, Saint John of the Cross, Madame Guyon, and Francis of Assisi.[17] Quaker spirituality sought a deeper encounter with Christ the inner light. It emphasized that Christ is living and we need to open our hearts to fully experience Christ in the innermost depths of our being. Through experiencing the light of Christ, we can open ourselves up to the light of others. Quakers have always been sensitive to the pain and suffering of others. They were important leaders in the abolition movement, the antiwar movement, the women's rights movement, and the civil rights movement. Yet, in all their political actions, their steps were very measured; they walked in the Spirit. Through his sojourn with the Quakers, Thurman learned the importance of meditation in hearing God's voice and receiving God's love.

Love was at the heart of Thurman's theological vision. We see the love motif come out strongly toward the epic conclusion of his *Jesus and the Disinherited.* In addressing the obstacles to love (fear, deception, and hate) in the book, Thurman saves his treatment of love for the last chapter. "The religion of Jesus makes the love-ethic central. . . . Every man is potentially every other man's neighbor. Neighborliness is non-spatial; it is qualitative."[18] There was a universalism in Thurman's vision of love — we are called to love everyone as our neighbor. Love has to do with the quality of our attention to others and their experiences, dreams, suffering, and needs.

It is a continual challenge to love the other as our neighbor, especially the enemy. Loving the enemy brings one face-to-face with the power of fear, deception, and hatred in our hearts and psyches, and in the heart and psyche of the other, powers that can only be overcome through an active and disciplined emotional life. As Jesus wrestles with temptation in the wilderness, we, too, must honestly and courageously confront the principalities and powers in ourselves, so that we are prepared to enter the land of God's love where justice rolls down like a river. Thurman writes that "the disinherited must recognize fear, deception, hatred, each for what it is. Once having done this, they must learn how to destroy these or to render themselves immune to their domination. In so great an undertaking it will become increasingly clear that the contradictions of life are not ultimate."[19]

Love then becomes all the more a discipline of the Spirit, especially loving the enemy. Thurman argues that the "good feeling" of love and "preaching 'love one's enemies'" is not enough: "At the center of the attitude is a core of painstaking discipline, made possible only by personal triumph. The ethical demand upon the more privileged and the underprivileged is the same."[20] It is the call into this "painstaking discipline" as a key to loving the enemy that is Thurman's plumb-line exhortation for setting any future cornerstones.

As the book of Hebrews says, the people of God are in search of a city whose cornerstone and foundation are God (Heb 11:10). In a sermon entitled "He Looked for a City," Thurman commented on this passage from Hebrews: "The person concerned about social change must not only understand the materials with which he has to do, the things which he is trying to manipulate, to reorder, to refashion but again and again he must expose the roots of his mind to the literal truth that is the tutor of the facts, the orderer and reorderer of the facts of his experience . . . modeled and shaped in accordance to the innermost transformation that is going on in his spirit."[21] Thurman reminds us that the external struggle to achieve the beloved city must be driven by the internal struggle to flow with the Spirit. It is only through being first deeply rooted in the Spirit that we are in a position to not only discern our calling but also hear for ourselves Jesus' Spirit-aligned proclamation of release to those bound up in timidity, uncertainty, or whatever else may hinder us from responding, in jazzlike fashion, to God's call.

Like a jazz musician, an urban prophet is called to improvise, to create inspiring forms of broken beauty. The prophet's task is to "reorder" and "refashion" the urban environment to be more just and peaceable. Yet, Thurman reminds us that the work of social transformation must be based on a deep inner transformation. Personal and social transformation are inextricably linked.

Spiritual transformation takes place through listening to "the tutor" — the living God who quietly guides one to fulfill one's destiny through the social embodiment of divine intentions. Attentively listening to the songs of God in the Psalter of Scripture, in the spirituals in church, and in the silence of private prayer acclimates one to the voice of God's Spirit. Listening to the Spirit — the Holy Spirit — remains the cardinal spiritual discipline, energizing us for the works of love.[22] As it creates the space to connect with God the Creator, listening to the Spirit is the first step toward building beloved cities. Rooted and aflame, mystic-prophets' practice of listening to the Spirit is the everlasting fountainhead of their activism.

Martin Luther King Jr. and the Morehouse Gospel

Martin Luther King Jr. would follow Thurman's path in attending Morehouse College in Atlanta, where he began to develop his vision of beloved cities. The Morehouse legacy in King's family was long and lauded, and included his grandfather A. D. Williams and his father Martin Luther King Sr. Morehouse president Benjamin Mays mentored King Jr. during his undergraduate days, inspiring him to serve humanity with intellectual precision and spiritual vibrancy.[23] While many churches in Atlanta embodied the black social gospel (e.g., Ebenezer Baptist, Big Bethel AME, Wheat Street Baptist, and Friendship Baptist), Morehouse became the most strategic educational community, forming hundreds of leaders in this prophetic theological tradition.[24]

Throughout King's days at Morehouse he was an energetic advocate for the poor in Atlanta. In "Kick Up Dust," a letter to the editor of the *Atlanta Constitution* in 1946, the young Martin Luther King Jr. wrote, "we want and are entitled to the basic rights and opportunities of American citizens: The right to earn a living at work for which we are fitted by training and ability; equal opportunities in education, health, recreation, and similar public services; the right to vote; equality before the law; some of the same courtesy and good manners that we ourselves bring to all human relations."[25] In this letter to the editor, written during a period of white mob violence close to Atlanta, King takes a courageous public stand on behalf of the rights and opportunities of African Americans. Written while King was an undergraduate, the letter shows that proclaiming the prophetic imperative was part of his upbringing. He is also calling for a more beloved Atlanta, pointing out that African American citizens of Atlanta should have all the rights, privileges, and opportunities that the rest of American citizens have.

During his graduate studies, King was inspired by the moral vision of the Hebrew prophets. King often invoked the prophets to give specific content to the discourse on the justice and righteousness of God. Commenting on Amos 5:21-24, King writes, "This passage . . . reveals the deep ethical nature of God. God is a God that demands justice rather than sacrifice; righteousness rather than ritual. The most elaborate worship is but an insult to God when offered by those who have no mind to conform to his ethical demands. . . . God is a God that demands justice and sacrifice can never be a substitute for it."[26] In this passage King lifts up the "ethical demands" of the prophets, theologically grounding them in the nature and character of God, who is righteous and just.

The content of "justice" for King presupposes a *theological* account of prophetic public witness. For King, we work for justice because God is a merciful and just God. Through Thurman's *Jesus and the Disinherited,* King learned the way in which Jesus' teaching and performance of the kingdom of God were an improvisation on the prophetic imperative. King understood justice as God's righteous reign of shalom reflecting God's specific way of dealing with the world as created as good, bound in a covenant of love. It is from such a theological account of justice, grounded in the Hebrew prophets, with Jesus being chief among the prophets, that King sought to proclaim and embody the justice of God.

For King, building upon Thurman, the work of justice is a natural blooming of the mystical rootedness of the centered self, an outworking of the energies of love found in one's personal wilderness-solitude and grounded in the power of the living God. The church is called to continue Jesus' ministry of proclaiming and embodying release to the captives (Luke 4:18-19). As King writes, "Whenever Christianity has remained true to its prophetic mission, it has taken a deep interest in social justice. Whenever it has fallen short at this point, it has brought about disastrous consequences."[27] For King, Christianity was true to its prophetic roots when it engaged in the work of social justice, seeking to transform society through a collective embodiment of the prophetic imperative. Given America's legacy of slavery and segregation, racial justice should be central to the mission of the church.

The antiracist struggle in society has both an outer and an inner dimension. While King would work for social transformation, Howard Thurman emphasized inner transformation; both are essential to a full expression of authentic Christianity. Social transformation included the organized struggle to be able to sit anywhere on the bus and have the right to vote, but inner transformation was an embracing of one's deepest dignity and sense of self. For Thurman, inner transformation was "walking humbly with the Lord," through the dark valleys and across the mountaintops of life (Mic 6:8). Through opening ourselves up to the presence of God, we can find a special dispensation of inner peace and fiery courage to weather the storms of opposition and press on in the struggle to materialize beloved cities.

A "fire in the bones" burned in the bodies of each activist in the civil rights movement. Sheriff Jim Clark in Selma, Alabama, was trying to intimidate the African Americans that were trying to vote there. Every Monday morning a group of African Americans would stand on the steps of City Hall during the one time they were allowed to register to vote, and Sheriff Clark would arrive shortly after and tell the crowd to disperse and go home. This ritual of white supremacy became a weekly fixture in Selma.

One day, a lone African American woman refused to leave the steps. Sheriff Clark approached her and hit her; she hauled off and hit him back, knocking him flat to the ground. Dumbfounded, he got up and went at her again; she clobbered him and he fell to the ground once more. Humiliated on the ground, Sheriff Clark yelled out to three of his deputies to help him. With their help Sheriff Clark held her down and clubbed her. However, that day in Selma, Annie Lee Cooper won the hearts of the crowd; that day in Selma, not a single African American was scared of Sheriff Clark any longer. The bond of oppression had been broken by the heroic heart of a fiery freedom fighter. Social transformation was fired by the passion of inner transformation. Annie Lee Cooper's improvisational confrontation with the powers sounded a new song characterized, not by a blue note, but by a note of victory — "You will not take my dignity today!"

Howard Thurman was a mentor in the movement, always seeking to press leaders to go deeper and push harder on their journey of the heart. Thurman was one of the spiritual guides in King's life that helped him deepen his mystical union with God. King knew Thurman through his friendship with his father, but really got to know him during his doctoral studies at Boston University. King was inspired by Thurman's preaching and went to Thurman's home to watch the World Series. Thurman was always concerned about King's spiritual life. Through conversations, correspondence, and visits, Thurman encouraged King to allow the Spirit to flow more powerfully through him and his ministry. The movement of the Spirit was the lifeblood of the mystical-prophetic vision.

Thurman's discipline of love had a large impact on King's vision of the beloved city. The love of the neighbor is rooted in a mystical love for God. King's own strength to love was based on his pressing through persistent prayer to know God and discern the divine direction for his life. King writes, "So in the truest sense of the word, God is a living God. In him there is feeling and will, responsive to the deepest yearnings of the human heart: this God both evokes and answers prayers."[28] It was on the basis of a mystical experience with God's love that King was spiritually enabled to lead a social movement based on the nonviolent love of the enemy.

King was tested numerous times regarding this walk of nonviolent love, but a pivotal moment came on the evening of January 30, 1956. When King's home was bombed in Montgomery, Alabama, he had to decide whether or not to retaliate. King chose the path of nonviolence, embodying Christ's teaching to love one's enemies. This was a watershed moment in King's life that had a profound effect on the civil rights movement.

One night King could not sleep because the constant onslaught of death threats was putting his family in danger. He got out of bed and paced around the house.

> I was ready to give up. With my cup of coffee sitting untouched before me I tried to think of a way to move out of the picture without appearing a coward. In this state of exhaustion, when my courage had all but gone, I decided to take my problem to God. With my head in my hands, I bowed over the kitchen table and prayed aloud. The words I spoke to God that midnight are still in my memory. "I am here taking a stand for what I believe is right. But now I am afraid. The people are looking to me for leadership, and if I stand before them without strength and courage, they too will falter. I am at the end of my powers. I have nothing left. I've come to the point where I can't face it alone." At that moment I experienced the presence of the Divine as I had never experienced Him before. It seemed as though I could hear the quiet assurance of an inner voice saying: "Stand up for righteousness, stand up for truth; and God will be at your side forever." Almost at once my fears began to go. My uncertainty disappeared. I was ready to face anything.[29]

King's description of this night is very mystical — a passage through the fierce storm cloud of anxiety and dismay into the illuminating darkness of the presence of the Divine. It mimics the passage of Moses into the glory cloud on Mount Sinai, the original narrative in which Abrahamic mysticism is rooted. God's call to King was prophetic, to stand up for righteousness and truth. The mystical and prophetic streams of his deep spirituality converge in this moment.

Mohandas Gandhi and Nonviolent Love

The nonviolent tradition of prophetic protest was mediated to black Christianity through the philosophy and activism of Mohandas Karamchand Gandhi (1869-1948). King had heard Mordecai Johnson, the president of Howard University, deliver a moving lecture on Gandhi in 1950 during his last year at Colgate Rochester Theological Seminary (now Colgate Rochester Crozer Divinity School). After that he was drawn to Gandhi's vision of nonviolence and began to devour every book on Gandhi that he could get his hands on. Through Gandhi's writing, King became persuaded that nonviolent love could be a collective force for social transformation.[30]

Several generations of advocates of prophetic black Christianity had pilgrimaged to India to meet with Gandhi and other nonviolent Indian activists. Howard Thurman was the first to go, meeting with Gandhi in 1935, followed by Benjamin Mays and Mordecai Johnson in 1936, so Gandhi's vision of nonviolent love was a central part of prophetic black Christianity since the late 1930s.[31] King was also tutored in Gandhi's philosophy of nonviolence during the Montgomery and Nashville struggles, by a number of activists who were associated with the Fellowship of Reconciliation, including Bayard Rustin, Glenn Smiley, and James Lawson. Thus, King was following trails well traveled when he, Coretta Scott King, and Lawrence D. Reddick traveled to India in 1959 to deepen their understanding of the freedom struggle in India.

From the bombing of King's Montgomery home in 1956 on, Gandhi's philosophy of nonviolence was a primary guide to King's thought and activism:

> Then I came upon the life and teachings of Mahatma Gandhi. As I read his works I became deeply fascinated by his campaigns of nonviolent resistance. The whole Gandhian concept of *satyagraha* (*satya* is truth which equals love, and *graha* is force; *satyagraha* thus means truth-force or love-force) was profoundly significant to me. As I delved deeper into the philosophy of Gandhi my skepticism concerning the power of love gradually diminished, and I came to see for the first time that the Christian doctrine of love operating through the Gandhian method of nonviolence was one of the most potent weapons available to oppressed people in their struggle for freedom.[32]

With the principle of nonviolent protest we see that King develops a political strategy to inspire people to collectively embody love through a coalition dedicated to realizing social justice, including the full participation of all people in democratic life.

King implements Jesus' political teaching of love as he organizes the civil rights movement. King sees love as the most fundamental force for social change:

> When I speak of love I am not speaking of some sentimental and weak response. I am speaking of that force which all the great religions have seen as the supreme unifying principle of life. Love is somehow the key that unlocks the door of ultimate reality. This Hindu-Moslem-Christian-Jewish-Buddhist belief about the ultimate reality is beautifully summed up in the first epistle of Saint John: "Let us love one an-

> other; for love is God and everyone that loveth is born of God and knoweth God. He that loveth not knoweth not God; for God is love."[33]

King well understood the power of love as a prophetic power that binds all other powers — certainly the "strong man" of violence and oppression (Mark 3:17). King writes, "darkness cannot drive out darkness; only light can do that. Hate cannot drive out hate; only love can do that."[34]

The blues are always played by hands wearied by oppression, recollections of misfortune. Jazz dances on the fingertips in delighted exploration of a new song, reworking old melodies and inventing new ones. While violence led to destruction, leaving in its wake the wearied blue-noted blues, nonviolent love "jazzed things up" with a new song — a redemption song — for all humanity. King wrote, "The way of acquiescence leads to moral and spiritual suicide. The way of violence leads to bitterness in the survivors and brutality in the destroyers. But the way of nonviolence leads to redemption and the creation of the beloved community."[35] The path of nonviolence marked King's democratic *theologizing* — it was only through the theory *and* practice of nonviolent love that beloved community could be realized.

Jesus teaches that those who have provided for "the least of these" (Matt 25:40, 45) will be welcomed into heaven. Jesus ups the moral ante even more when he says: "Love your enemies, do good to those who hate you, bless those who curse you, pray for those who abuse you. If anyone strikes you on the cheek, offer the other also; and from anyone who takes away your coat do not withhold even your shirt" (Luke 6:27-29). Moreover, he makes it plain that these guidelines do not apply *merely* to people "just like us" (whoever that "us" may be) but to all — and totally indiscriminately. For, in Jesus' parable it is the *Samaritan* — clearly the "enemy" — who proves to be the one who finally helps the *Jew* in need. And Jesus concludes by saying: "Go and do likewise" (Luke 10:37).

For King, the call to love the enemy demanded a call to Christians, especially white Christians, who stood by silently believing they could avoid complicity in the matter. To these churches he raised an even more serious charge: spit out your tepidity and choose a side. In his famous "Letter from the Birmingham City Jail" (1963), King leveled a fierce critique of Christian leaders who refused to join the civil rights movement. He rarely answered the letters of his critics, but when King received a letter from eight white Alabama ministers who encouraged him to slow down and fight segregation in the courts, instead of taking the struggle to the streets through nonviolent protest, he penned his famous missive from prison. Like a fiery note from the underground, this prophetic volley boldly confronted the white moderates for not seeing the evil depths of segregation and the fierce urgency of now!

King wrote, "I have been so greatly disappointed with the white church and its leadership."[36] The white church in particular came into the crosshairs of King's prophetic denunciation. King was sick and tired of the silence and moderation of the white church, which he saw as "ineffectual," becoming "the arch-supporter of the status quo."[37] Calculated silence was betrayal of the prophetic ideals that drove the Christian-led, interfaith movement for love and justice. King's experience of the failure of the white church caused him to reflect more intentionally upon what it means to be the church amidst the oppression and suffering of the modern world.

King, with the tenacity of a Hebrew prophet, called the church to emulate the sacrificial boldness of the early Christian martyrs: "If the church of today does not recapture the sacrificial spirit of the early church, it will lose its authentic ring, forfeit the loyalty of millions, and be dismissed as an irrelevant social club with no meaning for the twentieth century." Martyrdom was the supreme expression of the "sacrificial spirit of the early church." Before Christianity was made a legal religion by Constantine, Christians experienced intense persecution by the Roman Empire and were often martyred by Roman authorities for their belief in a god other than Caesar. This sacrificial spirit, even unto death, was continued among enslaved African Christians who were often persecuted and killed by fellow white Christians. King called all Christians, black and white, to embody the prophetic imperative and a love as strong as death.[38]

By and large, King felt that the white moderates had abdicated their call to embody justice. King thus began to search for a faithful remnant within the church, writing, "Perhaps I must turn my faith to the inner church, the church within the church, as the true *ecclesia* and the hope of the world."[39] Like the pietists of old who argued for a true or genuine Christianity, King longed for the embodied achievement of the true church, one rooted in mystical peace and burning with an unconsuming flame of courage when it came to standing with and for the disinherited.

In his invocation of the *ecclesiolae in ecclesia,* King offers a clear example of a prophetic black Christian reinterpretation of a central trope of Lutheran pietism. King was familiar with this Lutheran theme, quoting Martin Luther in a theology paper at Boston University: "For the sake of brevity and a better understanding, we shall call the two Churches by different names. The first which is the natural, essential, real and true one, let us call a spiritual, inner Christendom. The other [which] is man-made and external, let us call a bodily, external Christendom."[40] Like Luther, King opted for the former — an "inner Christendom."

According to pietist teaching, the *ecclesiolae in ecclesia* was a call for Christians to "truly" follow Christ into a deeper experience of community. Together, radically obedient Christians embody a prophetic collective force for active neighbor love in the community. King's notion of the "inner church" echoes the formation of *collegia pietatis* in German pietism. These colleges of piety were earlier embodiments of the "inner church" in the history of Continental Protestantism, providing concrete examples of Christians who lived in intentional community to hold each other accountable to the high ideals of Christian life. Pietists sought to intensify the ethical dimension of the Christian life through the formation of fellowship groups and social institutions. The pietist movement in Germany encouraged many institutions of social outreach, including orphanages, hospitals, and schools like *Franckesche Stiftungen* in Halle. The pietist notion of communities of transformation took on a new form in the prophetic black Christian religion of the "New World."

In King's context, the "true *ecclesia*" in the United States comprised those prophetic Christians who were joining together to fight against injustice. The social struggle crystallized around concrete political goals, including overcoming segregation and securing the right to vote for all American citizens. Because of their position on the underside of history, black Christians had both prophetic perception and a noble destiny. King wrote, "I am grateful to God that, through the Negro church, the dimension of nonviolence entered our struggle."[41] While the black church came out of suffering, through nonviolent protest it sought to embody the Christian teaching of shalom justice, providing a robust theological horizon for social justice Christianity.

Forged in the fires of resisting slavery, prophetic black Christianity formed an "inner church," providing a fuller communal embodiment of the gospel's call to neighbor love and social justice. A form of *ecclesiolae in ecclesia,* slave religion itself functioned as a "church within a church," or what Albert Raboteau has called an "invisible institution."[42] As a result of being rendered invisible in the white antebellum South, enslaved African Christians had to develop a sense of "we-ness" that transcended their estate of slavery and suffering. The collective identity of African American

Christians had both a theological and a political dimension. Theologically they conceived of themselves as a "church within a church"; politically they thought of themselves as a "nation within a nation." To be a black American Christian meant inhabiting a conceptual and existential place at once within and without American Christianity and politics. This double consciousness meant that black Christians had critical leverage against the racist and colonial character of the American empire.

Prophetic black Christianity was a vital embodiment of the inner church in the Americas, because it was here, among a people who Thurman argued had their "backs up against the wall," that a form of community developed that overcame the suffering induced by oppression through creative, collective struggle. From their position on the underside of modernity, enslaved African Christians created the conditions through which prophetic Christianity in the Americas emerged so robustly in the civil rights movement. While finding its heart in the prophetic black Christian tradition, King's vision of the "inner church" included antiracist whites. For King the true church was a community of righteousness, whoever the righteous may be. The true church includes any people, black, white, or any shade in between, who are willing to join the struggle for love and justice.

Love in the Poor People's Campaign

King's political theology of love was put to the test during the final years of his life, 1966-68. During this time, he deepened his struggle for racial justice through a growing focus on economic human rights. Economic justice had always been central to King's ministry. The March on Washington in 1963 was called "the March on Washington for Jobs and Freedom." Ending racial discrimination was vital, but King also thought every able-bodied American should have access to a living wage job, regardless of race, creed, or color.

Theologically, King recovered the Hebrew vision of Jubilee justice, embodied in Jesus' teaching of the kingdom, understood as an economic reality. Specifically, the reign of God needs to be manifest in the material conditions of this world, including all people having access to education, affordable housing, health care, living wage jobs, just working conditions, and fair benefits. However, economic justice for all God's children was not the primary priority of the federal government, nor of most churches.

As King began to deepen his economic analysis, he began to question the amount of money the U.S. government was spending on the Vietnam War. On April 4, 1967, at the Riverside Church of New York, King spoke out against the triplet of sins, "racism, materialism, and militarism," that he saw as plaguing the American empire. He showed how these three issues were all interrelated. King was specifically concerned about the enormous amount of money being spent to fund weapons of destruction in the Vietnam War, instead of going to support governmental programs that could help lift up the poor from their plight.

Once King publicly renounced the Vietnam War, he began to experience stiff resistance from many quarters; however, King saw that to propel the movement for racial justice ahead, he was going to have to directly address poverty in America amidst growing militarisms. In May of 1967 King told the staff of the Southern Christian Leadership Conference (SCLC): "We have moved from the era of civil rights to the era of human rights, an era where we are called upon to raise certain basic questions about the whole society."[43] While King had focused primarily on racial justice in Jim Crow America earlier in his ministry, later on he broadened his prophetic antiracist hermeneutic to include a bold critique of the Vietnam War and a laser-sharp focus on economic human rights. The desegregation movement was only the beginning of the comprehensive social change that was needed. King called for a "revolution of values" and a "redistribution of economic and political power."[44]

How would this revolution of values and redistribution of power take place? Marian Wright told King he needed to start a Poor People's Campaign, inviting him to Marks, Mississippi, to view the dire poverty of the Mississippi Delta. Bertha Burres, an activist from Marks, describes King's visit to Marks:

> He stopped by the church where we were having the Head Start. He was trying to get a Head Start started in Marks, the time he stopped by was lunch time, and the teachers only had one apple but there were six children so they had to divide one apple between six children. They were out of crackers so they just had the apple. And when Dr. King saw this he just cried. After seeing that the children only had an apple to eat, and the streets were like a field of water, and the houses looking the way they were looking, and he finally got word about our health problems and the work conditions we had, so he said he was glad he had decided to stop by. And when he came back again he was gonna do something about it.[45]

Like Jesus, who was moved with compassion when he saw the suffering of others, King's heart was filled with compassion when he saw the deep hunger and potential fire in the eyes of the youth of Marks, Mississippi. At that moment he was moved to launch a nationwide movement to dramatize the plight of the poor in America for the whole world to see.

Out of Marks, Mississippi, we saw the emergence of a nonviolent movement of the poor. This poor-led movement for economic justice placed its sights on Washington, D.C. As Jesus had set his face to go to Jerusalem (Luke 9:51-56), the center of power in Israel, with full knowledge that this might entail his martyrdom, Martin Luther King Jr. set his face to go to Washington, D.C., the symbolic political center of the American empire. King gathered the leaders of the Southern Christian Leadership Conference to begin planning this nationwide campaign for economic justice.

Fighting for living wages became the new front in the struggle for racial justice. At the northern tip of the Mississippi Delta, Memphis was under siege. With the great migration of former slaves and sharecroppers to Memphis, a large African American working population struggled for economic survival. While the manufacturing and service sector jobs offered new economic opportunity for Mississippians downstream, upon moving to Memphis, the harsh working conditions, low pay scale, and stressful lifestyle in this Tennessee city proved to be an ongoing challenge, creating a whirlpool of poverty and debt.

On a stormy day in Memphis, February 1, 1968, the rain accidentally triggered the compactor mechanism of a trash truck, killing two African American sanitation workers, Echol Cole and Robert Walker. Concerned about unsafe work conditions and low wages, over 1,000 workers from the Memphis Department of Public Works went on strike on February 12. Unresponsive to the workers' demands, Mayor Henry Loeb ordered the Memphis police force to attempt to shut down the strike with mace and tear gas. These draconian tactics of suppression unveiled the unjust structures of the Memphis city government. Rev. James Lawson, pastor of Centenary Methodist Church, felt this was the time to move and lift up this economic injustice to the national spotlight. He helped to gather 150 ministers to form the Community on the Move for Equality to organize the resistance.

Martin Luther King Jr. was invited to come down and lead a March for Justice and Jobs. On March 22, 1968, thousands of people of faith, labor leaders, and community activists joined the March for Justice and Jobs. A challenging call was sent out to the community to join the march: "We ask you to stay away from work or school and walk with more than 10,000 people who want Memphis once and for all to learn that it must be a city for all people. A man is a man. God requires that a man be treated like a man. Memphis must do so in work, play, education, housing, by the police and in all other ways the rights of each man must be upheld. This will be a march of dignity. The only force we will use is soul-force which is peaceful, loving, courageous, yet militant."[46] The sanitation workers' strike would be the pivotal movement for the acceleration of awareness for the deplorable state of black America.[47]

King saw that sanitation workers in Memphis were underpaid and helped lead the strike. He also saw the way it was demoralizing these black men at the very heart of their humanity and masculinity. Thus, he helped frame the campaign around our common humanity. The striking workers wore "I Am a Man!" placards to visually assert their personal dignity and share their struggle with a curious, onlooking nation.

On March 18, 1968, King flew into Memphis to address a crowd of nearly 25,000 people, proclaiming, "You are reminding, not only Memphis, but you are reminding the nation that it is a crime for people to live in this rich nation and receive starvation wages. I need not remind you that this is the plight of our people all over America. The vast majority of Negroes in our country are still perishing on a lonely island of poverty in the midst of a vast ocean of material prosperity." King, the powerful prophet, began to elucidate the contradiction between American opulence and low wages.

That night in Memphis he ended his speech opening himself and those gathered to a baptism of the Holy Spirit. He acknowledged that the struggle for economic justice was constant and exhausting, and sometimes one can despair, but he turned in hope to the deep river of faith found in the black spirituals, quoting "There Is a Balm in Gilead":

> "There is a balm in Gilead to make the wounded whole. There is a balm in Gilead to heal the sin sick soul." Then they came to another stanza that means so much to me, "Sometimes I feel discouraged." I'm not going to be untrue to you tonight, sometimes I feel discouraged, having to live under the threat of death every day. Sometimes I feel discouraged having to take so much abuse and criticism, sometimes from my own people. Sometimes I feel discouraged, having to go to bed so often frustrated with the chilly winds of adversity about to stagger me. Sometimes I feel discouraged, and feel my work's in vain. But then the Holy Spirit revives my soul again. In Gilead, we make the wounded whole. If we will believe that, we will build a new Memphis, and bring about the day when every valley shall be exalted, every mountain and

> hill will be made low. The rough places will be made plain, and the crooked places straight, and the glory of the Lord shall be revealed, and all flesh shall see it together. We will be able to build right here a city which has foundations.

King's search for a beloved city took on concrete form in Memphis. "Right here, right now!" King demanded. If the workers of Memphis pull together, not only can they shut the city down with a strike, they can rebuild it to become a beloved city — together.[48]

On March 28 the Memphis strike erupted into violence. This was the first time in the movement that a march had resorted to violence on a large scale. Pressure mounted in Memphis. On April 3, 1968, King stood up in the pulpit of the Bishop Charles J. Mason Temple in Memphis and said,

> Well, I don't know what will happen now. We've got some difficult days ahead. But it doesn't matter with me now. Because I've been to the mountaintop. And I don't mind. Like anybody, I would like to live a long life. Longevity has its place. But I'm not concerned about that now. I just want to do God's will. And He's allowed me to go up to the Mountain. And I've looked over. And I've seen the promised land. I may not get there with you. But I want you to know tonight that we, as a people, will get to the promised land. And I'm happy, tonight. I'm not worried about anything. I'm not fearing any man. Mine eyes have seen the glory of the coming of the Lord.[49]

When Martin Luther King Jr. was assassinated the next day, on April 4, 1968, the world stopped for a moment. Shaken, confused, but searching for a way to continue the fight, civil rights leaders decided to carry out King's Poor People's Campaign. Some preliminary plans had been drafted, but the movement was without a leader. They were forced to *improvise.* Ralph Abernathy, Jesse Jackson, and Andrew Young had to step up and lead, but they had to improvise daily in order to pull together and propel the Poor People's Campaign along.

Resurrection City

The Poor People's Campaign and the building of Resurrection City were a collective improvisation — a strategy depicting the emergence of a mystical-prophetic vision of the voiceless — a chorale of hope, dignity, justice, and equality played out upon the hearts and minds of those in power in America, and across the nation. King had seen that in order to transform the system, he needed to help mobilize a broader poor-led coalition for justice across the nation to lift the veil of America, exposing the darkness of oppression and injustice. King wanted this movement to be the foundation for the construction of the beloved cities around the nation, where shalom and justice would be the social norms of the beloved community.[50]

SCLC had been planning the Poor People's Campaign when James Lawson called King to come to Memphis and help lead the sanitation workers' strike. During 1968 King became increasingly focused on the ways in which the whole economic system needed to be reconstructed. Local victories in Montgomery and Selma, Alabama, were important, but now the civil rights movement needed to go national, and turn its focus to ending poverty.

King decided that a Poor People's Campaign was the most strategic path of action because it captured the hearts and minds of the whole nation. When King was brutally assassinated, civil rights leaders decided to continue King's Poor People's Campaign by building a tent city on the National Mall in Washington, D.C. People from around the country converged on the nation's capital to bear communal witness to the ravages of poverty and homelessness. They called it "Resurrection City," a parable of a loving, equal, and just community.

During the summer of 1968, thousands of poor people from around the country occupied the National Mall between the Washington Monument and the Lincoln Memorial. On May 13, 1968, Rev. Ralph Abernathy drove the first stake in the ground to begin the construction of Resurrection City. Rev. Jesse Jackson, Sr., ever eager for the political spotlight, was named the mayor of the city. The first family chosen to occupy a shanty was that of Mrs. Minnie Lee Hill from Marks, Mississippi, who was the mother of seventeen children and whose husband earned $155 a month working for the city of Marks. Rev. Abernathy passionately preached to the crowd: "Here we will build a *koinonia,* a community of love and brotherhood. American Indians, Puerto Ricans, Mexican Americans, white poor Americans from the Appalachian area of our country and black Americans will all live together here in this city of hope." The city went up quickly. Caravans from around the country moved in to express their solidarity with this faith-rooted social movement that sought to fight poverty and injustice.

On May 23 the southwestern caravan arrived, which included a large group of Mexican Americans led by Reies Lopez Tijerina, a New Mexican leader of the Political Confederation of Free City-States in the Southwest. Tijerina's organization sought land settlements for their people, based on an alternative interpretation of the 1848 Treaty of Guadalupe Hidalgo, an agreement through which Mexico ceded a large portion of the Southwest to the United States. Abernathy and the SCLC tried to be responsive to the concerns of Tijerina, Rodolfo "Corky" Gonzales, and Native American leaders as they marched together on the Supreme Court on May 29, to protest a decision that limited the fishing rights of Native Americans in many of the rivers of Washington State.

The demand of the Poor People's Campaign was for an "economic bill of rights" that guaranteed all citizens a job or an income. The Poor People's Campaign made these six demands: (1) an end to hunger; (2) an end to bad housing; (3) an end to unemployment, and guaranteed incomes for those unable to work; (4) adequate health care for all citizens; (5) full equality of educational opportunity for all; and (6) an end to violence and repression at home and abroad. Through the urban experiment of Resurrection City, the agenda of the Poor People's Campaign was forced to become more comprehensive, including advocacy for land claims and fishing rights that were important to Mexican American and Native American members of Resurrection City. The struggle for solidarity across ethnic lines, given different ethnic groups' political agendas, proved to be an ongoing struggle in Resurrection City, whose population peaked at 2,500 on May 26.

The campaign that took on urban form in Resurrection City was unique because it was led by the poor. Every day delegations went to the House and Senate to advocate for their issues. SCLC organized these advocacy activities that targeted different government agencies. They also conducted prayer vigils at the State Department, the Agriculture Department, and the home of Wilbur Mills, chairperson of the House Ways and Means Committee. During these marches and protests, many of the residents of Resurrection City were arrested. The police force began to clamp down, patrolling the city and trailing all protesters.

In addition to the militancy of the police, Resurrection City also faced stormy weather. It rained cats and dogs during the first two weeks of June. During one twenty-four-hour period between June 12 and June 13, nearly 2.5 inches of precipitation fell. While the shanty town turned into what some referred to as "Mudville," the residents held the line and remained anchored in their vision.

On Wednesday, June 19, Solidarity Day, Resurrection City pulled together a large-scale rally, planned in part by Bayard Rustin, who had helped plan the massive 1963 March for Jobs and Justice in Washington, D.C., where Dr. King delivered his "I Have a Dream" speech. On Solidarity Day, Dr. King's wife, Coretta, called out the violence of poverty: "Poverty can produce a most deadly kind of violence. In this society violence against poor people and minority groups is routine. I remind you that starving a child is violence; suppressing a culture is violence; neglecting schoolchildren is violence; punishing a mother and her child is violence; discrimination against a workingman is violence; ghetto housing is violence; ignoring medical needs is violence; contempt for equality is violence; even a lack of will power to help humanity is a sick and sinister form of violence." Mrs. King unveiled the infrastructure of violence that sustained poverty.

Resurrection City stood strong throughout the weekend, but on Monday, June 24, a column of 1,500 police filed in and surrounded the city. While the police said protesters no longer had a permit, Rev. Abernathy said, "We will honor the permit granted us by the Indians," referring to the blessing from the Native American elders that the elders of Resurrection City had received before building the city, a spiritual attempt to break the chain of colonial oppression and restore the shalom of creation that Native Americans embody.

On June 24, many fled and many were arrested, but the Spirit of Resurrection had been released in prophetic ministers throughout the nation. As Rev. Bevel had stated with such prophetic insight a few weeks earlier: "Resurrection City cannot remain an island; it must become a church that goes out into Washington and moves Washington to fight for the poor. . . . We must demonstrate every day, but in the afternoon we must get out into Washington . . . we must come back and canvass, knock on doors, talkin' to people about the reality of poverty in this country." Prophetic ministry in America must entail both public advocacy with elected officials and popular education efforts — a pedagogy of the oppressed in the spirit of the Highlander Folk School. Prophetic education and advocacy led by the poor remains an unfinished dream for the prophetic church in the Americas to realize.

While Resurrection City was not without conflict, including racial strife, and was plagued with logistical problems, it became a symbol in our social history of occupying public space and transforming it into a space of hope. Resurrection City was a city of hope. From the freedom train to D.C.

to the advocacy to end poverty, Resurrection City showed the nation that it could begin to live into its democratic ideals.

One of the decisions that had to be made was who would lead the mule train to Washington, D.C., Bertha Burres was chosen. She was a single black activist from Marks, Mississippi, where King had found his original inspiration. Burres served as secretary for the civil rights groups when they would come through. The choice of Burres was intentional; she was marginalized in nearly every way: in terms of race, class, gender, age, and marital status.

The SCLC's strategy was to dramatize this poor people's movement following the narrative of Jesus Christ. As Jesus entered Jerusalem, a powerful center of that day, Bertha Burres entered Washington, D.C., the "Queen of the Mule Train." In this framing, it was a black woman who was the Christ figure.[51] Bertha Burres unveiled the promise of women leaders of the movement as it moved into the 1970s.

Gender Justice in the Social Struggle

The civil rights movement was first and foremost a struggle for racial equality, while questions of gender were often suppressed. Despite the prophetic power of love in the movement, patriarchy was both a hidden and an overt problem. Martin Luther King Jr. and other male civil rights leaders were not always supportive of women's leadership. SCLC staff member Septima Clark confessed, "You can work behind the scenes all you want . . . but don't come forth and try to lead. That's not the kind of thing the (black men) want. I sent a letter to Dr. King asking him not to lead all the marches himself, but instead to develop leaders who could lead their own marches. Dr. King read that letter before the staff. It just tickled them; they just laughed."[52] Clark's quote unveils the way in which the patriarchal culture of the Southern Christian Leadership Conference did not fully support women leaders. The civil rights movement's focus on racial oppression was so great that gender justice was often seen as a secondary concern. It was often viewed as a distraction to the overall goal of racial justice. Yet, injustice in any form is wrong; in patriarchy, wherever women are being dominated, damaged, or destroyed, there must be powerful resistance to dismantle this oppression.

While the men of the movement — King, Ralph Abernathy, Jesse Jackson — are the leaders who are best known, the lion's share of the faith-rooted organizing on the ground was done by women. Many women assumed leadership in the civil rights movement as activists, educators, and organizers, including Annie Devine, Ella Baker, Dorothy Cotton, Mae Bertha Carter, Prathia Hall, Fannie Lou Hamer, Septima Clark, Dorothy Height, Winson Hudson, Coretta Scott King, Eleanor Moody-Shepherd, and many others. It is time to begin to use these women's lives as a source for a prophetic, intercultural, womanist theology.[53] These female freedom fighters continue a nomadic spirituality of justice that was preceded by women such as Hagar in the wilderness, Deborah the great judge, Sojourner Truth, Harriet Tubman, and Ida B. Wells.

Prophetic Christianity has a mighty heritage of female freedom fighters, but dismantling patriarchy entails a reimagining of Christian theology and ethics. When Martin Luther King Jr. offered his systemic vision of sin — "the giant triplets of racism, materialism, and militarism," which he articulated in his "Against Vietnam" speech — he did not identify patriarchy as a sin. As feminist and womanist scholars have pointed out, King's idea of systemic sin must be further fleshed out to include gender injustice. The struggle for racial and economic justice should include a similar commitment to the flourishing and integrity of women. Post–civil rights prophetic Christianity must participate in disconnecting or interrupting patriarchy from its own theologies and churches, joining a growing movement for gender justice.

Eboni K. Marshall Turman argues that the inhumanity experienced by the African American community is gendered as much as it is raced and classed.[54] Marshall Turman sees the Jewish human flesh of the incarnate Christ as providing the basis for a womanist ethic of incarnation that might be employed to reconstitute African American communities of resurrection. Black women's bodies are seen as the starting point for the church's ethical reflection and moral resistance.

As part of her work, Marshall Turman critiques the ideal of black masculinity promoted at Morehouse College. She focuses this critique on Benjamin E. Mays as part of the black social gospel tradition, with King and Thurman being emblematic of the "Morehouse Man." She sees the ideal of black masculinity behind the ideal of the "Morehouse Man" as perpetuating the problem of inferior humanity that black women internalize. Marshall Turman writes, "[I]n order to claim that inherent equality, the extreme dehumanization and disenfranchisement (read imperfection) that had colored most of his students' lives prior to their enrollment at Morehouse had to be challenged with a specific counternarrative that asserted 'manhood' where white supremacy had posited inhumanity."[55] This perspective drove Benjamin Mays "to the grueling work of building men by instilling 'confidence and self-esteem' into the hearts of young black males whose bodies and souls had been broken, both literally and figuratively, by the remnants of enslavement and the everyday evil of Jim Crow."[56] While Mays espoused progressive views about women and women's rights, "black" and "women" operated as different categories, not necessarily overlapping.[57]

Many black women have resisted the commodification that occurs through these labels. Marshall Turman writes, "Others who diametrically oppose this sort of black male embodied normativity, namely, black women, are regarded as differentiated bodies that are *not-made* toward the end of religious leadership specifically, but rather are to be acted upon within the context of subaltern sacred space."[58] While Morehouse continues to fulfill its mission of *"making men,"* it suggests that the female bodies that fall outside of that scope are "*not-made.*" To do one's work in society, one must be *made,* and in the process certain bodies are left out completely. Marshall Turman writes,

> The moral consequences of "making men" are amplified expressly because while positing that the substance of black personhood has been jeopardized by the oppressive acts of *others* who are the arbiters of certain kinds of power in the world, it simultaneously suggests that this same personhood that has been imperiled by the dangerous politics of incarnation that breed violence, fragmentation, metanarratives of superiority and inferiority, and ethics of submission and invisibility, can only be reconstituted by way of others who are empowered to *make* men. The *making* of black men is prompted by the social historical reality of white supremacy that has already predetermined blackness as no-thing . . . certain male bodies have been endowed with divine authority to gaze and act upon those who are *not-made men.*[59]

The black masculine is a reaction to the white masculine that undergirds the plantation patriarchy of the antebellum South.

While Benjamin E. Mays was successfully forging self-confident black men who could move beyond their internalized inferiority within a white supremacist regime, within this economy of black identity, black women were often transferred to a secondary status in relation to black men. While black men became "made men" overcoming the white supremacist conception of black men as "not-made men," black women remained "not-made women" who were viewed as inadequate for leadership in the church and the movement. When black women's bodies were left out of the rituals of leadership formation with the black communities and the academy, they became vulnerable to being objectified and commodified. While Marshall Turman focuses the sights of her critique on the Morehouse model of manhood that produced Howard Thurman and Martin Luther King Jr., her concern is with the way this tendency to build up black men, often at the expense of black women, continues in African American institutional life, especially the church. Third-generation womanists like Marshall Turman, Teresa Delgado, Melanie Harris, and Malinda Elizabeth Berry are seeking to find new models of mutuality in theology, ethics, and leadership. This must include a reimagining of masculinity both black and white.

Since the black masculine is a reflexive response to the white masculine, patriarchal forms of white masculinity must also be interrogated. As we saw in chapter 4, all the institutions in the United States were built to legitimate white male power and privilege. White landowning men like Thomas Jefferson were the only people in the new republic that had political power. The Holy Scriptures became one of the sources that white men in the American republic used to maintain their power, deploying the writings of Saint Paul, who wrote, "slaves, obey your masters" and "women are not to teach or have authority over a man." In every period of American history, evangelical patriarchy would find a way to reassert itself.

The radical social movements of the 1960s called into question the white supremacist and patriarchal architecture of the evangelical church. A group of prophetic evangelicals heard Dr. Martin Luther King Jr.'s cry for racial justice and signed the Chicago Declaration in 1973, which expressed their concern for racial and social justice. Gender justice proved to be more difficult to effect in the evangelical church. The women's movement in the 1970s offered new and needed perspectives on gender justice, but was met by stiff resistance, within both conservative black and white communities. Threatened by the women's movement, many conservative white evangelicals began to get concerned about what they perceived as a threat to their male-controlled power regime. James Dobson started Focus on the Family in 1976 as a men's ministry to provide a supportive environment for men to become strong leaders, husbands, and fathers, since they were feeling increasingly threatened by the rise of women in the women's rights movement. Dobson said, "I know that women are extremely important to the family. No one can take anything away from the women, but they tend to be more motivated for the family. If you get the husband involved, you get the whole family and if you lose the father and the husband, then you lose a certain percentage of the kids as well." Dobson believes that patriarchy is biblical and the church should implement a theology of male headship. These patriarchal codes are rooted in the "honor culture" of the American South. Deploying the rhetoric of family, manliness, and civilization, Dobson and the Religious Right appealed to the populist impulses within American evangelicalism to forward a conservative political program.[60]

The deepest roots of the oppression of women in the United States lie in white patriarchy, while black patriarchy is a cultural reflex to this deeper problem. While black men may oppress black women, historically white men have oppressed white women, black men, and black women. We see this moral contradiction clearly unveiled in Thomas Jefferson's relationship with Sally Hemings. White evangelical men's defense of manhood always entails a defense of a set of cultural values that go beyond a mere defense of maleness, which oppresses women, black and white. White evangelical patriarchy perpetuates multilayered forms of oppression.

We saw how Benjamin E. Mays sought to form a new generation of black men who could embody moral courage as they resisted a white supremacist regime; decades later James Dobson would form a different sort of male leadership. Dobson's men — primarily white men — sought to become good husbands and fathers who were also linked to becoming strong culture warriors who employed their power to defend that project of Western civilization as embodied in the idea of America. But this project was from the beginning structured between the poles of patriarchy and white racial supremacy and thus was always already simultaneously a gendered/racial project.

Now this might appear to be an *ad hominem* attack on Dobson and by extension an unwarranted critique of late modern American evangelicalism. But it is not, for what is primary here is not merely Dobson or his culture warriors as individuals. Rather, at issue is the structural and cultural links between the American evangelical Christian world and the United States, indeed, the wider racial world as it operated by way of a discourse of American civilizational ambitions and cultural (sometimes called "manifest") destiny. Dobson is instructive because he exemplifies precisely the problem of how the project of Western civilizing has made use of Christian terms and thus at the cultural level or the level of social structures has been nothing less than a problematic project of salvation

— where salvation here is ordered around a false "God-man," the white masculine.[61]

It is against the backdrop of this problem that one must understand the rise of the Morehouse men. Indeed, it is this dynamic — the hegemony of the white masculine — that they are struggling against. The Morehouse men formed during the Mays era were antiracist patriarchs, who effectively interrogated and worked to dismantle America's original sin of white racial supremacy as they became powerful religious and civic leaders even if they were still ensnared, as Marshall Turman has demonstrated, by its gendered protocols or the patriarchal dimension of the Western civilizational project. Today we see that men, Christian men both black and white, and every shade in between, need to do more work, in open, deep, and sustained collaboration with women, to work toward a new prophetic masculinity.

Feminist, womanist, and *mujerista* theologies are transforming our understandings of gender and opening new spaces for dialogues about gender and sexuality. Through the growth of interracial marriage in the postwar twentieth century, we are witnessing a deepening of the work of racial reconciliation.[62] In this intercultural milieu we need to cultivate a masculinity of mutuality, where men and women can love, grow, and work together as equals. Rejecting centuries of a model of "power over," we need to develop models of "power with" in which women and men can use all their gifts together to build a lasting movement for love and justice. In our post–civil rights world, it is vital that we develop new pedagogies, from Morehouse College to Wheaton College, to form men into a masculinity of mutuality that is antiracist and gender-just at its heart.

Since men and male behavior have been one of the greatest sources of the oppression and suffering of women, the site of women's suffering is a vital source of prophetic theology in the twenty-first century. The renewal of theology today will take place only when it begins in these places of suffering, especially the suffering of women. One of those places of woundedness is the suffering of women of color. Sojourner Truth and Ella Baker inspire us to a womanist hermeneutic and theological vision.[63] Delores Williams's *Sisters in the Wilderness* speaks to the importance of a theology rooted in black women's lives: "In the midst of testifying about my own faith and marveling at the faith and courage of female progenitors, I reflect upon what it means to take seriously (as a primary theological source) the faith, thought, and life-struggle of African-American women."[64] Womanist theology is an important trajectory because of the way in which it simultaneously interrogates racism and patriarchy, offering an ethic of prophetic mutuality.

We need to move into a *postpatriarchal* world.[65] The women's movement and the civil rights movement joined together in the 1960s to challenge U.S. society to affirm the full equality and dignity of all people regardless of their gender, race, or ethnicity. While feminist and womanist critiques of modernity have exposed the way that rationality and social structures were and are used to suppress and oppress women, feminist and womanist theologians have revised Christian theological categories to insure that they speak to those who are over half of the world's population. Contemporary Christianity's universal affirmation of all humanity is deeply indebted to the tireless labor of women theologians, ministers, and activists. If we are going to have a justice movement, it must not only include women but also recognize and actively support their leadership, especially the leadership of women of color.

Conclusion

King's vision of beloved cities continues to inspire a new generation of mystic-prophets, academic-activists, to work with prophetic imagination, jazzlike improvisation, and stout hearts in creating the common good throughout the world. But as Marshall Turman reminds us, even King's vision has its blind spots. Mystical-prophetic theology of the twenty-first century must be gender-just.

It is up to a new generation of Christian leaders to proclaim and embody Jesus' teaching of the kingdom, God's righteous reign of shalom. Howard Thurman's advocacy of a "centered self" walking with the living God is the baseline of King's improvisational vision for justice. Deep spirituality and strategic activism must walk hand in hand in order for prophetic Christianity to live into its destiny. Our creative Christ-centered, Spirit-led efforts can be parables of the kingdom as we seek to embody a missional ecclesiology marked and molded by love, justice, and the mending of creation.

Like Gandhi's freedom struggles on behalf of the "untouchables," King recognized that the black freedom struggle had implications for a global movement of human rights. For King, "It really boils down to this: that all life is interrelated. We are caught in an inescapable network of mutuality, tied into a single garment of destiny."[66] Our common humanity, knitted together by the living God, is the reason that humanity will prevail. As King continued to struggle for radical democracy, he was assassinated in Memphis on April 4, 1968, leaving us heirs to a new season of struggle to achieve a truly radical democratic vision — the building of beloved cities.

In our post–civil rights era, Christian theology today must lift up women's voices, leadership, theologizing, and activism. Women like Ella Baker, Septima Clark, Fannie Lou Hamer, Dorothy Height, and Coretta Scott King were powerful leaders in the civil rights movement. Prophetic female leadership is vital to the future of the movement for justice today.

God's reign of shalom justice is only possible postpatriarchy. Resurrection City bears witness to gender-just relations, where women are as "made" as any man, where men are not driven by insecurity in the face of women's rights, but actively seek to embody an ethic of mutuality. We must move from a paradigm of "power over" to a paradigm of "power with," a society where women and men respect and love one another, listen and encourage the other, and inspire each other into roles of leaders in all sectors of the urban and global development.

In the second decade of the twenty-first century, we are witnessing new signs of a global awakening. The Occupy movement embodies much of the spirit of hope embodied in Resurrection City. There are parallels between Resurrection City in 1968 and the occupation on Wall Street in 2011. In the Resurrection City demonstration, people occupied the federally owned land on the National Mall in Washington, D.C., to protest racial and economic injustice. In the same manner, the nonviolent occupiers of Zuccotti Park in New York City sought to demonstrate against the raging capitalist machine that is heightening economic oppression and inequality.

The nonviolent struggle for true freedom and economic justice wages on. It is time for a reconstitution of the Poor People's Campaign. It is time for the church as an improvisational movement for love and justice to be more intentional in our struggle to build beloved cities. It is time for Resurrection City.

CHAPTER SIX

The Church as a Theater of the Oppressed

Do not neglect to show hospitality to strangers, for by doing that some have entertained angels without knowing it.

Hebrews 13:2

A solidarity rally for Occupy Wall Street was held on Saturday, October 29, 2011, in New York City, and I was asked to deliver the opening prayer. Since this invocation would kick off the rally, I made my way down to City Hall early. It was pouring rain, which soon turned into sleet, and then snow. Within ten minutes I was sopping wet. As my hands turned red and I began to shake from the weather, I became preoccupied with a desire to run into one of the too-many nearby Starbucks, buy a cup of joe, and warm up. As I turned my gaze to the green singing siren of Starbucks, my heart was reminded of the activists in Zuccotti Park sitting in their tents despite the freezing cold, warmed by something deeper than a mere cup of coffee.

As I stood there, conflicted and cold, an African American man approached me, gave me a hug, opened his enormous umbrella, and commented on the frigid sight of me. This gentleman was my own council member, Robert Jackson, representing District 5 in Harlem where my wife Sarah and I live. Shielded from the sleet and warmed by his presence, I began discussing with him the Living Wage NYC campaign and how to persuade Speaker Christine Quinn to push the Fair Wages for New Yorkers Act through the City Council with a supermajority in order to override the veto of Mayor Michael Bloomberg.

I was interrupted midsentence: it was "time for the invocation." While we'd been scheming, a large crowd had gathered and was ready to march. It's often the case that, as an ordained minister, I feel as if I'm onstage before a crowd, a kind of liturgical performer, a lead actor before an audience. Not here; as I picked up the microphone and began to pray, I felt very much as a player among many, one of the ensemble. Out in the snow and sleet, as I prayed for God's Spirit of justice to "roll on like a river, righteousness like a never-failing stream," I had a deep soul-warming sense that this Occupy Wall Street solidarity rally was indeed a liturgy, but a liturgy of the street, a liturgy of deep mystical union with the God of the oppressed, and thus a powerful, prophetic act of interruption. Just as Council Member Jackson and my scheming had been interrupted, so that we could all be centered on the God-Who-Gathers, this rally was an act of interruption in the scheming of them-who-scatter. The "amen" that concluded my prayer was not mine, but the "amen" of the whole troupe. The players took their places, curtains were drawn; the show had begun. Council Member Jackson and I marched down to Zuccotti Park with Council Member Jumaane D. Williams, of District 45 in Brooklyn, and leaders from all over the city. On that day, members of labor unions, community action groups, and faith communities who were inspired by the occupation on Wall Street joined the historic mobilization of Americans around the country demanding economic justice for all God's children.

When we arrived at Zuccotti Park, we were met by the New York Police Department, which was trying to usher us down another road away from the Occupy encampment. Thinking this was strange, I turned to Council Member Williams. He signaled me to follow him into the encampment. Amidst the tents, we searched for his friend and made our way toward the Occupy Kitchen, a mere fold-up table under a tent with some kitchenware behind. It looked like something between a picnic cookout and a tent of Israel in the wilderness. I dropped some cash in a silver "donation" jar and struck up a conversation with the young bushy-brown-haired radical behind the table. He shared with me that he was heading to a working group concerned with feeding the occupiers hosted by Juan Carlos Ruiz of Colors, a worker-owned cooperative restaurant. "Father Juan Carlos," I said. "I've known him for years! He used to work for Youth Ministries for Peace and Justice in the Bronx and has been a prophetic leader in the movement for comprehensive immigration reform." "Wow! You should come with me to the Occupy Kitchen working group and say hello to Juan Carlos." And with that, we were off.

When we arrived at Colors Restaurant in the East Village, we drank some robust coffee and then gathered in a circle of about fifty people. Anyone who wanted to talk raised his or her hand and got the opportunity to speak. If you liked what the person said, you would stick your hand in the air and move your fingers. Within the circle you got the feeling that everyone's voice was respected and each would have an opportunity to share if he or she chose to.

The principal issue raised in the meeting was who to feed at the encampment. Because the kitchen was outdoors, this *very* limited operation was attracting the homeless and hungry. We wrestled with whether the Occupy Kitchen ought to feed everyone who came to the table or just the occupiers who were in Zuccotti Park. Arguments went back and forth, with good points being made for both sides. At one point a young man stood up and boldly proclaimed, "Let's feed them all!" There was a deep sense of release in these words. We sat in silence and smiled. The Quakers call this a "sense of the meeting," that ripe moment when everyone recognizes what is good, what is right, what is just, and a decision is made — *together.*

The occupation's commitment to feeding all God's children reminded me of the radical communal habits of the early church described in the Acts of the Apostles: "All who believed were together and had all things in common; they would sell their possessions and goods and distribute the proceeds to all, as any had need. Day by day, as they spent much time together in the temple, they broke bread at home and ate their food with glad and generous hearts, praising God and having the goodwill of all the people. And day by day the Lord added to their number those who were being saved" (Acts 2:44-47). Through their life together, the early church embodied God's love as an egalitarian community, a doxological, social, and economic *koinonia.*

While Acts describes the early church as a unified fellowship of worship, love, and justice, its unity is centered around a reciprocity of exchange, a ritual rooted in a vision of Jubilee justice. Abraham had shared his best land with Lot; Moses had shared the wisdom of YHWH with Israel; the prophets had shared their heart for the poor; Jesus had proclaimed release to the captives, shared his power to heal, and fed the hungry. As disciples of Jesus, the early church was called to do likewise and to follow in the footsteps of Jesus and the prophets.

Corporate worship and collective just action were all of one piece in the early Christian community. The early churches' commitment to the common good is demonstrated through their practice of economic democracy: "All who believed were together and had all things in common; they would sell their possessions and goods and distribute the proceeds to all, as any had need" (Acts 2:44-45; cf. 4:32-35). They ordered their economic relations in a manner that served the needs of all the members of the community, privileging those who had the greatest need. The mutual interdependence and spirit of sharing of these early Christian egalitarian communities stood in quiet defiance of the hierarchical economic structure of Rome.

The Roman Empire was governed by a colonial logic of oppression. Through heavy annual taxation where money was funneled back to the imperial coffers, Jews in Palestine were often squeezed into dire poverty, leaving impoverished villagers to be both aggressive and creative in how to make ends meet. The Christian resisters in Acts disrupted this timeline of taxation through the rhythm of liturgical time that propelled a fledgling economy of sharing. In every dimension of life together, the church bore prophetic witness to God's care for the marginalized and the unable-to-pay, and unveiled a warning that trying to save one's life via wealth and power would only lead to its loss. Day by day, these revolutionaries broke bread in the homes of each other and shared their bounty with the community; together they enjoined themselves to *eucharistia,* true charity, with glad and generous hearts. Many of the early congregations gathered in private homes, some of which were even the residences of wealthy women like Lydia, to share these holy feasts.

On Pentecost, God graciously and generously poured out the Holy Spirit upon children, women and men, people from all nations. In the rhythm of Rome, Jerusalem was preparing for another day of extortion in the marketplace, bribery in the courts, and ignorance of the orphans and widows, when there was a mighty rush of wind like the sound of a mighty river. People of the *koinonia* began to speak in the tongues of any and all visiting the city. This sudden and unnatural ability to understand the meaning of the message of these early followers of Jesus brought the marketplace to a halt, disrupting the day's usual rituals of commerce. The many languages of Pentecost demonstrate that God's shalom is multiethnic, multiracial, multilingual, and multicultural — an international *koinonia.*

Koinonia witnessed to the contours of the early Christians' lives together, their rituals of gathering, egalitarian economics, and common walking in "the Way" (Acts 9:2; 19:9, 23; 22:4; 24:14, 22). This radically democratic spiritual movement was named "the Way," pointing to a new way of being in the world, a nomadic existence, always being on a journey but never fully reaching the destination. Exiting the oppressive logics of the Roman Empire, "the Way" offered an alternative manner of living as a community committed to embodying God's love and justice in the concrete details of economic life together.

"The Way" was a community on the move. Never a static community, early Christianity was a dynamic, moving, missional fellowship. As the disciples followed Jesus across the Galilean countryside, this grassroots Jewish messianic movement sought to usher in a new socioeconomic order. The early Christian movement dramatically disrupted the colonial pretense of the *basileia tou Romes* through its preaching of the *basileia tou theou,* its healing-exorcisms, and its celebration of holy feasts.

In surveying the Christian terrain today, especially in the United States, it seems clear that there has developed a clear divide between the doxological activities of "the church" and its economic activities, including its participation in the global economic order. By segregating holy space within urban places to sanctuaries, built and enclosed locations, the prophetic voice of the liturgy is all but locked up in a corporate prayer closet where none hear the message but those who already know. Meanwhile, outside the prayer closet, it's another day of extortion in the marketplace, bribery in the courts, and intentional ignorance of the orphans, widows, immigrants, and prisoners. The church today needs a fresh in-breaking of the Holy Spirit.

The way forward is a restoration of the spirit of dramatic disruption and economic democracy established at Pentecost. As we reimagine the church through the lens that dramatic disruption makes in society, we need to turn to theater. Brazilian playwright Augusto Boal's call to break the fourth wall through spect-actors can unleash the creative power of the church today. Thinking about how to take the segregated liturgies of the church into the open-air markets of the city is one of the most pressing tasks for the church. The church in the power of the Holy Spirit can transform urban places of despair into spaces of hope, especially when reimagined as a musical theater of the oppressed that moves to the cadence of festival time. Youth Ministries for Peace and Justice, where Father Juan Carlos worked, is one example of how, even when the church seems divided, there is still a remnant, a church within the church, who are mystically rooted, and prophetically illumined, who follow a way forward, the way of Jesus.

Augusto Boal's *Theatre of the Oppressed*

Theater director Augusto Boal (1931-2009) developed the theater of the oppressed to speak to the people of his beloved Brazil. Boal was concerned that classical theater of the West was used by the bourgeoisie to quell the revolutionary impulses of the people. So he started writing plays and staging theatrical productions that sought to unmask the power and privilege of the elite, while empowering writers from the Brazilian underground to claim their own distinctive artistic voice.

In his manifesto, *Theatre of the Oppressed*, Boal critiqued the ways in which the ruling class had taken possession of the theater.[1] He called for Brazil to reimagine theater *by* and *for* the people. Reclaiming theater as a space of freedom could unleash the creative powers of the audience, inspiring them to become subversive moral agents in the struggle for liberation. The oppressed themselves would have to take the lead, liberating themselves, creating their own theater, and transforming the world.

Theater began as festivals celebrated by free artists in the streets of the city. "In the beginning the theater was the dithyrambic song: free people singing in the open air. The carnival. The feast. Later, the ruling classes took possession of the theater and built their dividing walls. First, they divided the people, separating actors from spectators: people who act and people who watch — the party is over! Secondly, among the actors, they separated the protagonists from the mass. The coercive indoctrination began!" writes Boal (119). Boal's prophetic task was drawing back the curtain on the strategy of indoctrination deployed by the ruling class, ushering in the prophetic possibilities of the theatrical festival, where spectators are transformed into revolutionary political actors.

Boal develops a "poetic of the oppressed" to critique the conventional theater, while creating the conditions for the emergence of a new theater of revolution. Analyzing classical theater from the subject position of the oppressed unveils the strategies it uses to sedate the populace into utter passivity, including creating a divide between the audience and the actors. Inspired by Aristotle's writings on tragedy, classical theater aspires to instill virtue in the citizenry, but in most instances these theatrical productions are deployed as coercive systems that legitimate the status quo. Boal writes, "the coercive system of tragedy can be used before or after the revolution . . . but never during it" (46). The audience member "lives *vicariously*" through the experiences of the protagonist, while remaining a passive spectator (34). Through their empathetic identification with the protagonists, the audience has a collective, cathartic experience of the transfiguration of tragedy. However, they are neither inspired nor energized to join the struggle for the liberation of the oppressed in the polis, but are subtly coerced into complicity. In this way classical theater is a sentimental theater.

In contrast to the sedation of classical theater, Boal desires the transformation fostered by the theater of the oppressed. Karl Marx was one of Boal's muses, writing, "The philosophers have only *interpreted* the world, in various ways; the point, however, is to *change* it."[2] It was Marx's desire to *change* the world that inspired Boal. Theater should add a log to the fire of the revolution. Boal was interested in theater that did not merely *interpret* the human experience through theatrical performance, but inspired the audience to *change* their community through just action. In this way, theater of the oppressed provides a way forward for the liturgical rhythms of *koinonia* in interrupting oppression and providing a means of transformation in the city.

In contrast to classical theater, Boal advocates a theater of the oppressed. Boal was concerned about the way that the ruling class was economically exploiting the oppressed, while the theater made them feel good about it. Classical theater had to be disrupted, reimagined, and reconstructed. Boal saw the transformation of the theatrical arts as integral to the transformation of the socioeconomic system. In solidarity with the freedom dreams of the oppressed, Boal believes that the theater of the oppressed offers an important pathway toward liberation.

Boal's dramaturgy was influenced by his friend Paulo Freire's classic work *Pedagogy of the Oppressed.*[3] The material circumstances of the poor and oppressed are the starting point for Freire's educational philosophy. He developed a pedagogy that raises consciousness in the oppressed about their plight and provides a pathway to their empowerment and liberation. In this work Freire posited an educational paradigm through which the "teacher-student contradiction" is overcome as teachers and students work together in the struggle for liberation.

For Freire the telos of the liberation struggle is *transformation.* "Liberation is praxis: the action and reflection of men upon their world in order to transform it."[4] What is transformation? Manfred Halpern has described transformation as seeking the social embodiment of the "fundamental new and better."[5] I would like to deepen this definition theologically by giving it the moral content of the prophetic imperative in Holy Scripture — social justice *(mishpat)* and steadfast love *(hesed).* Transformation is personal and political. It is more than a personal process, but it is simultaneously a social one. Transformation as socially embodied is fundamentally just and loving, rooted *and* aflame in the life of a community. To choose to make life fundamentally more just and loving is to *improvisationally* collaborate for the collective well-being of the community of creation.

Transformation becomes a category that can deepen Boal's theater of the oppressed, as it is a call not only to the liberation of the oppressed but also for the collective repentance of the oppressors. Thus, I will refer to Boal's theater of the oppressed as transformational theater, as its ultimate aspiration is the transformation of society. Boal suggests that the primary practice for changing the theater to change the world involves transforming spectators into "spect-actors." In theater the audience is never completely passive, but has an ever-present role to play in the drama. Boal's transformational theater creates the space for not just formal interaction between the actors and audience, but even improvisational play between them.

Improvisation is not limited to actors and musicians; it is a dynamic process that includes all people that are part of an artistic performance and its reception. While improvisation is usually associated with the performers, members of the audience should also be seen as "improvisers." When audiences begin to engage their own agency through creative performance, they become better equipped to exercise their moral agency in the theater of political affairs.[6]

This unleashing of the creative power of the audience has multiple political implications. Transformational theater offers spect-actors tools so they can take action in artistic performance, personal life, and the political realm. As spectators become actors, the conditions become ripe for lasting cultural revolution. The threat of transformational theater lies in the indirect, yet precise, unveiling of the oppressive logics of the ruling class. When Brazil experienced a takeover by a military coup in 1964, progressive writers and playwrights were seen to be a threat. That same year Paulo Friere moved into exile in Chile after being forced out of Brazil by the new government. Improvising to survive, Boal was eventually arrested in 1971 and forced into exile in Argentina.

In 1986 Boal returned to Rio de Janeiro and founded the Center for Theatre of the Oppressed. Wanting to have a broader political impact on Brazil, he was successfully elected as a councillor in Rio de Janeiro in 1993. He developed a legislative theater to explore political ideas in the form of drama. This provided citizens with a transitional space to discuss and act out different political problems in order to find creative solutions. Building on his work of transforming spectators into spect-actors, Boal sought to empower voters as legislators. While theater of the oppressed blurred the line between actors and spectators, legislative theater blurred the line between the arts and politics. It is not enough to disrupt business as usual; it is also necessary to create the conditions, structures, and policies that inaugurate a new way of doing business, a socioeconomic order that is fundamentally new and better, more just and loving.

Boal's pushing the theater to be more politically engaged is a great inspiration to Christian leaders today who are seeking to lead their churches in transforming the institutions of urban life through the arts and prophetic activism. Within the history of the church, the medieval mystery plays were one example where the dividing wall between actors and audience was dissolved. During these dramatizations of the scriptural narratives everyone participated in the collective mystical experience of Christian faith in festival time.

Festival Time: The Cadence of the Church as a Musical Theater of the Oppressed

The Feast of Corpus Christi is a festival celebrated every year in Orvieto, Italy, that played an important role in the emergence of the medieval mystery plays in Europe. Sarah and I began visiting Orvieto in 1998 and were initiated into the wondrous spectacle of a Christian festival first staged in the third century of the second millennium. In 1263, Peter of Prague, a priest from Germany, stopped at Bolsena, Italy, while on a pilgrimage to Rome. A doubting Thomas, Peter had deep reservations about the reality of the real presence of the risen Christ in the consecrated host in the Eucharist. It was doubt that had driven him on a pilgrimage to Rome in search of answers. During Holy Mass at St. Christina Church in Bolsena, while lifting up the host to heaven, Peter spoke the words of consecration. In that moment blood began to trickle down upon a corporal, a piece of linen on which the chalice and paten rest when on the altar. Peter was surprised by grace, and at that moment his doubt was transformed into faith.

Peter took the corporal to the neighboring city of Orvieto, where Pope Urban IV was living. The pope and other church officials authenticated this miracle and decided to house the relic in the Duomo of Orvieto. Inspired by this miracle, Pope Urban IV asked Saint Thomas Aquinas to compose a mass honoring the Holy Eucharist as the body of Christ. The following year, 1264, the Feast of Corpus Christi was instituted through a papal bull; this living tradition has continued every year in Orvieto in unbroken succession.

On the feast day each year, Orvieto celebrates a citywide procession through the streets of the Etruscan fortress town on a high hill in Umbria. The cloth from the miracle is brought outside the church and paraded through the streets of the city. Dressed in a historic medieval costume, the bishop carries the relic as he processes through the streets. This festival celebrates the Eucharist outside of the gates of the church. On that festival day the dividing wall between clergy and laity, sacred and secular, is brought down as all the residents of Orvieto join the dynamic, dancing movement through the streets of their beloved town.

The Feast of Corpus Christi ensures that everyone in Orvieto can have a personal encounter with the risen Christ in the streets of the city. Feasts and festivals are the bread and wine of human life together. It is during times of festival that we experience a way of being in the world that moves beyond the rushed rhythm of our temporal existence and into an experience of time that is mystical in its sense of timelessness. Hans-Georg Gadamer asks that we see the festival behavior of celebration not merely as the negation of that-which-scatters, the division of labor called work. For, if this is all a celebration is, then it is simply recovery for the self from the aches and stress of work for the purpose of being scattered again. Gadamer asks that festival celebration be more than a break from being scattered and instead a being-gathered, for a renewal of the soul of the community. In humans gathering together for festival, Gadamer acknowledges a shift in our relation to time, a transformation he calls *festive time.*[7]

Festive time is a pregnant pause within our daily routine, when we experience "community in its most perfect form." Gadamer writes, "If there is one thing that pertains to all festive experiences, then it is surely the fact that they allow no separation between one person and another. A festival is an experience of community and represents community in its most perfect form. A festival is meant for everyone."[8] Within festive time there is a collective sense of unity among all participants in the festival. In these moments there is the cathartic collective realization that each belongs not to time, that is, a work schedule, but to a deep experience of the collective other, a form of communal catharsis through self-transcendence.

Gadamer qualifies festive time as "autonomous time," meaning that it operates free of chronological time, and is not so easily regimented as chronological time. Gadamer's festive time is similar to *kairos* in the New Testament literature. *Kairos* is one of two Greek words used to describe time. *Chronos,* the other word, refers to chronological time, sequential time. In the New Testament, *kairos* refers to God's time, a sort of time that is independent of *chronos* time, a moment in history when God intervenes and change occurs. The transcendent also erupts in festive time, but the weight is often on the way the wisdom of the past breaks into the present, while Christian eschatology is oriented toward an ontology of the future.

Gadamer does not develop a sense of an eschatological future in his conception of festive time. For Gadamer, festive time is a collective moment of pregnant pause to join with the past, commemorate some event or story, and bring it into the present. Within eschatological time there is always an equal eye on the future, along with the past and present. Festive time, when conceived eschatologically, is grounded in the living God who has promised to come again. We are to live today in light of the coming of God from the future to resurrect the body and restore shalom in the community of creation.[9]

When Jesus inspired the people of Israel to imagine the reign of heaven, he described it as a banquet to which many will come, from east and west (Matt 8:11). The great and future feast was always in Jesus' field of vision. Since heaven is conceived as a great feast, it is wise for us to reimagine time as a place for celebrating the process of this growing union between the *basileia tou theou* and the world, which is to be fully realized at the eschaton, the end of time. This eschatological destination of all time — the Great Feast — is why I prefer to speak about *festival* time. A festival in Resurrection City is our great hope. Let us keep the feast.

We can see the rhythm of festival time in our weekly celebration of the Holy Eucharist; when "we proclaim the mystery of the faith," it is always "Christ *has* died, Christ *is* risen, and Christ *will* come again." Liturgical time is thus a festive sharing in the call-and-response of the eschaton, the end of all time, and the great cloud of witnesses from the beginning of time. When we gather for weekly worship of the living God, as a community of singing selves we join our voices with angels and archangels and with all the company of heaven, a kind of cosmic *koinonia.*[10]

Festivals, as social celebrations, tap into the depths of our humanity, our grief and surprise, our mourning and wonder. They invoke and inspire our playful, joyful, precocious self in the context of a larger communal celebration of life. Festivals are richly poised to perform two transformational acts. First, they invoke *koinonia,* whether with food, stories, or even the same table; they facilitate a culture of camaraderie and sharing, even charitable giving. And second, they bring the community to the threshold of *kairos,* for they bring into a single moment the legacy of the festival as well as a newness of expression. Each time a feast is kept, "each repetition is as original as the work itself."[11] Every time a festival is celebrated, it is celebrated anew, bringing the community together in a new social form through its collective experience of nonidentical repetition.

Strangers and Other Angels

Every Christmas in New York City, the Compagnia de' Colombari theater troupe performs *Strangers and Other Angels,* a wild, joyful reimagination of the centuries-old *Second Shepherd's Play,* a medieval mystery play about the birth of Jesus. In this rendition the Christmas story is brought to life on the streets of New York City through a raucous mix of alternately bawdy and reverent dialogue, music, dance, song, food, and drink. The play dramatizes the exhortation in the epistle to the Hebrews: "Do not neglect to show hospitality to strangers, for by doing that some have entertained angels without knowing it" (Heb. 13:2). Combating the commercial nature of the holidays, *Strangers and Other Angels* embraces humanity with a performance that celebrates the abundance and togetherness that should mark the season. By bringing communities together and crossing boundaries of race, class, and gender, Colombari celebrates beauty as a gift given back to the community.

An annual street festival in New York City, its location moves every year. Manhattan's Morningside Heights was the backdrop for the play in December 2010. *Strangers and Other Angels* engages the talents of a wildly diverse mix of artists, including actors, opera singers, step and tap dancers, "angels" with spectacular wings, steel drummers, accordionists, trombonists, and guitarists. As the performance unfolds, it moves, with different scenes being played in different locations. Actors and musicians take the play to their audience in the streets and weave through the crowd, using the city as a stage and presenting scenes and music that invite everyone to participate.

Like the procession during the Feast of Corpus Christi in Orvieto, the entire performance processed from Sakura Park, east on 122nd Street and south on Broadway, through the front entrance of Union Theological Seminary and into the quad. The actors led the procession, playing and singing along the way. Colorful dramatic angels blocked traffic as the audience walked across the intersection of 122nd and Claremont and down the hill toward Union. The performance culminated with a celebratory dance, involving the entire company and audience, ending with the arrival of food and drink for all to share.

Festival time leads us to the feast. Colombari embraces this fundamental theological logic in its street dramas. Like Augusto Boal, Colombari shares a commitment to staging theater that transforms spectators into active participants, or what Boal calls spect-actors. Creating prophetic faith-rooted theater for a new century, Colombari views every public place as a space for the sacred architecture of theater experience, and actively seeks to break the "fourth wall" (the barrier) between the performer and the audience, creating a community out of strangers, and inspiring a celebration of our city's spectacular abundance. By occupying the streets of New York, Colombari transforms places of despair into spaces of hope.

Spaces of Hope

Jesus' resurrection inaugurates a space for hope. When Jesus bursts forth from the tomb, he breaks open the place of ultimate oppression — the place of death. Suddenly — as never before achieved in cosmic history — the laws of nature, the wages of sin, and our inevitable fate were all opened like the drawing of a curtain between stage and house. The tomb was now, of all places in the universe, a space of hope; its reputation as the place for the end of being had been transformed to a space where one could arise, walk out, and live again.

Michel de Certeau approaches the dichotomy of place and space from the rubric of a spatial philosophy. He writes, "a place is the order (of whatever kind) in accord with which elements are distributed in relationship of coexistence." In other words, everything has its place, and that place in relation to other places. Consider a holy sanctuary, and how, from high church to low church, everything has its place in it. The piano goes here, the pulpit there, the paschal candle here, and so forth. Place is also commensurate with rest, a trajectory ended. This may apply to a stone tossed along the shore, or the span of a life drawn close.[12]

Space, however, is the "consideration of vectors of direction, velocities, and timelines." Space is dynamic, it's open, providing room to roam. The moment the relocation of the pulpit is considered, there holy place is acknowledged to have space. The moment the stone is lifted from off the ground, there is hope in where it might land. When a person dies, and that life seems to have come to its place of rest, the community gathers to celebrate life, to hope against despair that though the cadaver is placed in a tomb, this body is a symbol of a hope in coming resurrection, transforming this place of death into a space of everlasting life.

According to de Certeau, while place is seen as a relationship between static members, space is a vector, a relationship of motion. It is time to transform places of despair into what David Harvey calls "spaces of hope."[13]

When de Certeau describes ritual as the "performance of place into space," he does not describe a way of merely anesthetizing the dynamism of open space, but brings cohesion and intention to the abysmal qualities of too much space. When liturgy remains agile with improvisational curiosity, when it bears responsibility — is able to respond — to the wonders unveiled by time, it proves a deeply transformative practice of place as space, and open spaces of hope as an affirming place to be.

So liturgy initiates us into a new experience of time and space. While the streets of the city have been co-opted and commodified by capitalism, it is time for the poet to come now! We need to take back the streets to create a new global common. It is time for an age of rebel cities![14]

Rebellion begins in church. The liturgy calibrates us into festival time and gives us another experience of space in the sanctuary where each Sabbath we transform places of despair into spaces of hope. The doing of liturgy enacts *koinonia* among those who are participants. *Koinonia* is the context for engendering eucharistic love, justice, and truth among the gathered people of God. If the gathered are the oppressed, people in despair, especially social despair, like poverty, the festival nature of liturgical time disrupts that despair, introducing through the ritual of eucharistic feasting the festival agenda of the eschaton.

Sacraments play an integral role in creating the conditions for social transformation. Theater is sacramental in that it makes visible an invisible reality. Through *transformational theater* we can begin to preenact the outlines of a vibrant prophetic urbanism — a Resurrection City — a new space of *dynamos* being realized by the Spirit amidst the seemingly established places of urban oppression. To release the captives in these places of despair, we'll need people with eyes to see and hearts to act — spect-actors.

Like the audience in a jazz club, the members of the church have a vital role to play in the theo-drama of redemption. The arts play a crucial role in transforming place into space. Jazz must be performed to create jazz space. Theater must be performed to create dramatic space. The gospel must be embodied to create spaces of hope narrated by festival time.

As actors bring a script to life in live theater, so, too, do Christians bring the script of Scripture to life through their creativity in the liturgical and prophetic life of the church. The possession that takes place among players and audience is in the exchange of personhood, the abundance of the presence of people who are fully alive. The discourse of "possession" that takes place among all those who participate in theatrical production bears witness to the "liminal states" of existence that mark the boundaries of life. The church performs *koinonia* through ritual. The prophetic church today needs to design rituals that can be street performances. This will mean that the church will have to move outside of the gates, outside of its building, outside of its institutional strictures and structures. Liberation theology offers a powerful expression of bearing witness to Christ outside of the gates of the church.

Liberating the Church

The fires of revolution blazed in Latin America in the 1960s. In 1968 Latin American bishops met in Medellín, Colombia, to discuss how the church could respond to rampant poverty and seek peace in a culture of violence. Gustavo Gutiérrez was an active participant in those early conversations on liberation. Gutiérrez and other young liberation theologians sought to break the cycle of violence, seeking creative ways of ending institutional violence. The ethics of responsibility was not enough because it often took the current social structures for granted, legitimating the status quo.

Liberation theologians called for social disruption, the construction of new and more just social structures. The discourse of liberation captured the imagination of the theologians from the South, gradually leavening the theological conversation in the North. Through grassroots community organizing among the poor, these Latin American activists inaugurated a movement of *comunidades de base* that would seek to embody communal equality and justice at the most local level possible.

A church of the oppressed requires active participation and not spectatorship. The transforming move is to get people from pew/spectator to disciple/witness. The structures that are oppressive within the church need to be undone by helping congregants "act out" their experiences received in the church. Historically, the transformation of places of death into spaces of hope through their life together is witnessed in the *comunidades eclesial de base,* "base ecclesial communities," of Latin America. These were small gatherings of Christians who would worship and conspire creatively to dismantle injustice in their communities. These base ecclesial communities embodied the spirit of the early church and stood in critique of the excesses of the bureaucracy of the institutionalized Roman Catholic Church. Base ecclesial communities sought to embody the gospel in the concrete details of communal life in a specific city. Cities offer a spatial matrix through which the church can achieve its prophetic vocation.

To be prophetic urban ministers, we need to understand the city that we minister in. The church is called to a musical movement for love and justice in and for the city; however, cities are places with lengthy, twisted histories, complex social structures, and networks of back-office politics. Prophetic theology today must self-consciously analyze the *place* or social location from which it theologizes, including the ever changing city.

Youth Ministries for Peace and Justice

Today we need to reimagine the church as a theater of the oppressed. The members of the church need to awaken from their slumber as mere audiences to the machinations of priestcraft and become spect-actors in the struggle for social transformation in the local community. It is time to take the liturgy outside of the gates of the church and into the streets and into the community to disrupt business as usual and usher in the shalom justice of God.

Youth Ministries for Peace and Justice in the South Bronx is a youth social justice ministry that is an example of the church understood as a theater of the oppressed. Founded by Alexie Torres-Fleming, a Roman Catholic Latina, the ministry represents a prophetic, feminist, intercultural Christian-led movement for justice. Founded by a woman of color, the organization is doing the hard work of seeking to redeem the "powers and principalities" in the South Bronx, the poorest congressional district in the country. Youth Ministries for Peace and Justice is effectively using different forms of Boal's theater of the oppressed to dramatize the environmental injustices of the South Bronx.

Torres-Fleming was initiated into the movement for justice through her involvement in antidrug activism in the Bronx. A leader in the youth group at Holy Cross Catholic Church, she was mentored into the movement by Father Mike Tyson, and into a mystical-prophetic theology that flows through the Roman Catholic tradition, especially within the streams of Franciscan monasticism and liberation theology.

During the 1980s there was a growing crack epidemic in the South Bronx. Father Tyson began to organize prayer marches in front of crack houses. In retaliation to these prayers, drug dealers broke into Holy Cross and burned the church in November 1992. Instead of retreating in fear in the face of this violence, Father Tyson and the community committed to marching again to acknowledge that God's true sanctuary was the bodies of those being destroyed by drugs in the community.

When discerning a way to move ahead, Torres-Fleming said, "Let's march again!" She worked with Father Tyson and helped to organize local youth to mobilize 1,200 people to march against the drug trade in the neighborhood.

The march was successful. Crack houses were shut down, some becoming new homes in the community. Many of the youth realized that faith could move beyond the walls of the church, and that they had agency and could effect change together. With this taste of victory the youth of the South Bronx were ready for a new challenge, and Alexie was ready to lead them.[15] Coming from the margins, from invisibility, they were coming to the center. This led to Torres-Fleming envisioning a space of hope where young people could be formed into prophetic leaders. Torres-Fleming spent the next year planning a ministry to youth, and in 1994 Youth Ministries for Peace and Justice was launched. They got space at St. Joan of Arc Church, where they began to respond to the many issues of injustice in their neighborhood.

To build Resurrection City, we need to identify the places of death and transform them into spaces of hope. When Torres-Fleming's son Patrick was diagnosed with asthma, the struggle for justice got personal. Torres-Fleming began talking to other mothers and discovered that many of their children had asthma too. These mothers wanted to get to the bottom of their children's sickness. A search for answers to this growing health crisis led them to the sources of particle pollution in the Bronx. One source was the massive number of automobiles that traveled through the Bronx every day.

The South Bronx is crisscrossed by four highways. During the postwar period, urban planning in New York City under the leadership of Robert Moses focused on the efficiency of automobiles moving through the urban matrix. It was cars and capital, not poor people and the land, that were the primary foci of this urban planning paradigm. Through efficient channels of transportation, Moses sought to ensure the efficient flow of labor and capital throughout the New York metropolitan area. Poor neighborhoods like the South Bronx became the target for the construction of highways. Moses' urban-aesthetic ideal was order and efficiency; however, it was ultimately a white supremacist urban planning model that effectively segregated people into "their place," especially the black and brown bodies of the South Bronx.

To begin to take the land back in the South Bronx, Youth Ministries for Peace and Justice deployed strategies from the theater of the oppressed. Their theatrical campaigns for justice had two foci: the Sheridan Expressway and Concrete Plant Park. While the Sheridan Expressway had purportedly been built as a necessity because of massive traffic, there was not as much actual traffic as had been envisioned. To dramatize the situation, some Youth Ministries for Peace and Justice staff and volunteers lay across the expressway during rush hour. A photograph was taken and then circulated through the media to show New York City that the Sheridan Expressway was a highly underutilized transportation route. On another occasion, the community coalition organized a picnic on the highway, putting out blankets to dramatize what it would be like to have a park along the Bronx River. Both of these dramatic interventions unveiled an alternative vision of what the land could be used for. The highway that is a place of despair and pollution could be transformed into a space of hope and health. Theater of the oppressed visualizes what we are moving toward, not just what is wrong.

Another example is the Concrete Plant Park. There was an old, abandoned concrete plant that was owned by the city and sat dormant for over a decade. It was one of two pieces of public land that had access to the Bronx River. Youth Ministries for Peace and Justice attended community board meetings and filed petitions for the land to be officially turned over to the Parks Department to become waterfront park land and clean, open green space for the community.

In the process, they discovered that New York State had $11 million in federal money to build a truck route from the Cross Bronx Expressway into Hunts Point Market. They needed to dramatize the injustice, so several young people climbed to the top of the concrete plant and hung a sign that said, "Replant the Concrete Plant." They would also perform guerrilla theater. In a community where not everyone reads and writes and many do not speak English, theater is an effective way to communicate to the people. They would go to the corner with a group of young people and do a drama about the death of the river. They would take a portable radio and drums, and would conduct a funeral procession about the concrete plant. They tapped into people's hearts and their emotional memory. They made a casket and had a mock funeral for the concrete plant and put the casket in a canoe with flowers, letting it float downstream.

Congressman José E. Serrano took the $11 million and reallocated it for a greenway to be established for the park. Instead of a route for trucks, a route for pedestrians was built. The dramas performed by Youth Ministries for Peace and Justice effected social change. Ultimately there was a $30 million grant; there were domino tables, seats organized in a circle for reading, and a serpentine pathway to walk and bike. The struggle for green space for the whole community was successful. It is now a beautiful waterfront park.

Along the way theater was consistently used to dramatize the needs of the community. During Lent, the various injustices in the community were "crucified" during a procession called the Way of the Cross; canoes were baptized and christened in the "holy" waters of the Bronx River, and a Jewish atonement ritual was conducted to ask forgiveness for sins of environmental degradation.

Some would say their greatest achievement is a restored river and access to new waterfront open space, but the theater of the oppressed is more powerful than that. It is a process of transformation that happens among the people who are able to move and speak and emboldens them and creates the conditions in which they can claim their own voice and power. Social change does not occur solely on the energy of resistance. Theater of the oppressed requires an alternative energy that offers a vision of what can be and how we can get there, together and with joy. There now exists an empowered people with collective memory of being able to create change.

The environmental justice movement provides a new paradigm for Christian political theology in the twenty-first century. It clearly unveils the ways in which environmental degradation negatively impacts communities of color. While it focuses on adverse environmental impacts on poor populations, the environmental justice movement offers a holistic approach to environmental problems that has respect for all life-support systems, including human and nonhuman life. It envisions the conditions through which we can see the full integration of racial justice, gender justice, economic justice, and environmental justice. It translates the church-based model of faith-rooted organizing into the environmental movement. By tapping into the activist energies of the people most directly affected by environmental racism, the environmental justice movement redirects mainstream environmentalism to seek environmental protection in concert with the struggle for social justice in poor communities.

The environmental justice movement provides a model of privileging the perspective of the poor in Christian ethics. It begins with the concrete conditions of the neighborhoods that we live in, especially poor neighborhoods. It presses us toward a deeper analysis of our local ecologies in order to understand the pathways of injustice. Since all humans are ecologically vulnerable, the environmental justice movement affirms our common humanity.

Martin Luther King Jr. argued that every individual human being is a child of God made in the *imago Dei*. King appealed to the metaphor of a world house to describe the predicament that humanity finds itself in today. King writes the following in his essay "The World House": "Some years ago a famous novelist died. Among his papers was found a list of suggested plots for future stories, the most prominently underscored being this one: 'A widely separated family inherits a house in which they have to live together.' This is the great new problem of mankind. We have inherited a large 'world house' in which we have to live together . . . a family unduly separated in ideas, culture, and interest, who because we can never again live apart, must learn somehow to live with each other in peace."[16] In this passage King deploys the metaphor of a "world house" to convey the deep interconnection of the community of creation. King challenged the world to seek a deeper understanding of the interrelated dynamics that make up our common life on planet earth. Protecting the earth and caring for our neighbors go hand in hand as humanity seeks to live together in shalom justice in a world riddled with violence and conflict. Like King's vision of a "world house," the environmental justice movement shares a commitment to the dignity of all humans and the integrity of creation, foregrounding the experiences of the marginalized who suffer the most from environmental degradation.

The environmental justice movement challenges both liberal and evangelical Christians to actively respond to the physical suffering and ecological vulnerabilities of poor communities. While liberal theology and activism constituted one stream that informed the environmental justice movement in the 1980s, environmental justice stands in critique of the liberal sustainable community strategy. Willis Jenkins writes, "By tracing racist and sexist logics of domination, environmental justice laid open the way to an entirely distinct practical strategy."[17]

The environmental justice movement's distinct contribution comes from its subject position within communities of color, focusing especially on women of color who are disproportionately affected by environmental degradation. Furthermore, since women of color largely lead the environmental justice movement, the movement stands as a critique of the largely white male power structures at play in most mainline, evangelical, and Catholic institutions.

By pressing us to develop critical race and gender analyses of existing Christian environmental activism, the environmental justice movement can open up new possibilities for social transformation and ecological renewal. Rather than a top-down leadership style, the environmental justice movement seeks to promote the *self-determination* of local communities of color, developing local leadership capable of creatively and prophetically engaging the problems of environmental racism through organic, local community organizing.

Foregrounding the experiences of women of color provides a hermeneutical lens for developing a prophetic Christian social ethic, a prophetic intercultural, ecofeminist hermeneutic that engages environmental and economic problems from the perspectives of communities of color and their grassroots organizing efforts, particularly those of women of color. This prophetic intercultural, ecofeminist hermeneutic offers the world Christian movement an important resource for self-critique, social transformation, and environmental renewal.

This feminist hermeneutic should be complemented by an "interactionalist" social analysis that considers the deep interconnections of race, class, gender, theology, and ecology. Martin Luther King Jr. modeled this form of social analysis when he named the "giant triplets of racism, materialism, and militarism" in his "A Time to Break Silence" speech at the Riverside Church in New York City on April 4, 1967.

Since Dr. King was brutally murdered a year to the day later on April 4, 1968, while leading a protest of sanitation workers in Memphis, Tennessee, we could add environmental injustice to the list of oppressive evils. For in his advocacy on behalf of sanitation workers who were collecting other people's trash and taking it to the dump, King anticipated the poor-led environmental justice movement's interrogation of where those dumps were located and how these urban spatial configurations revealed what Emilie Townes calls "contemporary versions of lynching a whole people."[18]

Today the prophetic church must continue to end the lynching of black, brown, and female bodies, struggling to embody the beloved community.

Conclusion

Shortly after Occupy Wall Street began on September 17, 2011, in Zuccotti Park, a group of ministers gathered to work in solidarity with the protest movement called Occupy Faith. When the occupiers were thrown out of Zuccotti Park, several congregations took them into their fellowship halls, including Judson Memorial Church and Riverside Church.

On Wednesday, March 7, 2012, a group of clergy from Occupy Faith met to enact parables of an immoral budget in front of Governor Andrew Cuomo's Manhattan office. As political leaders in Albany finalized the details of New York State's budget, nearly fifty faith leaders from across New York engaged in a theater of the oppressed intervention to expose the immorality of the proposed budget that harmed poor, working-class New Yorkers.

Using beds to illustrate the crisis of record homelessness and increased poverty in New York, faith leaders demanded that budget cuts to human services be restored. In their prayers, they highlighted the unjust tax loopholes that permitted corporations like Goldman Sachs, Verizon, and News Corporation to earn billions in New York State but pay less in tax than a working-class family of four. The act of prophetic, public theater unveiled that it is sinful to balance the budget on the backs of "the least of these" while we permit wealthy corporations to evade their responsibilities to our communities.

Clergy laid the beds in front of Governor Cuomo's office and lay in them, blocking the entrance to the 633 Third Avenue office building. Business as normal was interrupted in the city. The ministers were arrested and the governor heard the protest of the people.

Throughout his ministry, Jesus Christ reached out and *touched* the sick and marginalized. This is no secret. As the *body* of Christ, the church is called then to find ways to also make physical contact with those in the world, usually outside the gates of the established church, who suffer the layers of colonization through neoliberal capitalism. It is time for the people of God to courageously, creatively, and compassionately respond to the cries of the oppressed. Thus the task of reimagining the church as a musical theater of the oppressed is urgent. This will involve deep thought about liturgical reform and renewal, thought that makes physical connections and interrupts the actual politics of the marketplace. Churches today need to learn how to translate the liturgical performance saved for Sunday worship into street theater freely performed throughout the week. When the church has the courage to open its doors to all God's children in the community of creation, the Spirit of justice will flow through the streets of our city like a mighty stream of salvation and the streets will burn bright with shalom as if made of gold.

Today we need to build on the best of prophetic black Christianity, while seeking to break the black-white binary. While blues music is about the pain of the past, jazz music speaks to a new future, a future we can create together through improvisation. To live into a prophetic, intercultural, feminist, jazzlike future, prophetic Christians need to open up new spaces of truth telling, develop an ear for hearing the sounds of a blues people, and learn to work collectively and improvisationally for more culturally and gender diverse leadership teams, churches, and schools.

While Christ is the head of the church, we are the body. We are Christ's hands and feet, which are supposed to reach out to love and serve the world. In the North American context, this will entail intentional solidarity with the freedom struggles of people of color who have been oppressed in this land for centuries.

We need to imagine new communities of resurrection. Because Jesus Christ is a crucified and *risen* Lord, we need to pray for and seek to embody communities of resurrection. We need to create new spectacles that unveil the colonial pretense of the city's controlling powers while embodying an alternative reality.

The power of the resurrection manifests itself in the Christ-centered community striving to embody love and justice. Dietrich Bonhoeffer writes, "Only Christ in his love tells me what love is."[19] Christ's call is a call to love, for only through Christ showing us how to love are we even in a position to love God and love our neighbor. Yet, this call is made amidst the struggle of great suffering in the world.

CHAPTER SEVEN

A Love Supreme

The Lord *God said, "It is not good that the man should be alone; I will make him a helper as his partner."*

Genesis 2:18

It is time for love to learn some lessons from jazz. Jazz and love are languages with much in common. Becoming fluent in these languages takes discipline and creativity. Through the disciplined study and practice of these languages, we are able to more freely express ourselves. Jazz musicians master the chord progressions of a tune in order to be fully free to improvise within its harmonic-rhythmic structure. With an intimate knowledge of the music's structure, a musician can take a song to a new place.

Improvisation is not just a principle for music and theater alone; it is a principle for life and love. Living *is* improvising. Analyzing the art of improvisation in jazz music can help deepen our understanding and practice of love. Individual jazz musicians learn the jazz tradition and different musical practices so they are ready to sing their own song. In addition to their technical knowledge of music and their performance experience, jazz musicians learn how to *listen,* to become part of a community where they seamlessly integrate their musical voices in an ensemble.

Like the Delta blues, jazz has a call-and-response structure. When a jazz ensemble plays, one musician's solo is a call and the next musician's solo is a response. Each musician's song inspires the next musician to venture out to a new space of musical freedom. The call-and-response structure of soloing propels the group on their musical journey, until they meet back at the end of the song with a reprise of their theme.

Jazz musicians need to be in tune and attuned to each other. There is a subtle form of communication that goes on between the players in a jazz ensemble. Sometimes they begin to quiet their instrument; sometimes this is done through eye contact, at other times by a hand signal, and sometimes by voice; but they develop highly attuned forms of communication to stay in sync with each other during performances.

Jazz songs are musical conversations. Like all conversation, they are essentially improvised on a theme. Improvisation is creative collaboration. Agile and attentive, improvisation entails openness to new possibilities. When jazz musicians creatively collaborate with each other, they unleash the creative power that comes from the synergy between the players.

Love is like jazz. Like jazz, personal relationships of love also move forward through conversations. We are designed to be in communion with each other. Through heart-to-heart conversation, a deeper, lasting bond is built. When we share our innermost thoughts and feelings with others, we extend a trust that is hopefully met with safety and deeper intimacy. With time these friendships can become revolutionary, when we are united by a common goal — transforming the world to be more just and loving.

A good lover is a good listener. As musicians listen closely to each other's solos, we need to listen intently to each other to really get to know each other. There is a time to talk and a time to listen. Attentive listening is the path to deeper intimacy and more loving relationships. As we really get to know the other person, we will be in a better position to love that person with a love language that speaks to his or her soul.

As good jazz musicians, lovers need to open their hearts to the other, not holding anything back. This is true jazz love — listening, sympathizing, quoting, sharing, playing, creating — together. It's collaborative and reciprocal, and as a result, intimate.

Jazz Love: A Love Supreme

John Coltrane's album *A Love Supreme* is a crescendo in American imagination as he gives musical form to the flow of love. This musical meditation on love offers a new horizon for a politics of love today. *A Love Supreme* was a transformative moment in the history of jazz. Recorded by the Coltrane Quartet at a studio in Englewood, New Jersey, in December of

1964, the album dropped in February 1965. The music was made by what has come to be known as the classic Coltrane Quartet, including Coltrane on saxophone, McCoy Tyner on piano, Jimmy Garrison on bass, and Elvin Jones on drums. Coltrane treats the love theme through a four-part suite with four titled tracks: "Acknowledgment," "Resolution," "Pursuance," and "Psalm." After briefly discussing this album, I will use the four headings to improvise on the theme of love.

I. Acknowledgment

With malleted strikes, feathered with Tyner's piano chords, *A Love Supreme* breaks into the aural sphere. This is not a violent interruption, but gentle and smooth. As the gong-strike decays, Coltrane introduces the love motif, a few bars of a smooth arpeggio with his saxophone while the drummer holds the space with the sparkling dance of drumstick upon cymbal. For a measure or two, the ride cymbal continues alone, building tension. At exactly the right moment, the snare clicks in, setting the groove. It is a rim shot — the drumstick is held sideways and the rim of the snare is hit, instead of the surface. This creates a sound like a hollow block, clear and percussive. Most of the direct strikes of the stick happen upon the tom-toms, generating the darker, rolling sounds behind the ride cymbal and the click of the snare. The groove allows the piano to step in with chords that dance delicately with the drums.

As Coltrane begins to build his melody, the piano pulsates with the rhythm section. Supporting both the drums in the percussive habits of the chords, the piano dances with the melody, in key and on step. The sound opens up into a classic jazz sound, with seeming chaos fitting seamlessly together in sonorous sound. Halfway through the song, the chords of the piano seem to have moved up the register and become slightly more prominent. In that prominence, they appear to hold a pattern, which Coltrane's saxophone links into. It's this pattern, this melodic meditation on love, that then turns into the chant of two bass-baritone voices:

A love supreme
A love supreme
A love supreme

This rhythmic chanting sounds like the beating of human hearts. A love supreme is the heartbeat of the universe. After the chanting, as the piano and the drums finish their parts in the song, dissolving or stopping altogether, the bass emerges from deep in the background, bringing the momentum to a more gentle stop. The bass ends curiously, with a syncopated break from the groove, signaling the end of the movement. The final note — a chord.

II. Resolution

Where "Acknowledgment" ended with the still, small, but deep voice of the bass subtly multiplied from a single note into a chord, this movement starts with the chorded bass, as if to connect the two songs, a turn from acknowledgment to resolution. The theme that Coltrane introduces on his sax stands clear and confident.

In "Resolution" the tempo picks up and sweeps you away. The piano solo starts simple but becomes more chromatic and complex. The whole time the drummer presses into the rhythm, picking up the intensity.

Coltrane's presence in "Resolution" is radiant. There is a freedom in the top of his tenor sax — a simple clarity. In his second solo, Coltrane takes things a little lower, with a heartier, warmer sound.

Throughout "Resolution" the main voices are the saxophone and the piano, a musical conversation energized by tension. When the instrumentalists depart from the progression's initial key, they work to dramatically increase harmonic tension. During the movement the pianist ascends a spiral of chords, creating a dark and cloudy atmosphere. The saxophone follows suit, exploring territory in midflight. On an adventure of exploration, Coltrane simply avoids the dominant note while he spirals around the theme. Finally, with a return to the initial key in the end, Coltrane brings us an experience of resolution, tension turned to harmony.

Jazz is about resolving conflict through harmony. Throughout the resolution the distinct solos and cross-rhythms create a dramatic tension that is resolved into harmony at the end of the movement, with smaller harmonizations throughout. Tension is resolved through convergence in the same key, as two voices become one. Two beating hearts beat as one. It's only through engaging real difference that true musical unity can be experienced. Harmony is reached through fully embracing conflict, then creatively resolving tension.

III. Pursuance

"Pursuance" opens with drums, setting a much faster pace to the song than the first two movements. A large part of the solo hovers around the snare, with rolls, strikes, and other polyrhythms hearkening back to the African rhythms of old. When the solo falls back onto the ride cymbal, the band enters, keeping up the much faster tempo.

Coltrane comes in with the love motif, followed by an up-tempo piano solo with the drummer quickly and lightly keeping pace on the cymbals. The pianist and drummer do a musical dance together, deepening the texture of the love theme, but all the while with a fierce urgency and driving rhythm.

"Pursuance" pulsates. It is forward-moving with explosive energy. The high-speed tempo of the drums is met by the quick, fluid piano playing. Both the drums and the piano are in a full sprint, each one darting ahead as the other runs quickly to catch up.

In the midst of this high-speed chase, Coltrane comes in playing swiftly in the same tempo, playing almost every note on his saxophone, from its lowest note to its highest top. He shows the extension, versatility, and range of his musical voice.

Overall, this movement remains much more scattered, full of dissidence and counterpoint, seemingly erratic jumps in the scales, that, when taken as a whole, blend into a complex and energetic movement. When Coltrane breaks in, it feels like a breaking into a full-tilted run, as if what started off as a scattered scramble has now found its destination — a place to be.

What is curious is that the song unfolds just as it opens. The sax and the piano cut out fairly suddenly, leaving the drums to crash and sputter to a stop, unveiling the serene but full-bodied bass. And when it seems like the song is over, a bass solo dances along for another couple of minutes. It's almost as if the bass is the only instrument to finish the song, that there is a difference between hot pursuit and steady pursuance. Though the energy of the piano and drums is exhilarating, they are unable to maintain their energy to the end of the movement. It is the bass, and the bass alone, that embodies a slow and steady pursuance. The reliable and rhythmic presence of the bass provides a musical foundation for Coltrane to launch his saxophone ascent.

IV. Psalm

In "Psalm" we see Coltrane move toward a contemplative jazz that seeks to hearken the spiritual possibilities and transformative potential of the very nature of jazz itself. From the very first note, "Psalm" is distinct from the previous three movements.

The vibe of "Psalm" feels smoky, misty, and ethereal. One might describe it as a lounge song, save that the drums are malleted, producing a deep, rolling, timpani sound. This keeps the listener from getting too comfortable, too calm. There is smoothness, but also an epic quality here.

"Psalm" doesn't have nearly as much variation as "Pursuance." The notes are but a handful. Instead the character here is found in the percussive qualities in the melody of the sax and piano.

The melody parallels a psalm printed in the album notes. The psalm is full of short concussive sentences, punctuated in beatnik style. In this poem Coltrane includes key words like "acknowledgement" and "resolve" but never "a love supreme."

Help us to resolve our fears and weaknesses.

The fact that we do exist is acknowledgement of Thee, O Lord.

What makes "Psalm" melodically congruous with the whole album is a small musical phrase right at the tail end of the movement, where Coltrane reprises the opening riff from "Acknowledgment," bringing the whole piece full circle. This reprise thus reveals the whole of "Psalm" to be a riff on that one theme. In such a move, "Psalm" is an unusual piece of jazz, in that the song is, in a way, backward. When the quartet enters into this piece, there is not the distinct jazz behavior of setting a theme then riffing upon it, sharing solos and then returning. Instead, the whole ensemble plays as if they have already heard the theme, which they only reveal in the end, and only then as a mere glimmering hint.

The unique structure "Psalm," a jazz riff on jazz itself, illustrates the kind of dynamic this book puts forth, that of improvising upon a theme that actually comes at the end of the song. In a similar dynamic, the mystic-prophet plays a melody directed toward the end of all things — an eschaton. We musically move toward a destination — the great banquet — while our prophetic imagination and improvisation in the Spirit lead us to the feast. The meaning of love supreme lies not in a conceptuality, but in the concrete, embodied practice of loving, making space for each one to join in *koinonia*. While we daily meditate on a love supreme in our inner life, we need to embody it in our outer life. Like passionate jazz, passionate love is moved not merely by sentiment, but by the sacramental presence of God's supreme love.

Music Is a Common Language

Coltrane, as a musician, spoke of this love with all his heart, in a voice and vocabulary nearest his soul — jazz music in an African American idiom. Rooted in the spiritual chants and ring shouts of their African ancestors, the enslaved Africans of antebellum America gave voice to a common language that, though culturally distinct, was universal in its vocabulary. Music sustained the souls of enslaved Africans as they traveled the Middle Passage from Africa to the New World. Music became the common language that held the African diaspora together in the Americas. Music was a vehicle for spiritual renewal, communal bonding, political resistance, and psychic survival. Through the rituals of music, Africans in the diaspora began to subvert the logic of commodification, retaining their moral and cultural agency, despite being enslaved in an economy that not only valued them as little more than bodies fit for manual labor, but also claimed theological validation from Holy Scripture.

Christian theology provided the social imagination for the Western project of colonization in the Americas. From Jesuit theologian José de Acosta Porres' Thomistic racial hierarchies to Puritan theologian Jonathan Winthrop's Calvinist "city on a hill" vision, the theologies of European Christendom were blind to the racism and genocide underlying their stories of providential colonial expansion. European and North American Christianity often willingly accepted and promoted the benefits it gained as the religion of the political superpowers. From the genocide of native peoples to the transatlantic slave trade, the logic of colonization turned the God-given goodness of creation and difference into tools for producing exploitation, fear, and the infrastructure of empire. Given this stubborn legacy of colonization and white supremacy, the rehabilitation of Christian theology in the Americas begins with confession and repentance of these sins of a white, colonialist past.

Naming the idols of whiteness, colonization, and patriarchy is the beginning of transforming Christian theology in the Americas today. Through the long, hard work of dismantling these idols, Christian theology can begin the process of living into a new prophetic, intercultural, womanist future. Prophetic theology today must deconstruct the white, Western, and male character of modern theology.

The colonial, white, patriarchal theology provides the architecture of much of hierarchical church life in North America today. While women and people of color are increasingly placed in positions of leadership, white, Western men continue to have the most political power within the ecclesial establishment. White men need to relinquish their power and be open to new configurations of power that are based on racial and gender justice. This is the only way the North American church can live into the future that God is calling it toward.

A politics of love demands confession of sins. In America, white folks need to confess their complicity in social structures of white supremacy that give them power and privileges not shared by people of color. Furthermore, they need to actively work toward dismantling these racist structures through changing the policies, programs, and personnel of their places of work and houses of worship. Antiracist whites should follow the lead of antiracist leaders of color in embodying new institutions that are fundamentally just and loving.

Following the *Jewish* Jesus, who is leading an intercultural, improvisational movement of love and justice, we each must also confess our own culpability within the power struggle of race. While the colonial imagination viewed white Europeans as God's elect in the New World, the Scriptures repudiate this exceptionalist logic. Christian identity, to which Christian theology bears intellectual witness as a churchly identity, is forged and ever exists within God's election of the Jews.

Following in the footsteps of the Jewish Jesus, Christianity today should form a politics of love that draws deeply from the tradition of Hebrew prophecy but leans into a new and transformational future. In the Hebrew prophetic imagination, *hesed,* or the steadfast love of God, was the basis of Jewish life together.

Prophetic ministers are called to inspire and equip Christians to build beloved cities today. The love that expresses both justice and faithfulness is marked by God's particular concern for the suffering, the vulnerable, and the oppressed. The prophets lift up care of all God's children, especially the marginalized — widows, orphans, strangers, and the poor — as one of the central practices reflecting our love for God (Zech 7:9-10).

There is a *lingua franca* that is not beholden to race or creed, politics or class — it is music. *Linguae francae* are usually developed for assisting in the intercommunication of numerous political/cultural entities. French, at the height of the colonial expansion of Europe, was used to aid diplomatic negotiations between various European thrones, often for carving up the "unexplored" continents of Africa, Asia, and South America. In the early twentieth century, this language slowly shifted to English, along with a drift from colonialism to capitalism. English has become the language of our age of global cities.

But an essential division remains; without the *lingua franca,* one person cannot understand another. Yet with music, division is subverted. Sure, there may be apparent oddity at first encounter, but with keenness of perseverance and love, the deep universal grammar and syntax of music break forth and the equally deep commonality of humanity is ratified.

Unfortunately, a binary dialectic is often maintained, a jazz that is not cooperative but competitive, an oppressive music that holds the city in despair. This has happened, in due part, because of the ways in which the song of Israel has been co-opted over the years to allow for a belief that the city, as a place outside the sanctuary, as an audience of "unbelievers," is not the concern of the church. Even the lyrics of this song — *mishpat, sedaqah, emet,* and *hesed* — have been altered to ensure that the focus be upon the church as cloistered theater, a segregated sanctum.

Dismantling this segregation is the beginning of gathering the beloved community through truth telling and practices of justice, walking together on a path toward deeper intimacy. James Cone has shown us that blacks and whites in America have been bitter enemies and intimate lovers. Blacks and whites have expressed and experienced the intimacy of hate. But, by the grace of God, we can also find the deeper intimacy of love; any gulf between blacks and whites can be bridged by the power of justice and love. This will demand open conversations and confessions, as well as collective repentance and collaboration. A love supreme must press beyond the black-white binary toward a prophetic intercultural future that is inclusive of all people, black, white, and every shade in between. We must listen deeply, earnestly, for a love supreme amidst the travail of our life together.

Acknowledgment: In God We Live and Move

Creator is calling. Creator called the world into existence. We acknowledge that we would not be without the one in whom we live and move and have our being. The fact that we exist is acknowledgment. At the very start, "when God created," the earth was a "formless void and darkness covered the face of the deep" (Gen 1:1-2). Creator forms the world from the formless void and deep darkness. Shaping the materials available, Creator improvises to create a new world. *Creatio ex improvisatio* unveils that improvisation is integral to life.

The fact that we are made in the *imago Dei* acknowledges that we are improvisers. Humans are called to emulate God's creativity as an acknowledgment of the call-and-response between earth and heaven, the *basileia tou theou* and the *malkut shamayim.*

Our improvisation is guided by shalom justice. We are to seek the well-being of the whole community of creation, which is interdependent. A human being is only fully human insofar as he or she is in relationship with an Other. We bear God's image as we love God and one another. We need to acknowledge those who have loved us, like our parents, our beloved, our children and friends.

Imago Dei is connected to the *civitas Dei.* We become human in our life together in cities. This is why Jeremiah instructed the exiled Jews to seek the shalom of the *city* (Jer 29:7). In Saint Paul's letter to the church in Philippi, he said, "I want to know Christ and the power of his resurrection and the sharing of his sufferings by becoming like him in his death, if somehow I may attain the resurrection from the dead" (Phil 3:10-11). Since Jesus was raised from the dead, we should continue with this resurrection power in our work to cultivate communities of resurrection in our cities. Building beloved cities is one of the ways that we image God.

Before the initial acts of creation, "a wind from God swept over the face of the waters." From this scenario we read of how the creation continually unfolded. If we are to resolve to create anything, we must understand, must first acknowledge, that one thought can produce millions of vibrations, and they all go back to God. Our origin, existence, and future is the living God. So, then, do we choose to create out of fear and hate, or out of love and charity?

Resolution: Harmony Is Created through the Resolution of Conflict

Loving is dangerous. It cuts deep. It demands risk. It lays us bare, open and vulnerable.

In loving, there is the possibility of loss. In loving, there is the possibility of heartbreak. In loving, one never has the option of turning away, regardless of what is uncovered. There may be weaknesses we have not accepted or overcome. We may carry disfigurements from childhood that are difficult to understand. From any of these may emerge fresher, open wounds — disappointments, accidents, errors, failed relationships, pain, and emptiness. All this can cause confusion, or worse, repulsion. Loving — and being loved — is as great a risk as we can face.

Loving unloosens our deepest fears. We fear not having what we desire, and then in having it we fear losing it. To love someone fully is to risk losing that person and his or her love one day, but to not love that person is to close oneself off from a deeper, richer life. It's crucial that we face these fears head-on. We must take heart and have the courage to plumb the depths of our heart and the hearts of others.

To love others and minister to them in their own suffering, we must first boldly enter into our own pain. To do so requires a journey through the valley of the shadow, entering into the places of utmost darkness and despair. The flames of our first love for God are fanned through transforming our fearsome loneliness into festive solitude. T. S. Eliot's *Four Quartets* unveils the paradox of love that transforms darkness into light and stillness into dancing.

When the courageous task of examining one's wounds is undertaken, it is wise to learn both honesty and charity. No matter how deep or painful the wound, we can begin the process of healing if we are both charitable and honest: *Ubi caritas et amor, Deus ibi est.* As we heal, we become freer and freer, reaching, ready, toward a more robust life-centered ethic. Hearing our own cries sensitizes us to the cries of others. Facing our own pain allows us to empathize with the pain of others. And the more we heal, the more we are able to accompany others toward healing, health, wholeness, and service. Being present to others requires, following the kenotic path, emptying our ego's desire for the desire of God; "not my will but yours" (Luke 22:42). As Jesus is the One *pro nobis,* we, too, are called to be for the other. "Being for the other" means to have the courage to enter into the pain of others, while being honest about our own pain, trauma, and struggles. Being compassionate means being "com-passionate," actually feeling what others are feeling in order to intercede for them and support them through a difficult time.

In light of trauma, the pastoral and prophetic vocations must go hand in hand. We can't rush to join the struggle for liberation; it makes no sense, spiritual or otherwise, to try to move forward while leaving our own and others' crushed spirits behind. The intensity of our social justice ministries must be matched by our intensity in creating communities of healing and hope for the emotionally wounded.

When the church gathers around victims of trauma for fellowship, healing, and hope, a new horizon is opened up for the ongoing healing of the whole community of God. Because of the radical disruption in victims' lives and psyches, pastoral psychotherapy becomes one service that the church, as a graced community, can offer to victims of trauma and other people who seek a deep engagement with their issues.

The graced community becomes a conversation and a fellowship; one could also liken it to jazz improvisation. With the materials we have at hand (our pain, our depths, our healing), we are equipped to listen more deeply to the songs of others, and to sing with them, offering harmonies and the encouragement of familiar refrains reimagined in a new context.

Attentive listening is vital to resolution. We have restless hearts, and thus must seek to hear God's voice as we discern our course of action. The primary purpose of discernment is to listen to the voice of the living God. "The sheep follow him because they know his voice" (John 10:4). Hearing the voice of the living God often comes through quieting our souls, preparing our hearts to hear the still-small voice of God. Listening to God is the work of the church. Yet there is a very subtle difference between listening as passive act and acknowledgment as active face-to-face engagement. Each has the means to listen to the voice of God, but as is so often the case, we each hear something similar yet also different. In voicing the things we hear, we gather in community to discuss and share; it is very possible that these different strains of the same song are in conflict or discord. What is needed is resolution.

Theologically, God affirms the need to confront the shadow side. God does not turn from pain and trauma, but rather enters headlong and fully into it through the full humanity of Jesus of Nazareth. God affirms the need to embrace humanity and to improvise in love. God becomes fully human because God is love.

Erotic love exceeds the dyad of the lover and the beloved. For Luce Irigaray, love between two includes a third. A woman and a man making love transcend the circle of their subjectivity. Through a shared outpouring of love, blurring the boundaries of bodies, they pass into the porous fluidity of mucous membranes into a new time and space that exceed our normal reality. The lover and the beloved are three through the ecstasy they share. Prior to any child, the third is the ecstasy of becoming one, while being two, the ecstasy of being one in the other.

What is the third that is created in the ecstatic love between the two? Theologian Sarah Coakley sees the bodies and souls of lovers and the love they share as a reflection of the image of the triune God, a communion of love. The love between lovers opens a channel of participation in the divine communion of love. While human love images the love of the triune God, the mystery of the triune God always exceeds our human ability to fully comprehend or commune with God. While seeking God with all our heart, we are often left lonely, longing for noetic and ecstatic communion with God.

Sexual desire is a gift from God; it reveals the singing self as one who longs. Ecstatic, embodied, and faithful sexuality images God's loving presence in our lives. We as three reflect the triune God, the *imago Trinitatis*. We should channel, intensify, and unify our desires into a prayerful and intimate encounter with the living God. Our love for God overflows in loving our neighbor and even our enemy (Matt 5:43-44).

Pursuance: Seeking the Shalom of God

Like a rhythm section in a good jazz band, a rocking rhythm pulsates through life. We have to hear that rhythm and flow with it. Feeling it in our heart and soul, we must move with the music. If we can hear the music and roll with the rhythm, we can dance through life. As Coltrane's "Pursuance" thrives on cross-rhythms, we need to walk with the Spirit in our own path of pursuing the kingdom of God.

We all crave intimacy. We long for connection, for closeness, for togetherness. We want to be known and loved by those who cherish our sparks and quirks, our strengths and weaknesses, our scars and beauty marks. We long to share our wildest dreams and deepest desires with others. We yearn to embody, be embodied, and join our bodies with an other.

Our quest for intimacy is driven by our deepest desires, not least the erotic; the arrow's wound drives us mad. Boundless energy propels us into each day. Raw desire is at the heart of our humanity, flowing through our social and political interactions as a ubiquitous subtext. The infinite longing in each human heart is what propels us to make music, make love, make theater, and work toward making a more loving and just city.

While thinkers like Anders Nygren have seen agape love and erotic love as separate types of love, theoretical distinction does not play out so well in the world of making. Instead of viewing erotic love as a love that draws us away from agape love, properly ordered erotic love can inform and energize our agape love. They are not separate, but are all of the same piece.

Desire compels us into love, and to fully live, to suck the marrow out of life. For early Christian theologian Gregory of Nyssa, eros was agape stretched out in longing toward the divine goal. Shaped by Platonic thought, the Cappadocian school of love understood erotic love more capaciously than sexual love; it overflowed into agape, reflecting the gracious excess of the Holy Trinity.

Gregory describes this process as *epektasis. Epektasis* comes from the term *epi-ek-teinomai,* meaning "to reach out after." It is the creature's constant forward motion or journey beyond itself into the boundlessness of God's fullness as the creature's capacities are stretched by what it receives. Gregory of Nyssa was inspired by the motif of pressing on toward God as proclaimed by the apostle Paul in his letter to the Philippians: "Beloved, I do not consider that I have made it my own; but this one thing I do: forgetting what lies behind and straining forward to what lies ahead, I press on toward the goal for the prize of the heavenly call of God in Christ Jesus" (Phil 3:13-14).

Gregory's *Life of Moses* is the story of Moses' entry into a dark cloud as the height of spiritual illumination. We can imagine no limitation in an infinite nature. That which is limitless cannot by its nature be understood. Desire for the beautiful draws our soul ever onward toward God. We are never fully satisfied but desire to see more and more of God. No limit can be set on our journey toward God. The infinite spiritual growth of creatures is based on the infinite power and mercy of God. The triune God is morally beautiful; no limitation can be placed on God. Moreover, our desire for God is never satisfied, and so no limits can be set as the creature seeks deeper and deeper knowledge of God. In like manner, Coltrane's longing and aspiration in *A Love Supreme* lure listeners to pursue God and truth with all their heart.

Gregory's whole theological program is an ascetical transformation of desire into dynamic participation in the triune life. Gregory grounds the limitlessness of one's desire for God in the infinite nature of God. Since we are made in the image of God to pursue God and goodness and since God is absolute goodness, our desire for God itself necessarily has no stopping place, but stretches out with the limitless.

The boundlessness of God's omnipotent love is the basis of our sanctification in the power of the Holy Spirit. Our spiritual growth into God knows no limit. Thus, we must press on. Our desire beckons us on. Gregory of Nyssa calls us to channel, intensify, and unify our desires into a prayerful and intimate encounter with the living God. For God is the source of a Love Supreme.

God is love, according to John's Gospel, as a person. This love is not just that which binds, but that which is binding all things; there is a verb. God transcends our notion of what love is, while being the source of all the love we are able to conjure through words and experience. We all have felt love in different ways — we have felt the love of our lover, the love of parents, the love of friends; however, our human experiences of love do not fully disclose the depths of God's love for us. Even these words, pulled like stray threads from the cosmos, fail to fully speak the dread splendor, the illuminating darkness that is love.

Love often feels like a flaming desire, a passion or "suffering" of want that does not consume yet is all-consuming. Mystic-prophetic Christianity must always have this fire burning at its source; this is the flame that mystic-prophetic Christianity must carry into the public sphere. Be not afraid of the redeeming fire of God's love; remove your shoes; fall upon your face and listen to love's voice.

Psalm: In the End is the Beginning

[1]I waited patiently for the LORD;
he inclined to me and heard my cry.
[2]He drew me up from the desolate pit,
out of the miry bog,
and set my feet upon a rock,
making my steps secure.
[3]He put a new song in my mouth,
a song of praise to our God.
Many will see and fear,
and put their trust in the LORD. . . .

[16]But may all who seek you
rejoice and be glad in you;
may those who love your salvation
say continually, "Great is the LORD!"
[17]As for me, I am poor and needy,
but the Lord takes thought for me.

In the Mennonite and Friends tradition the church seeks to reach consensus through a "sense of the meeting." When any issue is raised, it is discussed by all. When the questions dissipate, the leader asks whether the group has a "sense of the meeting" on the issue. If someone says no, then the discussion continues until consensus is achieved. People can still oppose a decision, but they get to speak their peace. Once the decision is made, the community must move ahead with grace to seek God's discernment for the next major decision that awaits them. Discernment as mutually individual and communal is a vital spiritual discipline because it makes the community attentive to the voice of the living God as sounded through a person and a collective of people.

Discernment is opening our eyes and ears to God's move of the Spirit in our lives and in the world. To love is also a discipline, a training work of the soul. The fullness of love does not merely happen extemporaneously. Loving is a way of life. The life of love is deepened through the practice of spiritual exercises that open within us the capacity to listen and acknowledge love, to resolve toward justice and pursue humility with our God. Psalms, like the one above (Ps 40), provide an example of reaching deep within as a means of reaching out, waiting patiently for the Lord as a means of finding, in one's mouth and body, a new song to share.

Through a mystical rootedness in the Word of Scripture and contemplative prayer, we can begin to sense the gates of the kingdom and embody agape love; by praying the Psalms, we hear the melody of love from the eschaton. The songs of the eschaton lure us into *kairos* moments, into festival time.

Yet, as the Mennonite tradition shows, personal rootedness finds fullness in community. Loving God is always coupled with loving the neighbor, thus one can only be accomplished through active participation in the other. The church provides the sacramental and communal traditions through which disciples can grow like "oaks of righteousness" (Isa 61:3). While the Christian life is rooted in love and charity — God's perpetual and unfettered favor — because of our sinful nature, the spirit of the world, and sinful social structures, human beings, especially the poor, are oppressed.

To live as Christian disciples in an age in which America is the new empire, it is vital that disciples corporately practice spiritual disciplines. These disciplines create conditions through which we can continue to walk together in the gospel pattern.

There are many spiritual disciplines, but two that are key to a life in pursuance of the shalom of any city are acts of prayer and acts of justice. As noted above, prayer is an internal rootedness, a deep mystical acknowledgment of a psalm of love and mercy that always fills the air around us. It's like hearing a faint sound of a musical troupe in the midst of Times Square, and from the middle of the vast crowd, trying to discern the direction from which the sound flows.

The next are acts of justice. Once the music is acknowledged, and the resolution to find its source made, and then pursued, what is the response to the psalm? Do we merely sit in a sort of staid consumption of this theater? Do we remit ourselves to the chaos of Times Square feeling blessed by a song? How are we changed and challenged? For the songs of heaven are not merely lovely, they are also imperatives, sacramental shouts for an egalitarian distribution of wealth and power, a recalibration of the roots of our own humanity, be we black, white, brown, citizen, immigrant, female, male, poor, rich, gay, lesbian, transsexual, or straight. Power, after all, is the fulcrum of all politics. Thus it seems logical that God's move of love would address the politics of love.

Embodying the Politics of Love

The character of any political order can be understood by examining what it loves. In *The City of God,* Augustine argues that the city of God, *civitas Dei,* is distinct from the city of man, *civitas terrena.* As Augustine put it, "Accordingly, two cities have been formed by two loves: the earthly by the love of self, even to the contempt of God; the heavenly by the love of God, even to the contempt of self. The former, in a word, glories in itself, the latter in the Lord."

Martin Luther King Jr. wrote similarly about the twofold character of the church. For him it was a church within the church — the outer layer, that loved being the church and the inner core that loved seeking justice for and in the city. People gathered together in a polis, a prophetic community within its broader political community. The inner church is the prophetic church.

In both of these models, the fulcrum of pursuance is the power of love. While Saint Augustine's model inspired a segregation of the two (who, in love with God, would want to live in a city not also in love with God?), King's model called out an *ekklesia* that interrupted the love of self with the transformative love of God. Thus, the church as Christ's body in and for the city always has to negotiate the ways in which it remains a distinct community, seeking to embody love among its own members and likewise working for urban transformation.

The city of God is marked by the politics of love and justice, not a quest for personal power and prestige. The earthly city, as seats of governance and market exchange, is so easily enamored by the spirit of power. It is easy for the church, as God's voice on earth, to also become enamored by such spirits. Therefore the imperative is all the more strong: to love God is to love justice! The cities of the earth are beloved, and in them the church is called to seek shalom, to transform them into beloved cities.

To transform our cities into communities of resurrection, in order to enter into politics, we need a power analysis. To transform our communities, we need to release the mechanisms of power that function outside, below, and alongside the state apparatus and structures of the capitalist economy. We need a new urban ecology to understand the nature of the powerful institutions in the city — the mayor's office, the city council, the police department, the corporations, the insurance companies, and the real estate developers. We play our prophetic role in confronting these "powers and principalities" when we understand them.

For the church to be a site of prophetic resistance, it must understand that the channels connecting civil society to the state have been reordered. The distinction between state and civil society has rapidly become misleading in North America. Whereas civil society once operated as a mediator between the immanent forces of capital and the transcendent sovereign, all three are now collapsed into an imperial matrix of power. The work of disciplining and normalizing the subject is no longer done by the state alone, but also by the global institutions of capitalism that shape our consumer lifestyle.

The civil subject is now disciplined and normalized by those institutions that make up civil society. The schools, the workplace, the hospital, the prison, and the church have all become disciplining institutions that do the work of creating docile subjects. Power does not hover over us in an abstracted state but is all around us, in the fissures of the social terrain. In empire, the walls between the various disciplinary institutions have broken down; their logics of subjectification are now generalized across the social field.

As those walls have collapsed, so have the walls between nations and between self and other, black and white. Exclusion of minorities has been replaced by a finely calibrated attention to the nuances of different market niches. As a world in which difference is celebrated, empire is a world of fluidity and hybridity. Instead of maintaining essential identities, and binary divisions, empire does away with them to create a smooth terrain upon which commodities can travel unimpeded. Here it's not clear whether empire is a good thing or not. To evaluate empire we must understand its flows of power.

Society is a living organism, and power circulates throughout it. Power cannot be localized here or there; it can never be held in anybody's hands, never appropriated as a commodity or piece of wealth. Power is exercised through an open source network. Our individual subversive moral agency is expressed within a broader matrix of power.

We need to move beyond the binary of domination and subjugation. All people, even the oppressed, have some power because power functions like a network, and we all can play a role in its netlike organization.

Power is not held just by the victors and oppressors, but by all people in various degrees, even the oppressed. If we aggregate power, we can have a larger impact in transforming society. Faith-rooted organizing is an important strategy for embodying the politics of love today. Faith-rooted organizing is gathering people together to create comprehensive community change in a way that is completely shaped and guided by faith and is designed to enable people of faith to contribute all their unique gifts and resources to the broader movement for social and economic justice.

While love has a global, universal ambition, it must incarnate itself in the prophetic practices of urban dwelling and urban development. Love must be incarnated in the ways in which we live in the city. The city of God calls us to create the conditions for the establishment of cities of love. They will know we are Christians by our love; however, the way love is manifest is not just in a fellowship of love, but also in a Christ-led, Spirit-filled, wild, and festive movement for love that seeks to create the conditions for the emergence of a just city.

The prophetic call for justice brings God's call to love into political form. While our neoliberal capitalist order is shaped by ego-driven competitive relations, the church has the opportunity to model another way of being in the world. We are called to embody a living community through noncompetitive relations. Again, we are called to love through the Great Commandment: "Love the Lord your God with all your heart, and with all your soul, and with all your strength, and with all your mind; and your neighbor as yourself" (Luke 10:27; cf. Matt 22:37-39; Mark 12:29-31).

The Jesus way is the way of love — a life lived for the neighbor and the good creation. Our actions demonstrate our deepest spiritual passions. To pursue such a love, how could we not seek to transform our social and economic relations?

The gospel is grace incarnate. Jesus incarnates what love really is. Dietrich Bonhoeffer argues that ultimately we only understand what love is through Christ, who in his love shows us what it is. Christ's call is a call to love, for only through Christ telling us what love is and showing us how to love are we even in a position to love God and our neighbor. Yet, this call is made amidst the struggle of great suffering in the world. His vision of binding the brokenhearted is our call today. While Christ is the head of the church, we are the body. We are Christ's hands and feet, which are supposed to reach out to love and serve the world.

In his discourses, Jesus reaches back into the Hebrew Scriptures (Lev 19:18 and Deut 6:5) for source material. As an improviser he goes further — love your enemy. "Love your enemies, do good to those who hate you, bless those who curse you, pray for those who abuse you. If anyone strikes you on the cheek, offer the other also; and from anyone who takes away your coat do not withhold even your shirt" (Luke 6:27-29). Here, Jesus the Jewish improviser opens up new possibilities for prophetic Christianity today. He plays upon a jazz standard and injects it with new poignancy.

Martin Luther King Jr. is an example of one who walked boldly in love, improvising, dancing to the rhythms of the gospel. King is drawn to Matthew 25, where Jesus describes those who will be welcomed into heaven, precisely because they have provided for "the least of these" (Matt 25:40). From this call came King's response: the Poor People's Campaign, the mobilization of his last, most ambitious campaign to embody Christ's love for poor people — all poor people. This included poor whites in Appalachia. It was an echo of the scandal of a Samaritan helping a Jewish stranger on the roadside. It was a creative vision of Resurrection City.

While Barack Obama's election as the first African American president was one concrete fulfillment of King's dream, building the "beloved community" is an unfinished task in America and throughout the world. King's dream of a beloved community was driven by an idealism that another world is genuinely possible — a social order based on love and justice, where active citizens work together to end poverty and war. As we live through today's deep economic crisis, the church is erupting as a musical movement for justice and love.

The politics of love flow from a jazz approach to theology, grounded in the standards along with the infinite possibilities that emerge through improvisation. Clearly we have struggled to extend God's love and justice throughout the world; however, Americans carry the shame of slavery, a history of economic oppression, and segregated cities. From this country came the blues, thousands of primal wails from many tortured souls.

Yet it was also in America that jazz emerged, from found materials, all-colored and bold, with creativity, with intimacy. If the church could be like jazz, the call-and-response of the oppressed, loving, responding, just imagine the beautiful melodies that would emerge. Perhaps they would be like those melodies that find their way into the back of your mind and emerge, familiar but new. Never again would a blue note call out with nothing but another blue note. Never would a woman's clear, plaintive tone remain unaccompanied. Nor would a man's angry, distorted cry find only numbness in return. Modern-day spirituals would take shape, as would songs of celebration and hope. Imagine the music — a multicolored church, guided by the Holy Spirit, inspired and challenged by each other, taking part in a grand performance, a shared composition, an embodiment of loving God and loving the neighbor, including your enemy.

The politics of love lead us to a moment of awakening. They make our theology come alive; they set our souls free. I know this because I have lived it.

When I was a boy, I was a novice musician, learning to appreciate the classics. One of my favorite days of the year was Easter Sunday, when my dad Sam would take me to the sunrise service on Fort Hill at the Vicksburg Military Park in Mississippi. A graduate of Virginia Military Institute and a captain in the army, my father always woke up at the break of day. But this day was different. Standing on the high bluff with Christians from all around my hometown, my dad and I waited patiently, quietly, for the sun to rise. I was waiting for the music of heaven, something like *A Love Supreme.*

And then I heard it. With malleted strikes, girded with cloud-chords, *A Love Supreme* broke into the heavenly sphere. Yet this was not a violent interruption, but gentle and smooth. Suddenly the music came alive, and I acknowledged something more than just theory or memorization. As the gong-strike of night upon day faded, a few bars of a smooth arpeggio rose up from the horizon, while the drummer held the space with the sparkling dance of drumstick upon cymbal ride. This was new — creative; this was the stuff of the soul. With the morning light came joy and the glory of day, even as our bodies still longed for darkness and sleep. But there, upon the side of that ridge, I heard the music of resurrection, and I was forever changed.

The brilliance of daybreak is always at the margins of darkness; hope comes at the edge of despair. The liberated prisoner becomes an attentive watchman at the edge of the city, waiting patiently and perceptively for the dawning of a new day (Hab 2:1). When teaching at the New York Theological Seminary northern campus in Sing Sing Prison, Ossining, New York, I realized that in front me were prisoners who, when freed, would be watchmen, not in a tower with a rifle watching for escaping prisoners, but as preachers with eyes peeled for any sign of Christ's coming. After the black darkness of solitary confinement, any ray of light can be like a gong-strike. When prisoners are freed, their senses are alive in a way that those of the numb people on the outside are not.

In Sing Sing Prison, I witnessed interruption, not violent, but gentle and smooth. I saw men locked away in a place of iron and concrete get caught up in singing songs of hope; there I sensed I was part of a space of transformation, full of vectors and velocity. These men, darkened by a belief in power as a brutal fight for love of self, were haloed with love for their neighbors, emptying and giving themselves away in care for their fellow prisoners. Though chronologically bound to this place for some time, they rested in the freedom of festival time and waited patiently for the coming of Resurrection City.

> I will stand at my watchpost,
>   and station myself on the rampart;
> I will keep watch to see what he will say to me,
>   and what he will answer concerning my complaint.
> Then the Lord answered me and said:
> Write the vision;
>   make it plain on tablets,
>   so that a runner may read it.
> For there is still a vision for the appointed time;
>   it speaks of the end, and does not lie.
> If it seems to tarry, wait for it;
>   it will surely come, it will not delay. (Hab 2:1-3)

The Final Refrain: The Beloved City

The future calls. Can you hear it? Jazz. A Love Supreme. We hear echoes in the music of Coltrane or Duke Ellington, Louis Armstrong or Billie Holiday, but it's more than that. It might not even be "jazz," but it's music, the song of heaven. Coltrane's "Psalm" tucked the clearest expression of the theme at the end of the movement, forcing us to listen for it, allowing us to listen back on the rest of the song and understand. It is a mystical meditation forward, a deep listening into time for the songs of the festival, the liturgies of heaven.

In our liturgies we sing the Sanctus. Isaiah's riff on the song of the angels around the throne of God — "holy, holy, holy" — is the utmost in justice and righteousness, steadfast love and truth. Isaiah also shares a vision of the heavens being opened, and God entering earth. Isaiah is not taken into the city of heaven, but heaven enters into Isaiah's city. The prophet witnesses this theater of the Spirit because the fourth wall between heaven and earth is rent by God's own intent.

In the book of Revelation, John relates a similar image, the city of God coming down out of the heavens from God. There is a clear motion out of the place of abstraction and into the realm of creation. But, and here is a curious thing that John also records, the place where the city of God arrives, where the saints are gathered, is referred to as "the beloved city" (Rev 20:9).

There is a clear emphasis upon the city. But why the city? What do urban environments have that rural ones do not? Is God not for the pastures and farmlands? The prophets used countless images from agrarian life to communicate the essential call for *mishpat* and *sedaqah.* What a city has that a rural environment doesn't are seats of governance and market exchange. In short, cities are places of centralized power.

Power is the acidic catalyst that perverts righteousness into privilege, justice into favoritism, steadfast love into lust, and truth into selectivity; power is the *dynamos* that drives dominating, marginalizing, corrupting, and creates places of oppression.

The power of Pharaoh over cities of Egypt caused him to oppress the Jews. The power of the scribes and the Pharisees caused them to oppress Jesus. The power of the European explorers caused them to oppress the indigenous peoples they encountered. The power of Thomas Jefferson caused him to continue to oppress his slaves, despite writing otherwise. The power of whites in American cities causes them to oppress African Americans, Hispanics, and Asian Americans. The power of the financial global institutions and the people who oversee them continues to oppress the majority of middle- and working-class people across the globe.

Yet in all these cities movements of justice arose. In Egypt it was the great exodus; in first-century Palestine it was the messianic movement of

Jesus; and in European colonies there arose deeply suppressive folk communities of song and story. In the nineteenth century, alongside Jefferson, there arose the abolition movement, with prophets like Sojourner Truth. Amidst the flagrant segregation of the twentieth century there arose the civil rights movement with Martin Luther King Jr. and Howard Thurman. And now, under heavy financial oppression, the Occupy Wall Street protest movement gathers in public places in the city to create just the sort of vector and velocity needed to generate a space of hope for those oppressed by markets and unjust legislation.

The double sin on Wall Street is that it's a seat of governance over market exchange, two levels of power compacted into one. In this way the New York Stock Exchange (NYSE) serves as the heart of the American financial system, and even the world, the right and left ventricles, where stocks, bonds, and hedge funds for many of the world's leading corporations and banks are bought and sold, a staid and settled box that retains power and thus becomes a place of oppression. It can be likened to the image of whitewashed tombs Jesus used to critique the self-righteous piety of the Pharisees, emblems of great wealth and mighty power that house the most putrid rot and decay. How could there ever be any hope of resurrection for something so far gone?

But, declares the Lord, I am singing a new song. Do you not perceive it? Starting at the front door of the NYSE, people are gathering, people whose houses are foreclosed, who have not found mercy from banks despite a poor job market; people who are weary of the ability of the superwealthy to affect the political discourse. There are groups forming that feel in their bones, the roots of their body, a deficit of justice in the governance of markets, and a disproportionate doling out of mercy in the governance of corporations.

Spreading from city to city, the Occupy movement's tactics are to take a central public place, a park or a square, close to where many of the levers of power are centered and, by putting human bodies in that place, to convert public places into a space for political commons — a space for open discussion and debate about what power is doing, and how best to oppose its reach, and to build solidarity and alternative configurations of power. Through the Occupy movement, be it in Seattle, Oakland, Detroit, Austin, or New York City, we smell the sweet scent of resurrection coming from those tombs. The gathering in public spaces and the streets is an icon of a world that is fully saturated with the shalom of heaven.

A place of oppression becomes a space of hope, not just for the poor in America, but for the poor around the world. When places of oppression are occupied, they become spaces of hope. Hope is not a pie-in-the-sky abstract future; it is face-to-face. When a place of oppression is occupied, the oppressor and the oppressed, the actor and the spectator, Moses and Pharaoh, Jesus and Death, come face-to-face. Looking into the face of the other, we can see the infinite possibilities of peace and justice.

Opposition is a tricky path to tread. How to oppose systemic power structures and not fellow humans, especially when systems of oppression are the labor of human individuals? Banks don't just foreclose on homes; they destroy families. The people the banks are foreclosing on are collectives of people, fathers and mothers, lovers and beloveds, misguided as any about making decisions.

This is where the task of the church enters, the great struggle that none but the wisest among us have managed to achieve. The revolutionary who is truly great, who has risen within the global consciousness as a visionary architect of the beloved city, has been the one who has given himself or herself to nonviolent resistance, to the point of death. Consider what makes Jesus great outside of Christianity, what inspired Gandhi and later Martin Luther King Jr. All these people insisted upon a way of life greater than that of the way it was, to the point of living as if the world of nonviolent love was a reality.

They each knew the rules of their culture intimately, knew how to play the songs of their cities. They were not blues players, pining for the old ways — they were jazz musicians, creating a new future. They weren't committed to love simply as a way of surviving, but a love supreme that bent the vector of their imaginations beyond the here and now. And when they played for the people, it made the oppressed shake and the oppressor quake.

When they gathered in concert, it was not to destroy the orchestra or to break the blues guitar, but to proclaim release, to bring the world face-to-face, ear-to-ear with a new song, the song of Israel, a song that has been ringing in the heavens since before the time of humanity. Jazz singers don't gather to condemn the classical musicians and the blues singers, but to *invite* them into a new jazz age. In this theater of liberation, the oppressed dance and the mute sing. Hope, option, new possibility open up. Those in power see that it's not their power the church wants, but to do *mishpat,* and to love *hesed,* and to walk humbly with God.

The church then opposes, not by pushing back face-to-face, but by improvising, creating new options, looking at a third way, one without an oppressive hierarchy. This is creation, thinking outside the box, finding hope, attending to love, playing jazz in the beloved city.

Open to the Spirit's improvisations, prophetic Christianity today must work strategically, interreligiously, and internationally. A broad array of African, Latino, Asian Protestant, Pentecostal, Orthodox, and Roman Catholic traditions shares a deep commitment to the common good. Moving away from old binaries, American Christianity is in transition. When the churches work together with other religious communities, labor unions, community groups, and the government, they show that the love of God as worship is not different from love of justice as action. Mobilizing for justice from the deepest roots of our faith creates a new soul force in politics today, one that is capable of generating global social change not only rooted in Scripture but also described by it.

Open to the Spirit's improvisations, mystic-prophetic Christianity today must engage the interpersonal, interreligious, and international dimensions of the city. The work of love is political, but also personal. Power is at stake, but also people, human faces, traumatized, scrutinized, marginalized people. From the kitchen table to the city hall, the politics of love never loses sight of the essential woundedness of even the worst oppressor.

A politics of love yearns to sing songs of peace, to share the music of heaven; it understands that every earthly love reflects a greater love — a love supreme. As jazz musicians improvise together to make music, so, too, should prophetic Christians improvise for justice today. Through improvisation, jazz players are able to make new music in new places — *together.* Embracing a jazz consciousness, it is time for Christians to gather up the theater of the oppressed, imagining and improvising love and justice in the city, amongst the powers and principalities. In doing this we lay foundations with rejected stones; we garden where no growth could happen, where rivers flow freely in dry, paved places. Only when each member of Christ's body creatively uses his or her gifts to build the beloved city will we see justice roll like a river, and righteousness like an ever-flowing stream.

A Love Supreme

Behold, I am singing a new song
It rings forth from the heavens
Can you not hear it?

See, I am coming soon!
watch and wait
swim in the river, plant trees
Love and be fruitful
Rebuild the beloved city
In light of the City of God
The Alpha and Omega
The First, the Last, the Beginning, the End

A Love Supreme

The End, the Beginning, The Last, the First
Omega and Alpha
In the light of God's city
Beloved rebuild
Be fruitful and love
Eat of the Tree, drink of the Water
Wait, watch
See, I am coming soon!

Notes

Notes to Chapter 1

1. Christopher Morse, *The Difference Heaven Makes: Rehearsing the Gospel as News* (New York: T. & T. Clark, 2010).

2. All quotations from Scripture in this book are from the New Revised Standard Version, unless otherwise noted.

3. "And the LORD God made garments of skins for the man and for his wife, and clothed them" (Gen 3:21). I learned of the way in which the garments of skin represent God's merciful providential care of Adam and Eve from Gordon Paul Hugenberger, "A Neglected Symbolism for the Clothing of Adam and Eve (Gen. 3:21)" (paper read at the Annual Meeting of the Evangelical Theological Society, Jackson, Mississippi, November 22, 1996).

4. William Stringfellow, *An Ethic for Christians and Other Aliens in a Strange Land* (Waco, Tex.: Word, 1973).

5. Orlando E. Costas, *Christ Outside the Gate: Mission Outside the Gate* (Maryknoll, N.Y.: Orbis, 1982), 192.

6. Martin Luther King Jr., "I See the Promised Land," April 3, 1968, Memphis, Tennessee, in Martin Luther King Jr., *I Have a Dream: Writings and Speeches That Changed the World,* ed. James W. Washington (New York: HarperSanFrancisco, 1968), 282.

7. Works on race and religion that have shaped my thinking include the following: Cornel West, *Prophesy Deliverance! An Afro-American Revolutionary Christianity* (Louisville: Westminster John Knox, 1982); Anthony B. Pinn, *Terror and Triumph: The Nature of Black Religion* (Minneapolis: Fortress, 2003); Dwight Callahan, *The Talking Book: African Americans and the Bible* (New Haven: Yale University Press, 2006); Eddie S. Glaude Jr., *Exodus! Religion, Race, and Nation in Early Nineteenth-Century Black America* (Chicago: University of Chicago Press, 2000); Colin Kidd, *The Forging of the Races: Race and Scripture in the Protestant Atlantic World, 1600-2000* (Cambridge: Cambridge University Press, 2006); Michael Omi and Howard Winant, *Racial Formation in the United States: From the 1960s to the 1990s* (New York: Routledge, 1994); Emilie Townes, *Womanist Ethics and the Cultural*

Production of Evil (New York: Palgrave Macmillan, 2006); Gayraud S. Wilmore, *Black Religion and Black Radicalism: An Interpretation of the Religious History of Afro-American People* (Maryknoll, N.Y.: Orbis, 1994).

8. See Brian Bantum, *Redeeming Mulatto: A Theology of Race and Christian Hybridity* (Waco, Tex.: Baylor University Press, 2010); J. Kameron Carter, *Race: A Theological Account* (Oxford: Oxford University Press, 2008); Willie James Jennings, *Christian Imagination* (New Haven: Yale University Press, 2010).

9. Richard A. Bailey, *Race and Redemption in Puritan New England* (New York: Oxford University Press, 2011); Joy Gilsdorf, *The Puritan Apocalypse: New England Eschatology in the Seventeenth Century* (New York: Garland, 1989); Andrea Smith, "Rape of the Land," chapter 3 in *Conquest: Sexual Violence and American Indian Genocide* (Cambridge, Mass.: South End Press, 2005), 55-78; George Hunston Williams, "Fleeing to and Planting in the Wilderness in the Reformation Period and Modern Times," in *Wilderness and Paradise in Christian Thought: The Biblical Experience of the Desert in the History of Christianity and the Paradise Theme in the Theological Idea of the University* (New York: Harper and Brothers, 1962), 65-97.

10. Robert Allen Warrior, "A Native American Perspective: Canaanites, Cowboys, and Indians," in *Voices from the Margin: Interpreting the Bible in the Third World*, ed. R. S. Sugirtharajah (Maryknoll, N.Y.: Orbis, 1991), 287-95.

11. Luis N. Rivera, *A Violent Evangelism: The Political and Religious Conquest of the Americas* (Louisville: Westminster John Knox, 1990); George Tinker, *Missionary Conquest: The Gospel and Native American Cultural Genocide* (Minneapolis: Augsburg Fortress, 1993).

12. Richard Slotkin, *Regeneration through Violence: The Mythology of the American Frontier, 1600-1860* (Middletown, Conn.: Wesleyan University Press, 1973), 5.

13. Russell Bourne, *Gods of War, Gods of Peace: How the Meeting of Native and Colonial Religion Shaped Early America* (New York: Harcourt, 2002); Yasuhide Kawashima, *Igniting King Philip's War: The John Sassamon Murder Trial* (Lawrence: University Press of Kansas, 2001); Jill Lepore, *The Name of War: King Philip's War and the Origins of American Identity* (New York: Vintage Books, 1999); Neal Salisbury, *Manitou and Providence: Indians, Europeans, and the Making of New England, 1500-1643* (New York: Oxford University Press, 1982); Alden T. Vaughan, *New England Frontier: Puritans and Indians, 1620-1675* (Oklahoma City: University of Oklahoma Press, 1995).

14. Cornel West, "A Genealogy of Modern Racism," in *Prophesy Deliverance!* 47-68.

15. Howard Thurman, *Jesus and the Disinherited* (Boston: Beacon Press, 1976).

16. For some examples of the growing theological literature on the relationship of Christianity and Judaism, see Chris Boesel, *Risking Proclamation, Respecting Difference: Christian Faith, Imperialistic Discourse and Abraham* (Eugene, Oreg.: Cascade Books, 2008); Mary C. Boys, *Christians and Jews in Dialogue: Learning in the Presence of the Other* (Woodstock, Vt.: SkyLight Paths Publishing, 2006); Mary C. Boys, *Has God Only One Blessing? Judaism as a Source of Christian Self-Understanding* (New York: Paulist, 2000); Carl E. Braaten and Robert W. Jenson, *Jews and Christians: People of God* (Grand Rapids: Eerdmans, 2003); Tikva Frymer-Kensky et al., eds., *Christianity in Jewish Terms* (Boulder, Colo.: Westview, 2000); Norbert Lohfink, *The Covenant Never Revoked: Biblical Reflections on Christian-Jewish Dialogue* (New York: Paulist, 1991); R. Kendall Soulen, *The God of Israel and Christian Theology* (Minneapolis: Fortress, 1996); Clark W. Williamson, *Way of Blessing, Way of Life: A Christian Theology* (St. Louis: Chalice, 1999); Marvin R. Wilson, *Our Father*

Abraham: Jewish Roots of the Christian Faith (Grand Rapids: Eerdmans, 1979); Michael Wyschogrod, *Abraham's Promise: Judaism and Jewish-Christian Relations,* edited and introduced by R. Kendall Soulen (Grand Rapids: Eerdmans, 2004).

17. On the theological connection between anti-Judaism and white supremacy, see Carter, *Race.* I am indebted to Carter and Clark Williamson for the ideas in this paragraph.

18. See Stefan Arvidsson, *Aryan Idols: Indo-European Mythology as Ideology and Science,* trans. Sonia Wichmann (Chicago: University of Chicago Press, 2006); Zygmunt Bauman, *Modernity and the Holocaust* (Cambridge: Polity, 1988); Robert P. Ericksen and Susannah Heschel, eds., *Betrayal: German Churches and the Holocaust* (Minneapolis: Fortress, 1999); Susannah Heschel, *The Aryan Jesus: Christian Theologians and the Bible in Nazi Germany* (Princeton: Princeton University Press, 2008); Susannah Heschel, "Transforming Jesus from Jew to Aryan: Protestant Theologians in Nazi Germany" (Albert T. Billgray Lecture, University of Arizona, 1995); George Mosse, *Nationalism and Sexuality* (Madison: University of Wisconsin Press, 1985); Leon Poliakov, *The History of Anti-Semitism,* vol. 1 (Oxford: Oxford University Press, 1985); Leon Poliakov, *The Aryan Myth* (London: Sussex University Press, 1974); Paul Lawrence Rose, *Revolutionary Anti-Semitism in Germany from Kant to Wagner* (Princeton: Princeton University Press, 1990); Gershom Scholem, *From Berlin to Jerusalem: Memories of My Youth,* trans. Harry Zohn (New York: Schocken, 1980).

19. Some thoughtful discussions of whiteness include "Forum: American Religion and Whiteness," *Religion and American Culture* 19, no. 1 (2009): 1-35; Matthew Frye Jacobson, *Whiteness of a Different Color: European Immigrants and the Alchemy of Race* (Cambridge: Harvard University Press, 1998); Nell Irvin Painter, *The History of White People* (New York: Norton, 2010); David R. Roediger, *Working toward Whiteness: How America's Immigrants Became White; The Strange Journey from Ellis Island to the Suburbs* (New York: Basic Books, 2005).

20. See Peter Goodwin Heltzel and Corey D. B. Walker, "The Wound of Political Theology: A Prolegomenon to a Research Agenda," *Political Theology* 9, no. 2 (2008): 252-55.

21. For a thoughtful discussion of the contributions of African American and Creole musicians to the origins of jazz music, see David Ake, *Jazz Cultures* (Berkeley: University of California Press, 2002), 10-41; James Lincoln Collier, *Jazz: The American Theme Song* (New York: Oxford University Press, 1993), 183-202; Alan Lomax, *Mister Jelly Roll: The Fortunes of Jelly Roll Morton, New Orleans Creole and "Inventor of Jazz"* (Berkeley: University of California Press, 2001); Charles B. Hersch, *Subversive Sounds: Race and the Birth of Jazz in New Orleans* (Chicago: University of Chicago Press, 2008).

22. See Edward Blum, *Reforging the White Republic: Race, Religion, and American Nationalism, 1865-1898* (Baton Rouge: Louisiana State University Press, 2005).

23. See James Cone's insightful discussion of the lynching era in relation to Christianity and its theological claims. See James H. Cone, "'Nobody Knows de Trouble I See': The Cross and the Lynching Tree in the Black Experience," in *The Cross and the Lynching Tree* (Maryknoll, N.Y.: Orbis, 2011), 1-29. Cf. Michelle Alexander, *The New Jim Crow: Mass Incarceration in the Age of Colorblindness* (New York: New Press, 2010). The metaphor of a deep river is an allusion to the spiritual "Deep River." This was a powerful symbol in the African American cultural experience, as witnessed in the writings of Langston Hughes, Howard Thurman, and James H. Cone. See Langston Hughes, *The Negro Speaks of Rivers* (New York: Disney Jump at the Sun Books, 2009); Howard Thurman, *Deep River: The Negro Spiritual*

Speaks of Life and Death (Richmond, Ind.: Friends United Press, 1975); James H. Cone, *The Spirituals and the Blues: An Interpretation* (Maryknoll, N.Y.: Orbis, 1991).

24. See Paul Gilroy, *The Black Atlantic: Modernity and Double Consciousness* (Cambridge: Harvard University Press, 1993), esp. 1-40, 72-110. Alan Lomax has demonstrated the Senegalese influence on American slave songs through recordings of intercutting Senegalese and Mississippi singers on "African and American Field Songs," on the LP *Roots of the Blues* (New York: New World Records 252, 1977); Georges Niangoran-Boiuah introduces the concept of "the talking drum" as a way to describe the power of African rhythm in mediating the sacred in "The Talking Drum: A Traditional Instrument of Liturgy and of Mediation with the Sacred," in *African Traditional Religions in Contemporary Society,* ed. Jacob K. Olupona (New York: Paragon House, 1991), 81-92.

25. On the exodus motif in black religion, see Glaude, *Exodus!*

26. Albert J. Raboteau, *Slave Religion: The "Invisible Institute" in the Antebellum South,* 2nd ed. (Oxford: Oxford University Press, 2004).

27. For more on the call-and-response, see Bruce Ellis Benson, "Call Forwarding: Improvising the Response to the Call of Beauty," in *The Beauty of God: Theology and the Arts,* ed. Daniel J. Treier, Mark Husbands, and Roger Lundin (Downers Grove, Ill.: InterVarsity, 2007), 70-83.

28. See Leroi Jones (Amiri Baraka), *Blues People: Negro Music in White America* (New York: Harper Perennial, 1999); Alan Lomax, *The Land Where the Blues Began* (New York: Dell, 1993); Paul Oliver, *The Story of the Blues* (Chicago: Northwestern University Press, 1998); Robert Palmer, *Deep Blues: Negro Music in White America* (New York: Viking Press, 1981); Gunther Schuller, *Early Jazz: Its Roots and Musical Development* (New York: Oxford University Press, 1968); Jeff Todd Titon, *Early Downhome Blues: A Musical and Cultural Analysis* (Chapel Hill: University of North Carolina Press, 1994); Elijah Wald, *Escaping the Delta: Robert Johnson and the Invention of the Blues* (New York: Norton, 1971).

29. For the notion of the underside of modernity, see Enrique Dussel, *The Underside of Modernity: Apel, Ricoeur, Rorty, Taylor, and the Philosophy of Liberation,* trans. Eduardo Mendieta (Atlantic Highlands, N.J.: Humanities Press, 1996).

30. Cornel West, "On Afro-American Popular Music: From Bebop to Rap," in *Prophetic Fragments* (Grand Rapids: Eerdmans, 1988), 5. Gilroy draws on Zygmunt Bauman's notion of "counterculture of modernity." See Zygmunt Bauman, "The Left as the Counterculture of Modernity," *Telos* 70 (Winter 1986-87): 81-93. While Cornel West emphasizes the ways that jazz is subversive as a *political* practice, Bruce Ellis Benson analyzes how jazz is a subversive *musical* practice; see Bruce Ellis Benson, "The Fundamental Heteronomy of Jazz Improvisation," *Revue international de philosophie* 60 (2006): 453-67. While jazz, especially in the 1960s, was subversive, it has also been complicit in maintaining the status quo in America in more commericalized forms. See Lisa E. Davenport, *Jazz Diplomacy: Promoting America in the Cold War Era* (Jackson: University Press of Mississippi, 2009).

31. Works that have shaped my thinking on improvisation in jazz music include the following: Bruce Ellis Benson, *The Improvisation of Musical Dialogue* (Cambridge: Cambridge University Press, 2005); Derek Bailey, *Improvisation: Its Nature and Practice in Music* (New York: Da Capo Press, 1992); Paul Berliner, *Thinking in Jazz: The Infinite Art of Improvisation* (Chicago: University of Chicago Press, 1994); Ingrid Monson, *Saying Something: Jazz Improvisation and Interaction* (Chicago: University of Chicago Press, 1996); John Murphy, "Jazz Improvisation: The Joy of Influence," *Black Perspective in Music* 18, no. 1-2 (1990): 7-19.

For an exploration of improvisation across disciplines, see George E. Lewis, ed., *Oxford Handbook of Critical Improvisation Studies,* vols. 1 and 2 (Oxford: Oxford University Press, forthcoming). Recent theologies of improvisation include Jeremy Begbie, *Theology, Music, and Time* (Cambridge: Cambridge University Press, 2000); Mary McClintock Fulkerson, "'They Will Know We Are Christians by Our Regulated Improvisation': Ecclesial Hybridity and the Unity of the Church," in *Postmodern Theology,* ed. Graham Ward (Oxford: Blackwell, 2001), 265-79; Anthony G. Reddie, "A Dialectical Spirituality of Improvisation: The Ambiguity of Black Engagements with Sacred Texts," in *Black Religion and Aesthetics: Religious Thought and Life in Africa and the African Diaspora* (New York: Palgrave Macmillan, 2009), 153-74; Anthony G. Reddie, "Dramatic Improvisation: A Jazz Inspired Approach to Undertaking Theology with the Marginalized," ed. Dawn Llewellyn and Deborah F. Sawyer (Aldershot: Ashgate, 2008); Kevin J. Vanhoozer, *The Drama of Doctrine: A Canonical-Linguistic Approach to Christian Theology* (Louisville: Westminster John Knox, 2005); Samuel Wells, *Improvisation: The Drama of Christian Ethics* (Grand Rapids: Brazos, 2004); Samuel Wells, "For Such a Time as This: Esther and the Practices of Improvisation," in *Liturgy, Time, and the Politics of Redemption,* ed. Chad Pecknold and Randi Rashkover (Grand Rapids: Eerdmans, 2006), 167-87; Samuel Wells, "Improvisation in Theatre as a Model for Christian Ethics," in *Faithful Performance: Enacting Christian Tradition,* ed. Trevor A. Hart and Steven R. Guthrie (Aldershot: Ashgate, 2007).

32. A Rogers and Hammerstein musical, *The Sound of Music* opened on Broadway on November 16, 1959. In 1965 it was adapted as a film musical starring Julie Andrews as Maria Rainer and Christopher Plummer as Captain Georg von Trapp. Richard Rogers and Oscar Hammerstein II, *The Sound of Music,* Irwin Kostal. RCA Victor LSOD-2005, 1965. Cf. Julia Antopol Hirsch, *The Sound of Music: The Making of America's Favorite Movie* (Chicago: Contemporary Books, 1993); Max Wilk, *The Making of "The Sound of Music"* (New York: Routledge, 2007).

33. Cornel West, "The Spirituals as Lyrical Poetry," in *The Cornel West Reader* (New York: Basic Books, 1999), 469.

34. See Lewis Porter, "John Coltrane's *A Love Supreme:* Jazz Improvisation as Composition," *Journal of the American Musicological Society* 38, no. 3: 593-621; Lewis Porter, *John Coltrane: His Life and Music* (Ann Arbor: University of Michigan Press, 1998).

35. The literature on the performative force of theology is growing rapidly. Hans Urs von Balthasar's conception of "theo-drama" has been one of the primary inspirations to this theological movement. *Theo-drama: Theological Dramatic Theory,* 5 vols. (San Francisco: Ignatius, 1988-98). More contemporary work includes Bruce Ellis Benson, "Improvising Tests, Improvising Communities: Jazz, Interpretation, Heterophony, and the *Ekklêsia,*" in *Resonant Witness: Conversation between Music and Theology,* ed. Jeremy S. Begbie and Steven J. Guthrie (Grand Rapids: Eerdmans, 2011), 295-319; Shanon Craigno-Snell, "Command Performance: Rethinking Performance Interpretation in the Context of Divine Discourse," *Modern Theology* 16, no. 4 (2000): 475-94; Shanon Craigno-Snell, *The Empty Church: Theatre, Theology, and Bodily Hope* (Oxford: Oxford University Press, forthcoming); Shanon Craigno-Snell, "Theology as Performance," *Ecumenist* 45, no. 2 (Spring 2008): 6-10; Trevor Hart and Steven Guthrie, *Faithful Performances: Enacting Christian Tradition* (Hampshire: Ashcroft, 2007); Nicholas Lash, "Performing the Scriptures," in *Theology on the Way to Emmaus* (London: SCM, 1986), 37-46; Kevin J. Vanhoozer, *The Drama of Doctrine;* Frances Young, *The Art of Performance: Towards a Theology of Holy Scripture* (London: Darton,

Longman and Todd, 1990); Wells, *Improvisation;* and N. T. Wright, "How Can the Bible Be Authoritative?" *Vox evangelica* 21 (1994): 7-32. For an introduction to performance studies, see Richard Schechner, *Performance Studies: An Introduction* (New York: Routledge, 2002).

Notes to Chapter 2

1. For theological introductions to the biblical concept of shalom, see Walter Brueggemann, *Living toward a Vision: Biblical Reflections on Shalom,* 2nd ed. (New York: United Church Press, 1982), and Perry Yoder, *Shalom: The Bible's Word for Salvation, Justice, and Peace* (Nappanee, Ind.: Evangel Publishing, 1987).

2. See Temba L. J. Mafico, "Just, Justice," in *The Anchor Bible Dictionary,* ed. David Noel Freedman, 6 vols. (New York: Doubleday, 1992), 3:1127-29. Cf. James L. Mays, "Justice: Perspectives from the Prophetic Tradition," in *Prophecy in Israel* (Philadelphia: Fortress, 1987), 144-58; Nicholas Wolterstorff, *Justice: Rights and Wrongs* (Princeton: Princeton University Press, 2008); Nicholas Wolterstorff, *Justice in Love* (Grand Rapids: Eerdmans, 2011).

3. For a theological analysis of the community of creation with reference to Native American theology, see Randy Woodley, *Shalom and the Community of Creation: An Indigenous Vision,* Prophetic Christianity, vol. 2 (Grand Rapids: Eerdmans, 2012). In this work Woodley persuasively narrates how Israel's ethic of shalom justice and Native American Harmony Way worldviews can create a new, just, and sustainable way of life for North American Christians. See Woodley's discussion of the "Harmony Way" in Native American culture in his "'The Harmony Way': Integrating Indigenous Values within Native North American Theology and Mission" (Ph.D. diss., Asbury Theological Seminary, 2010). Randy Woodley often uses the term "Creator" without the preceding definite article "the" to emphasize God's ongoing gracious activity in creating and sustaining the universe. To describe God as "Creator" expresses a more direct relation to God. Where I am able, I use Woodley's language of "Creator" without the definite article throughout the rest of this book.

4. James Barr, "The Image of God in the Book of Genesis — a Study of Terminology," *Bulletin of the John Rylands University Library of Manchester* 51 (1968-69): 11-26; Richard J. Middleton, *The Liberating Image: The Imago Dei in Genesis 1* (Grand Rapids: Brazos, 2005); Claus Westermann, *Genesis 1–11,* trans. John J. Scullion (Minneapolis: Fortress, 1994), 142-61.

5. Jeffrey Jay Niehaus argues that "the storm wind is the advancing presence of Yahweh." See his "In the Wind of the Storm: Another Look at Genesis III 8," *Vetus Testamentum* 44, no. 2 (April 1994): 263-67; Jeffrey Jay Niehaus, *God at Sinai: Covenant and Theophany in the Bible and Ancient Near East* (Grand Rapids: Zondervan, 1995), 157.

6. Thoughtful theological discussions of Abraham that have shaped my interpretation here include Paul Borgman, *Genesis: The Story We Haven't Heard* (Downers Grove, Ill.: InterVarsity, 2001); Martin Buber, "Abraham the Seer," in *On the Bible* (New York: Schocken, 1968); Gerald J. Janzen, *Abraham and All the Families of the Earth: A Commentary on the Book of Genesis 12–50* (Grand Rapids: Eerdmans, 1993); Marvin R. Wilson, *Our Father Abraham: Jewish Roots of the Christian Faith* (Grand Rapids: Eerdmans, 1979). Cf. John H. Sailhamer, *The Pentateuch as Narrative: A Biblical-Theological Commentary* (Grand Rapids: Zondervan, 1992).

7. My understanding of Christian theology's logic of promise is shaped by Jürgen

Moltmann, Christopher Morse, and M. Douglas Meeks. See Jürgen Moltmann, *Theology of Hope,* trans. James W. Leitch (Minneapolis: Fortress, 1993); Jürgen Moltmann, "Theology as Eschatology," in *The Future of Hope: Theology as Eschatology,* ed. Frederick Herzog (New York: Herder and Herder, 1970); Christopher Morse, "Hearing of Heaven as Promise," in *The Difference That Heaven Makes: Rehearsing the Gospel as News* (New York: T. & T. Clark, 2010), 44-48; Christopher Morse, *The Logic of Promise in Moltmann's Theology* (Minneapolis: Fortress, 1979). M. Douglas Meeks writes, "The future is the 'power of God' to realize his righteousness in everything that is. . . . The being of God is defined by his promise given in history, by his faithfulness and power to keep his promise, and by the future fulfillment of his promise." M. Douglas Meeks, *Origins of the Theology of Hope* (Philadelphia: Fortress, 1974), 86. Cf. Walter C. Kaiser, *The Promise-Plan of God: A Biblical Theology of the Old and New Testaments* (Grand Rapids: Zondervan, 2008); Claus Westermann, "The Way of Promise through the Old Testament," trans. Lloyd Gaston and Bernhard W. Anderson, in *The Old Testament and Christian Faith,* ed. Bernhard W. Anderson (New York: Herder and Herder, 1969).

8. The seven visits between God and Abraham in Genesis can be found at 12:1-3; 12:7; 13:14-17; 15:1-21; 17:1-22; 18:1-33; and 22:1-18. In addition to these seven visits, God also visits Hagar twice, in 16:1-16 and 21:9-21. I include the two times that God visits Hagar as part of a larger set of nine divine visits to Abraham's house.

9. Delores S. Williams uses Hagar and her wilderness experiences as the basis for a womanist theology grounded in the wilderness experiences of African American women. See Delores S. Williams, "Hagar's Story: A Route to Black Women's Issues," in *Sisters in the Wilderness: The Challenge of Womanist God-Talk* (Maryknoll, N.Y.: Orbis, 1993), 15-33; on the nomadic ideal in Hebrew Scripture, see John W. Flight, "The Nomadic Idea and Ideal in the Old Testament," *Journal of Biblical Literature* 42, no. 3/4 (1923): 158-226; on the subject position of women as "nomadic," see Rosi Braidotti, *Nomadic Subjects: Embodiment and Sexual Difference in Contemporary Feminist Theory* (New York: Columbia University Press, 1994).

10. For my understanding of the form of covenants in the ancient Near East I am indebted to my teacher Gordon Paul Hugenberger, *Marriage as a Covenant: Biblical Law and Ethics as Developed from Malachi,* Biblical Studies Library Series (Grand Rapids: Baker, 1998), 10-11 and especially chapter 6, "'Covenant [*Berit*]' and 'Oath' Defined," 168-215, and Hugenberger's teacher Meredith G. Kline, especially *Kingdom Prologue: Genesis Foundations for a Covenantal Worldview* (Overland Park, Kans.: Two Age Press, 2000). The paradigmatic article that explains the structure of covenants in the ancient Near East is G. E. Mendenhall, "Covenant Forms in Israelite Traditions," *Biblical Archaeologist* 1 (1954): 50-76. For explorations of Israel as the covenant people of God in biblical studies, see Walther Eichrodt, *Theology of the Old Testament,* trans. J. A. Baker, 2 vols. (Philadelphia: Westminster, 1961-67); Delbert Hillers, *Covenant: The History of a Biblical Idea* (Baltimore: Johns Hopkins University Press, 1969); G. E. Mendenhall, *Law and Covenant in Israel and in the Ancient Near East* (Pittsburgh: Biblical Colloquium, 1955); Ernest W. Nicholson, *God and His People: Covenant and Theology in the Old Testament* (Oxford: Clarendon, 1986).

11. See Jon D. Levenson's account of the binding of Isaac in *The Death and Resurrection of the Beloved Son: The Transformation of Child Sacrifice in Judaism and Christianity* (New Haven: Yale University Press, 1993), 3-31, 111-42.

12. Walter C. Kaiser Jr., *Mission in the Old Testament: Israel as a Light to the Nations* (Grand Rapids: Baker, 2000).

13. For an insightful theological interpretation of Exodus, see Brevard S. Childs, *The Book of Exodus,* Old Testament Library (Louisville: Westminster John Knox, 2004). For a thoughtful introduction to the source criticism and redaction criticism of the Hebrew Bible, see David M. Carr, *The Formation of the Hebrew Bible: A New Reconstruction* (Oxford: Oxford University Press, 2011), especially 3-101.

14. I am indebted to Vanessa L. Ochs for the notion of "prophets-in-collaboration." We see an earlier instance of this in Exod 1, when the Hebrew midwives did not obey Pharaoh's order to kill the boys and let the girls live. When Pharaoh asked the midwives why they did not kill the baby boys, they said that Hebrew women were stronger than the Egyptian women and gave birth before the midwives arrived (Exod 1:15-19). See Renita Weems, "The Hebrew Women Are Not Like the Egyptian Women: The Ideology of Race, Gender and Sexual Reproduction in Exodus I," *Semeia* 59 (1992): 25-34.

15. See Jan Assmann, *Moses the Egyptian: The Memory of Egypt in Western Monotheism* (Cambridge: Harvard University Press, 1997).

16. See Phyllis Trible, "Bringing Miriam Out of the Shadows," *Bible Review* 5, no. 1 (February 1989): 13-25.

17. Gerhard von Rad, *Old Testament Theology,* vol. 1, *The Theology of Israel's Historical Traditions,* trans. D. M. G. Stalker (New York: Harper and Row, 1962), 12, 13.

18. See Frank Moore Cross, "The Song of the Sea and the Canaanite Myth," in *Canaanite Myth and Hebrew Epic: Essays in the History of the Religion of Israel* (Cambridge: Harvard University Press, 1973), 112-44; Mark S. Smith, "The Poetics of Exodus 15 and Its Position in the Book," in *Imagery and Imagination in Biblical Literature: Essays in Honor of Aloysius Fitzgerald,* ed. Lawrence Boadt and Mark S. Smith (Washington, D.C.: Catholic Biblical Association, 2001), 23-34. The victory song of Moses (Exod 15:1-5) continues to be prayed in rabbinic morning prayer within the Jewish tradition, a spiritual practice that Peter Ochs argues nurtures relational modes of redemptive thinking and prophetic action for the purpose of healing the community of creation. See Peter Ochs, "Morning Prayer as Redemptive Thinking," in *Liturgy, Time, and the Politics of Redemption,* ed. Chad Pecknold and Randi Rashkover (Grand Rapids: Eerdmans, 2006), 50-90.

19. Gregory of Nyssa writes, "The light's grace was distributed to both senses, illuminating the sight with flashing rays and lighting the way for the hearing with the undefiled teachings." Gregory of Nyssa, *The Life of Moses,* trans. Abraham J. Malherbe and Everett Ferguson (New York: Paulist, 1978), 35.

20. Aryeh Cohen writes, "God articulates the explicit causality between being attentive to — *hearing* — the cries of the oppressed, and doing something about it — acting on it." Aryeh Cohen, "Hearing the Cry of the Poor," in *Crisis, Call, and Leadership in the Abrahamic Traditions,* ed. Peter Ochs and William Stacy Johnson (New York: Palgrave Macmillan, 2009), 111. We learn from this narrative of Hebrew Scripture that the God of Abraham, Isaac, and Jacob hears the cry of the poor and responds through divine rescue. The cry of the poor has performative force in Scripture, inspiring God and Israel to care for the poor. To be good readers of Scripture means to open our ears to hear the cry of the poor and the cry of the text of Scripture itself. Yet, this is not solely an exercise in attentive exegetical listening; rather it is an empathetic listening to prayer and acts of justice. Peter Ochs writes, "we who are in earshot of the cry are obligated to hear it and join in the work of healing." The work of healing

the creation is not optional; it is a task of utmost urgency. Peter Ochs, "Philosophic Warrants for Scriptural Reasoning," in *The Promise of Scriptural Reasoning,* ed. David F. Ford and C. C. Pecknold (Malden, Mass.: Wiley-Blackwell, 2006), 130.

21. Martin Buber, *I and Thou,* trans. Ronald G. Smith (New York: Charles Scribner's Sons, 1958), 135.

22. Frank Moore Cross, "The Priestly Tabernacle and the Temple of Solomon," in *From Epic to Canon: History and Literature in Ancient Israel* (Baltimore: Johns Hopkins University Press, 1998), 84-95; Victor Hurowitz, "The Priestly Account of Building the Tabernacle," *Journal of the American Oriental Society* 105 (1985): 21-30; Daniel E. Flemming, "Mari's Large Public Tent and the Priestly Tent Sanctuary," *Vetus Testamentum* 50 (2000): 484-98; Sarah Henrich, "Seen and Unseen: The Visibility of God in Exodus 25–40," in *"And God Saw That It Was Good": Essays on Creation and God in Honor of Terence E. Fretheim* (St. Paul: Word and World, 2006), 103-11; Mark K. George, *Israel's Tabernacle as Social Space,* Ancient Israel and Its Literature 2 (Atlanta: Society of Biblical Literature, 2009), 17-44.

23. Norman K. Gottwald rightly sees the steadfast love of God as a primary attribute of the God of Israel in the context of the religions of the ancient Near East. See Norman K. Gottwald, *The Tribes of Yahweh: A Sociology of the Religion of Liberated Israel, 1250-1050 B.C.* (Maryknoll, N.Y.: Orbis, 1979).

24. Imitating God is one of the primary ways that Israel understands the ethical task. See John Barton, *Understanding Old Testament Ethics* (Louisville: Westminster John Knox, 2003), 50-54.

25. Meredith G. Kline writes, "Moses' shining face was only a partial and passing qualification, but in this phenomenon there was a prophetic intimation of the ultimate resurrection-glorification of God's people in which the *imago Dei* attains full-orbed perfection." Meredith G. Kline, *Images of the Spirit* (Grand Rapids: Baker, 1980), 62. Moses has to veil himself as he comes down the mountain to protect Israel from the divine burn; however, through Christ and the Holy Spirit, God's glory is brought to the people of God, the veil is taken away, and God's people are free to worship God in radiant light. See Scott Hafemann, *Paul, Moses, the History of Israel: The Letter/Spirit Contrast and the Argument from Scripture in 2 Corinthians 3* (Peabody, Mass.: Hendrickson, 1996).

26. On the origins and function of the law in the religion of Israel, see Albrecht Alt, "The Origins of Israelite Law," in *Essays in Old Testament History and Religion,* trans. R. A. Wilson (Sheffield: JSOT Press, 1989), 79-132; Otto Kaiser, "The Law as the Center of the Hebrew Bible," in *Sha'arei Talmon: Studies in the Bible, Qumran, and the Ancient Near East Presented to Shemaryahu Talmon,* ed. Michael Fishbane and Emanuel Tov (Winona Lake, Ind.: Eisenbrauns, 1992), 93-103; Robert R. Wilson, "The Role of Law in Early Israelite Society," in *Law, Politics, and Society in the Ancient Mediterranean World,* ed. Baruch Halpern and Deborah W. Hobson (Sheffield: Sheffield Academic Press, 1993), 90-99.

27. Gregory of Nyssa writes insightfully about Moses' mystical encounter with God: "Since he was alone, by having been stripped as it were of the people's fear, he boldly approached the very darkness itself and entered the invisible things where he was no longer seen by those watching. After he entered the inner sanctuary of the divine mystical doctrine, there, while not being seen, he was in company with the Invisible. He teaches, I think, by the things he did that the one who is going to associate intimately with God must go beyond all that is visible and (lifting up his own mind, as to a mountain top, to the invisible and incom-

prehensible) believe that the divine is *there* where the understanding does not reach." Gregory of Nyssa, *The Life of Moses,* 43.

28. For more theological analyses of the Year of Jubilee, see John S. Bergsma, *The Jubilee from Leviticus to Qumran* (Leiden: Brill, 2007); R. H. Lowery, *Sabbath and Jubilee* (St. Louis: Chalice, 2000); Eric Nelson, *The Hebrew Republic* (Cambridge: Harvard University Press, 2010), 64-87; Robert North, S.J., *Sociology of Biblical Justice* (Rome: Pontifical Biblical Institute, 1954); and André Trochmé, *Jesus and the Nonviolent Revolution,* trans. Michael H. Shank and Marlin E. Miller (Scottdale, Pa.: Herald, 1956), 48-52.

29. For thoughtful theological accounts of God's economy, see M. Douglas Meeks, *God the Economist: The Doctrine of God and Political Economy* (Minneapolis: Fortress, 1989); Joerg Rieger, *No Rising Tide: Theology, Economics, and the Future* (Minneapolis: Fortress, 2009); Kathryn Tanner, *Economy of Grace* (Minneapolis: Fortress, 2005). For missiological developments of the biblical "household" motif, see Lesslie Newbigin, *The Household of God: Lectures on the Nature of God* (London: SCM, 1953), and Letty Russell, *Households of Freedom: Authority in Feminist Theology* (Philadelphia: Westminster, 1987).

30. It is vital that we recover the biblical language of oppression in our theological writing today. While it is ubiquitous throughout the biblical literature, it is curiously absent in much contemporary theology. For insightful biblical theologies of justice that respond to oppression, see Thomas Hanks, *God So Loved the Third World: The Biblical Vocabulary of Oppression* (Maryknoll, N.Y.: Orbis, 1983); Elsa Tamez, *Bible of the Oppressed* (Maryknoll, N.Y.: Orbis, 1982); Delores Williams, "Women's Oppression and Lifeline Politics in Black Women's Religious Narratives," *Journal of Feminist Studies in Religion* 1, no. 2 (1985): 59-71.

31. For an insightful analysis of the theme of justice for the poor in the literature of the ancient Near East, see F. Charles Fensham, "Widow, Orphan, and the Poor in Ancient Near Eastern Legal and Wisdom Literature," *Journal of Near Eastern Studies* 21, no. 2 (April 1962): 129-39.

32. Many contemporary scholars argue that the book of Isaiah has three different authors for three major sections of the prophecy, representing different historical periods: First Isaiah (1–39), Second Isaiah (40–54), and Third Isaiah (55–66). While acknowledging the distinctions in these three sections of Isaiah, I use a theological interpretation of Isaiah trying to understand it as a literary whole in the context of the theological vision of the whole scriptural canon. See Brevard Childs, *The Struggle to Understand Isaiah as Christian Scripture* (Grand Rapids: Eerdmans, 2004); Robert Wilken, *Isaiah Interpreted by Early Christian and Medieval Commentators* (Grand Rapids: Eerdmans, 2004).

33. See Walter Brueggemann, *Israel's Praise: Doxology against Idolatry and Ideology* (Philadelphia: Fortress, 1988).

34. For a theological analysis of temple in Zion as the space of the presence of God, see Ben C. Ollenburger, *Zion, the City of the Great King: A Theological Symbol of the Jerusalem Cult,* Journal for the Study of the Old Testament: Supplement Series 42 (Sheffield: Sheffield Academic, 1987).

35. See Jon D. Levenson, *Resurrection and the Restoration of Israel: The Ultimate Victory of the God of Life* (New Haven: Yale University Press, 2006), and with Kevin J. Madigan, *Resurrection: The Power of God for Christians and Jews* (New Haven: Yale University Press, 2008).

36. Gerhard von Rad, *The Message of the Prophets* (New York: Harper and Row, 1962), 121.

Notes to Chapter 3

1. Matt 5 is filled with such sayings (e.g., vv. 21-22, 27-28, 31-32, 33-34, 38-39, 43-44). My biblical Christology is indebted to Allen Dwight Callahan, A Love Supreme: A History of the Johannine Tradition (Minneapolis: Augsburg Fortress, 2005).

2. I interpret Mary's poem, 1:46-55, and John the Baptist's poem, from Isa 3:4-5, as songs. Cf. Stephen Farris, *The Hymns of Luke's Infancy Narratives: Their Origin, Meaning, and Significance* (Sheffield: JSOT Press, 1985). While the New Testament does not have a collection of hymns like the Psalms in the Hebrew Bible, it is full of canticles, confessions, hymns, and doxologies. Within these musical movements we see improvisations on the song of Israel as the early cadences and themes of Israel's song are increasingly focused on Jesus the Messiah. We see the christological focus on New Testament hymnody illustrated in the letters of Paul. While the Christ hymn in his letter to the Philippians (2:6-11) is the best known, other examples can be found in Col 1:15-20; Eph 1:3-14; 1 Cor 15:3-8; and 1 Tim 6:15-16.

3. Following Samuel Terrien, I interpret Mary's song as having a chiastic structure, with four strophes and core verses in the center of the song: "He has shown strength with his arm; / he has scattered the proud in the thoughts of their hearts." When viewed in this light, this song's prophetic thunder is directed clearly at the proud and affluent that actively resist the embodiment of shalom justice called for in the Law and the Prophets. Samuel Terrien, *The Magnificat: Musicians as Biblical Interpreters* (New York: Paulist, 1995).

4. Beverly Roberts Gaventa, *Mary: Glimpses of the Mother of Jesus* (Minneapolis: Fortress, 1999), 57.

5. Abraham J. Heschel, *The Prophets* (New York: HarperCollins, 2001), 213.

6. My narrative of Jesus' ministry focuses principally on Luke's Gospel and is indebted to recent attempts to interpret the Luke-Acts narrative as a whole theological document following Joel B. Green, *The Theology of the Gospel of Luke* (Cambridge: Cambridge University Press, 1995), and Paul Borgman, *The Way of Luke's Gospel* (Grand Rapids: Eerdmans, 2005). Cf. Hans Conzelmann, *The Theology of St. Luke* (London: Faber and Faber, 1960); I. Howard Marshall, *Luke: Historian and Theologian* (Grand Rapids: Zondervan, 1970).

7. For an insightful analysis of the ways in which John the Baptist interacted with and influenced Jesus, see J. Ramsey Michaels, "The Baptizer," in *Servant and Son: Jesus in Parable and Gospel* (Atlanta: John Knox, 1981), 1-24.

8. Virgilio Elizondo, *Galilean Journey: A Mexican-American Promise* (Maryknoll, N.Y.: Orbis, 1983), 53ff. Obery M. Hendricks Jr., "Galileans: Twice Marginalized," in *The Universe Bends toward Justice: Radical Reflections on the Bible, the Church, and the Body Politics* (Maryknoll, N.Y.: Orbis, 2011), 68-71. Cf. Richard A. Horsley, *Galilee: History, Politics, People* (Valley Forge, Pa.: Trinity, 1995); Gerd Theissen, *The Shadow of the Galilean* (Philadelphia: Fortress, 1987).

9. On the importance of Jesus' Jewish heritage in his prophetic ministry, see Elizondo, *Galilean Journey;* John P. Meier, *A Marginal Jew: Rethinking the Historical Jesus* (New York: Doubleday, 1991); Howard Thurman, *Jesus and the Disinherited* (Boston: Beacon Press, 1976); and Amy-Jill Levine, *The Misunderstood Jew: The Church and the Scandal of the Jewish Jesus* (San Francisco: Harper One, 2006).

10. For the etymology of *basileia tou theou,* see Gerhard Kittel, ed., *Theological Dictio-*

nary of the New Testament, vol. 1 (Grand Rapids: Eerdmans, 1969), 564-93. For recent treatments of Jesus' teaching of the kingdom of God in empire-critical studies, see John Dominic Crossan, *God and Empire: Jesus against Rome, Then and Now* (San Francisco: HarperSanFrancisco, 2007); Obery M. Hendricks Jr., *The Politics of Jesus: Rediscovering the True Revolutionary Nature of the Teachings of Jesus and How They Have Been Corrupted* (New York: Doubleday, 2006); Richard A. Horsley, *Jesus and Empire: The Kingdom of God and the New World Disorder* (Minneapolis: Fortress, 2003). Ada Maria Isasi-Diaz uses the term "kindom," emphasizing the "kinship" of all creation and the promise of a just future. See Ada Maria Isasi-Diaz, *Mujerista Theology: A Theology for the Twenty-first Century* (Maryknoll, N.Y.: Orbis, 1996), 103 n. 8.

11. Hendricks, *The Politics of Jesus,* 19-23.

12. Joel B. Green, "'To Proclaim Good News to the Poor': Mission and Salvation," in *The Theology of the Gospel of Luke,* 76-101.

13. Karl Barth, *Church Dogmatics* IV/3.1 (Edinburgh: T. & T. Clark, 1961), 180.

14. André Pascal Trocmé (1901-71) was a French pastor and theologian who helped to harbor Jewish refugees in France during the Shoah in World War II. André Trocmé, *Jesus and the Nonviolent Revolution,* trans. Michael H. Shank and Marlin E. Miller (Scottdale, Pa.: Herald, 1956). Trocmé's work on the politics of Jesus is deepened and developed by John Howard Yoder, *The Politics of Jesus: Vicit Agnus Noster* (Grand Rapids: Eerdmans, 1972), and Hendricks, *The Politics of Jesus;* cf. Sharon Ringe, *Jesus, Liberation, and the Biblical Jubilee: Images for Ethics and Christology* (Philadelphia: Fortress, 1985); Robert B. Sloan Jr., *The Favorable Year of the Lord: A Study of Jubilary Theology in the Gospel of Luke* (Austin: Scholars, 1977); Robert B. Sloan Jr., "Luke 4:16-30: Proclamation of the Messianic Jubilee," in *There Shall Be No Poor among You: Essays in Lukan Theology,* ed. Helen R. Graham (Quezon City, Philippines: JMC Press, 1978), 1-24.

15. Bruce J. Malina writes, "The proclamation of the kingdom of God meant at least that the God of Israel would be taking over the country soon." Bruce J. Malina, *The Social Gospel of Jesus: The Kingdom of God in Mediterranean Perspective* (Minneapolis: Fortress, 2001), 1.

16. Obery Hendricks Jr. writes, "Jesus' vision of the kingdom of God includes an egalitarian socio-economic order that takes responsibility for the well-being of all. It refuses to be hindered from the task of serving the needs of the dispossessed and the vulnerable by official sanctions, traditional narratives of social control, or even by edicts from on high, if they stand in the way of the kingdom's goal of ensuring that the basic elements of a healthy and secure life are available to all." Hendricks, *Universe Bends toward Justice,* 123.

17. The "politics of Jesus" is discussed by André Trocmé, "The 'Politics' of Jesus," in *Jesus and the Nonviolent Revolution,* 41-52. John Howard Yoder, *The Politics of Jesus;* Hendricks, *The Politics of Jesus.*

18. Crossan, *God and Empire,* 28ff.

19. Hendricks, *The Politics of Jesus,* 63-66; Hendricks, *Universe Bends toward Justice,* 65-66.

20. Ched Myers, *Binding the Strong Man: A Political Reading of Mark's Story of Jesus* (Maryknoll, N.Y.: Orbis, 1988).

21. My interpretation of this exorcism is indebted to Hendricks, *The Politics of Jesus,* 145-48.

22. René Girard, *I See Satan Fall Like Lightning* (Maryknoll, N.Y.: Orbis, 2001), 185.

23. Joel Marcus, "Entering the Kingly Power of God," *Journal of Biblical Literature* 107, no. 4 (1988): 663-75.

24. In developing the theme of Christ as victor over the principalities and powers of this world, I am following in the tradition of Johann Christoph Blumhardt, Karl Barth, and more recent theologians including Hendrikus Berkhof, Richard A. Horsley, John Howard Yoder, William Stringfellow, and Walter Wink. See Johann Christoph Blumhardt, *Blumhardt's Battle: A Conflict with Satan,* trans. Frank S. Boshold (New York: Thomas E. Lowe, 1970); Karl Barth, "The Lordless Powers," in *The Christian Life: Church Dogmatics* IV/ 4, *Lecture Fragments* (Grand Rapids: Eerdmans, 1981), 213-33; Hendrikus Berkhof, *Christ and the Powers,* trans. John Howard Yoder (Scottdale, Pa.: Herald, 1962); Richard A. Horsley, *Jesus and the Powers: Conflict, Covenant, and the Hope of the Poor* (Minneapolis: Fortress, 2011); Yoder, *The Politics of Jesus;* William Stringfellow, *An Ethic for Christians and Other Aliens in a Strange Land* (Waco, Tex.: Word, 1973); Walter Wink, *Naming the Powers: The Language of Power in the New Testament* (Philadelphia: Fortress, 1984); Walter Wink, *Unmasking the Powers: The Invisible Forces That Determine Human Existence* (Philadelphia: Fortress, 1986); Walter Wink, *Engaging the Powers: Discernment and Resistance in a World of Domination* (Minneapolis: Fortress, 1992).

25. See Amos Yong, "On Healing as Economic Justice," in *In the Days of Caesar: Pentecostalism and Political Theology* (Grand Rapids: Eerdmans, 2010), 276-80.

26. Graham, ed., *There Shall Be No Poor among You;* John Linskens, *Christ Liberator of the Poor: Secularity, Wealth, and Poverty in the Gospel of Luke* (San Antonio: Mexican American Cultural Center, 1976); Walter E. Pilgrim, *Good News to the Poor: Wealth and Poverty in Luke-Acts* (Minneapolis: Augsburg, 1981); S. John Roth, *The Blind, the Lame, and the Poor: Character Types in Luke-Acts* (Sheffield: Sheffield Academic, 1997).

27. On the social dimension of Jesus' ministry see Gerhard Lohfink, *Jesus and Community: The Social Dimension of Christian Faith* (Philadelphia: Fortress, 1984).

28. For an insightful account of Jesus' practice of faithful feasting that I am indebted to, see Greg Carey, *Sinners: Jesus and His Followers* (Waco, Tex.: Baylor University Press, 2009), especially 17-54. The Gospel of Luke describes many different feasts that Jesus participated in throughout his ministry: 5:29-32; 7:36-50; 15:1-2, 6, 9, 22-25; 16:19-25; 22:14-22; 24:30-31; 24:41-43. Cf. Dennis E. Smith, *From Symposium to Eucharist: The Banquet in the Early Christian World* (Minneapolis: Fortress, 2003).

29. Robert J. Karris, *Eating Your Way through Luke's Gospel* (Collegeville, Minn.: Liturgical Press, 2006), 97, as quoted by Carey, *Sinners,* 21.

30. N. T. Wright, *The Challenge of Jesus* (Downers Grove, Ill.: InterVarsity, 1999), 84, 85.

31. Dietrich Bonhoeffer, *The Cost of Discipleship* (London: SCM, 2001), 44.

32. I follow J. Carl Laney, who interprets this episode as Jesus' "Royal Entry" into Jerusalem, arguing that the donkey was not a lowly animal in the ancient Near East, but was "the mount of princes [Judg. 5:10; 10:4; 12:14] and kings [2 Sam. 16:1-2]." J. Carl Laney, *John* (Chicago: Moody, 1992), 225; see 222-25. 1 Kings 1:33 is another example in Hebrew Scripture of riding a colt being a symbol of kingship: in opposition to the royal pretender Adonijah, King David pointed to his son Solomon as the rightful heir to the throne by having him ride on his own mule. Gordon Paul Hugenberger introduced me to this interpretation of Jesus' royal entry into Jerusalem.

33. Myers, *Binding the Strong Man,* 296.

34. Paula Fredriksen, *From Jesus to Christ: The Origins of the New Testament* (New Haven: Yale University Press, 2000), 95, 110-11, 129ff., 144.

35. Stanley P. Saunders and Charles L. Campbell, *The Word on the Street: Performing the Scriptures in the Urban Context* (Grand Rapids: Eerdmans, 2000), 109.

36. Hendricks, *The Politics of Jesus,* 32-33, 51-55, 65, 77-78, 183.

37. Gregory of Nyssa, "An Address on Religious Instruction," trans. C. Richardson, in *Christology of the Later Fathers,* ed. Edward Hardy (Philadelphia: Westminster, 1954), 300, 301. Cf. Nicholas P. Constas, "The Last Temptation of Satan: Divine Deception in Greek Patristic Interpretations of the Passion Narrative," *Harvard Theological Review* 97, no. 2 (2004): 139-63.

38. Gregory of Nyssa, "Address on Religious Instruction," 302.

39. Gustaf Aulén, *Christus Victor: An Historical Study of the Three Main Types of the Idea of the Atonement,* trans. A. G. Herbert (New York: Macmillan, 1969). In biblical studies, I have found N. T. Wright's recovery of the Jesus is Victor tradition of theology in Christian theology instructive. See N. T. Wright, *Jesus and the Victory of God: Christian Origins and the Question of God,* vol. 2 (Minneapolis: Fortress, 1996); N. T. Wright, *The Challenge of Jesus* (Downers Grove, Ill.: InterVarsity, 1999); Dale C. Allison Jr., *The End of the Ages Has Come: An Early Interpretation of the Passion and Resurrection of Jesus* (Philadelphia: Fortress, 1985); Caroline Walker Bynum, *The Resurrection of the Body in Western Christianity* (New York: Columbia University Press, 1995); Christian T. Collins Winn, *"Jesus Is Victor!" The Significance of the Blumhardts for the Theology of Karl Barth* (Eugene, Oreg.: Pickwick, 2009); Rowan Williams, *Resurrection: Interpreting the Easter Gospel,* rev. ed (Cleveland: Pilgrim Press, 2002).

40. Aulén, *Christus Victor,* 32. On Irenaeus's creation theology, see Colin Gunton, *The Triune Creator* (Grand Rapids: Eerdmans, 1998).

41. Irenaeus, *Adversus haereses* 3.18.7, as quoted by Aulén, *Christus Victor,* 19, emphasis added.

42. N. T. Wright, *The Resurrection of the Son of God* (Philadelphia: Fortress, 2001), 587, as quoted by Kevin J. Madigan and John D. Levenson, *Resurrection: The Power of God for Christians and Jews* (New Haven: Yale University Press, 2008), 260. For works that describe the resurrection in Jewish thought, see Neil Gillman, *The Death of Death: Resurrection and Immortality in Jewish Thought* (Woodstock, Vt.: Jewish Lights, 1997); *Moses Maimonides' Treatise on Resurrection,* ed. Fred Rosner (New York: KTAV, 1982).

Notes to Chapter 4

1. James H. Cone, *The Cross and the Lynching Tree* (Maryknoll, N.Y.: Orbis, 2011), 158.

2. Cone, *The Cross,* 158.

3. Jon Sobrino talks about "the crucified people as the presence of christ crucified in history." Jon Sobrino, *Jesus the Liberator: A Historical-Theological Reading of Jesus of Nazareth* (Maryknoll, N.Y.: Orbis, 1993), 264.

4. As Dale T. Irvin argues, we need a "retraditioning" that is accountable to the ways in which Christianity has been complicit in colonial oppression. The subject position of the oppressed is vital to new narrations of Christianity in the Americas. Dale T. Irvin, "Accountable Retraditioning," in *Christian Histories, Christian Traditioning: Rendering Accounts*

(Maryknoll, N.Y.: Orbis, 1998), 50-52; Dale T. Irvin, "The Terror of History and the Memory of Redemption: Engaging the Ambiguities of the Christian Past," in *Surviving Terror: Hope and Justice in a World of Violence,* ed. Victoria L. Erickson and Michelle Lim Jones (Grand Rapids: Brazos, 2002).

5. This paragraph is indebted to Albert J. Raboteau's *Canaan Land: A Religious History of African Americans* (Oxford: Oxford University Press, 1999) and Paul Gilroy's *The Black Atlantic: Modernity and Double Consciousness* (Cambridge: Harvard University Press, 1993). For some other early treatments of transatlantic historiography, see Bernard Bailyn, "The Idea of Atlantic History," *Itinerario* 20 (1996): 19-44; cf. David Eltis, "Atlantic History in Global Perspective," *Itinerario* 23 (1999): 141-61. My thinking on the transatlantic character of evangelicalism and pietism is indebted to Jon Sensbach, *Rebecca's Revival: Creating Black Christianity in the Atlantic World* (Cambridge: Harvard University Press, 2005); Jon Sensbach, "'Don't Teach My Negroes to Be Pietists': Pietism and the Roots of the Black Protestant Church," in *Pietism in Two Worlds: Transmissions of Dissent,* ed. Jonathan Strom (New York: Ashgate, 2009), 183-98; Sylvia R. Frey and Betty Wood, *Come Shouting to Zion: African American Protestantism in the American South and British Caribbean to 1830* (Chapel Hill: University of North Carolina Press, 1998); William Reginald Ward, *The Protestant Evangelical Awakening* (Cambridge: Cambridge University Press, 1992).

6. Albert J. Raboteau, *Slave Religion: The "Invisible Institution" in the Antebellum South* (Oxford: Oxford University Press, 1978); cf. Peter Goodwin Heltzel, "Revival, Race, and Reform: The Roots of Modern Evangelical Politics," in *Jesus and Justice: Evangelicals, Race, and American Politics* (New Haven: Yale University Press, 2009), 13-44.

7. On the "encounter of black and white Christianity" model for the study of the history of world Christianity, see David W. Wills, "The Central Themes of American Religious History: Pluralism, Puritanism, and the Encounter of Black and White," *Religion and Intellectual Life,* no. 1 (Fall 1987): 30-41. In *Jesus and Justice,* I seek to tell a story of evangelicalism through the encounter between black and white Christians, drawing on perspectives from the historians of evangelicalism *and* the black church. As a theologian, I am interested in the ways that black Christians made theological interventions that redirected and transformed the white Christian experiences in the Americas and hearkened a prophetic, intercultural "blue-green" future. *Jesus and Justice: Evangelicals, Race, and American Politics* (New Haven: Yale University Press, 2009).

8. *Narrative of Sojourner Truth; A Bondswoman of Olden Time, with a History of Her Labors and Correspondence,* ed. Nell Irvin Painter (New York: Penguin, 1998), 89.

9. As a delegate from Virginia to the Continental Congress, Jefferson was asked to draft the Declaration, which was edited by John Adams, Benjamin Franklin, and himself.

10. As Robert Bellah has argued, it is the radical Baptist Roger Williams, instead of the Puritan Jonathan Winthrop, who is the founding political theorist of America. I read Jefferson out of this Williams line of political thought. Robert N. Bellah, "Is There a Common American Culture?" *Journal of the American Academy of Religion* 66 (1998): 613-26. For an analysis of this movement from the ideal kingdom of God to the ideal of the secular city, see Harvey Cox, *The Secular City: Secularization and Urbanization in Theological Perspective* (New York: Macmillan, 1965), 116ff. I am indebted to J. Kameron Carter for the idea of a "secular Jesus."

11. On this broader secularization trend from a Continental Christendom toward Deism, see William Cavanaugh, "'A Fire Strong Enough to Consume the House': The Wars of

Religion and the Rise of the State," *Modern Theology* 11, no. 4 (October 1995): 397-420; Thomas S. Kidd, *God of Liberty: A Religious History of the American Revolution* (New York: Basic Books, 2010); Theo Hobson, *The Rhetorical Word: Protestant Theology and the Rhetoric of Authority* (Burlington, Vt.: Ashgate, 2002); Mark A. Noll, *America's God: From Jonathan Edwards to Abraham Lincoln* (New York: Oxford University Press, 2002); and Charles Taylor, *The Secular Age* (Cambridge: Harvard University Press, 2007).

12. See Michel Foucault, *Discipline and Punish: The Birth of Prison,* 2nd ed. (New York: Vintage Books, 1995). Jefferson also thought the panopticon should be used for prisons. We see this in his first American architectural commission in 1797 of Benjamin Henry Boneval Latrobe (1764-1820), a neoclassical architect who designed the state penitentiary in Richmond, Virginia.

13. Willie James Jennings, *Theology and the Origins of Race* (New Haven: Yale University Press, 2010), 171-80.

14. *The Adams-Jefferson Letters: The Complete Correspondence between Thomas Jefferson and Abigail and John Adams,* ed. Lester J. Cappon, 2 vols. (Chapel Hill: University of North Carolina Press, 1959), 2:570. I am indebted to Corey D. B. Walker for this reference.

15. Robert J. C. Young, *Colonial Desire: Hybridity in Theory, Culture, and Race* (New York: Routledge, 1995). Racism and sex are inextricably linked in the colonial imagination. Colonial desire includes a sexual longing for the nonwhite other displaced and destroyed because of colonialism. Renato Rosaldo describes the white longings for lost dark races, destroyed by white conquest, as "imperialist nostalgia," providing a vehicle for affirming desire for a cultural other while simultaneously allowing white guilt about their own atrocious behavior to be subsumed into sorrow and longing that restore their sense of being good people. Renato Rosaldo, *Culture and Truth: The Remaking of Social Analysis* (Boston: Beacon Press, 1993); cf. Heltzel, *Jesus and Justice,* 23ff.

16. Colin Calloway, ed., *First Peoples: A Documentary Survey of American Indian History,* 2nd ed. (Boston: Bedford/St. Martin's, 1999), 220-56.

17. Grant Foreman, *Indian Removal: The Emigration of the Five Civilized Tribes of Indians* (Norman: University of Oklahoma Press, 1989); Barbara Alice Mann, *George Washington's War on Native America* (Westport, Conn., and London: Praeger, 2005); Max M. Mintz, *Seeds of Empire: The American Revolutionary Conquest of the Iroquois* (New York and London: New York University Press, 1999); Ronald N. Satz, *American Indian Policy in the Jacksonian Era* (Norman: University of Oklahoma Press, 2002).

18. Thomas Jefferson, *Notes on the State of Virginia,* in *The Declaration of Independence: Thomas Jefferson* (London: Verso, 2007), 82.

19. David Walker, *Appeal to the Coloured Citizens of the World, but in particular, and very expressly, to those of the United States of America* (1829; reprint, New York: Hill and Wang, 1965).

20. For treatments of the nineteenth-century Christian black imagination dreaming of a space of freedom outside of the circumscription of the nation-state, see Laurie F. Maffly-Kipp, *Setting Down the Sacred Past: African-American Race Histories* (Cambridge: Harvard University Press, 2010); Clarence Hardy III, "From Exodus to Exile: Black Pentecostals, Migrating Pilgrims and Imagined Internationalism," *American Quarterly* 59, no. 3 (September 2007): 747-67.

21. Walker, *Appeal to the Coloured Citizens of the World,* pp. 18-21, at http://docsouth.unc.edu/nc/walker/walker.html#n12 (accessed May 29, 2012).

22. This paragraph draws on Thomas S. Kidd, *God of Liberty: A Religious History of the American Revolution* (New York: Basic Books, 2010).

23. *Narrative of Sojourner Truth* (Mineola, N.Y.: Dover Publications, 1997), 4.

24. *Narrative of Sojourner Truth* (1997), 46-47.

25. Nell Irvin Painter cites from *Battle Creek Nightly Moon,* November 24, 1883, Sojourner Truth Brown Files, Willard Public Library, Battle Creek; "Memorial Chapter," p. 7 in *Sojourner Truth: A Life, A Symbol* (New York: Norton, 1996), 254.

26. *Narrative of Sojourner Truth* (ed. Painter), 48.

27. *Narrative of Sojourner Truth* (ed. Painter), 60.

28. *Narrative of Sojourner Truth* (ed. Painter), 239.

29. Helen LaKelly Hunt, "Sojourner Truth: Finding Your Voice," in *Faith and Feminism* (New York: Atria Books, 2004), 59, 64-65.

30. Valerie Charlene Cooper, *Word, Like Fire: The Biblical Hermeneutics of Maria Stewart* (Charlottesville: University Press of Virginia, 2011).

31. Allen Dwight Callahan, *The Talking Book: African Americans and the Bible* (New Haven: Yale University Press, 2006), 12.

32. *Narrative of Sojourner Truth* (ed. Painter), 74.

33. Rosi Braidotti, *Nomadic Subjects: Embodiment and Sexual Difference in Contemporary Feminist Theory* (New York: Columbia University Press, 1994).

34. *Narrative of Sojourner Truth* (ed. Painter), 95.

35. Joanna Brooks, *American Lazarus: Religion and the Rise of African-American and Native American Literatures* (New York: Oxford University Press, 2003).

36. See Katie Geneva Cannon, *Black Womanist Ethics* (Atlanta: Scholars, 1988); Katie Geneva Cannon, *Katie's Canon: Womanism and the Soul of the Black Community* (New York: Continuum, 2003); and Delores S. Williams, *Sisters in the Wilderness: The Challenge of Womanist God-Talk* (Maryknoll, N.Y.: Orbis, 1993).

Notes to Chapter 5

1. Howard Thurman, *Jesus and the Disinherited* (Boston: Beacon Press, 1976), 14-15. Thurman began a tradition within the black social gospel of traveling to India to meet and study with Gandhi and his circle, a tradition that would be continued by Mordecai Wyatt Johnson, Benjamin Mays, and Martin Luther King Jr. For a theological reflection on lynching in the United States, see James H. Cone, *The Cross and the Lynching Tree* (Maryknoll, N.Y.: Orbis, 2011).

2. Thurman, *Jesus and the Disinherited,* 11.

3. Howard Thurman, "Jesus — an Interpretation," in *Jesus and the Disinherited,* 16.

4. Martin Luther King Jr., "Who Was Jesus of Nazareth?" November 23, 1949, Crozer Seminary, in *The Papers of Martin Luther King, Jr.,* 2 vols. (Berkeley: University of California Press, 1992), 1:245.

5. For the influence of Thurman on King, see the following sources: Lerone Bennett, *What Manner of Man,* 2nd rev. ed. (Chicago: Johnson Publishing Co., 1976), 74-75; John J. Ansbro, *Martin Luther King, Jr.: The Making of a Mind* (Maryknoll, N.Y.: Orbis, 1982), 27-29, 272; Lewis V. Baldwin, "Understanding Martin Luther King, Jr. within the Context of Southern Black Religious History," *Journal of Religious Studies* 13, no. 2 (Fall 1987); Lewis V.

Baldwin, "Martin Luther King, the Black Church and the Black Messianic Vision," *Journal of the Interdenominational Center* 12, no. 1-2 (Fall 1984/Spring 1985); Walter E. Fluker, *They Looked for a City: A Comparative Analysis of the Ideal of Community in the Thought of Howard Thurman and Martin Luther King, Jr.* (Lanham, Md.: University Press of America, 1989); Walter E. Fluker, "Howard Washington Thurman and Martin Luther King, Jr.: Critical Resources in the Development of Ethical Leadership," in *Ethical Leadership: The Quest for Character, Civility, and Community* (Minneapolis: Fortress, 2009), 11-32. See Johnny B. Hill, "King and the Spirituality of Howard Thurman," in *The Theology of Martin Luther King, Jr. and Desmond Mpilo Tutu* (New York: Palgrave Macmillan, 2007), 66-69; Larry Murphy, "Howard Thurman and Social Activism," in *God and Human Freedom: A Festschrift in Honor of Howard Thurman* (Richmond, Ind.: Friends United Press, 1983), 154-55.

6. My conception of mystical-prophetic theology is indebted to David Tracy's "Dialogue and the Prophetic-Mystical Option," in *Dialogue with the Other: The Inter-Religious Dialogue* (Grand Rapids: Eerdmans, 1991), 95-123; cf. M. Shawn Copeland, "To Live at the Disposal of the Cross: Mystical-Political Discipleship as Christological Locus," in *Christology: Memory, Inquiry, Practice,* ed. Anne M. Clifford and Anthony Godzieba (Maryknoll, N.Y.: Orbis, 2003).

7. David Tracy, "Approaching the Christian Understanding of God," in *Systematic Theology: Roman Catholic Perspectives,* vol. 1, ed. Francis Schüssler Fiorenza and John P. Galvin (Minneapolis: Fortress, 1991), 146; David Tracy also discusses the claim that "God is love" (1 John 4:8) in *On Naming the Present: Reflections on Catholicism, Hermeneutics, and the Church* (New York: Orbis, 1994), 33-34.

8. My first engagement with the mystical tradition of the Eastern Christian tradition was in my dissertation, especially in my discussions of Gregory of Nyssa and Pseudo-Dionysius; see Peter Goodwin Heltzel, "The Triune Pantokrator: Jurgen Moltmann's Reinterpretation of Omnipotence in Light of Gregory of Nyssa's Trinitarian Theology" (Ph.D. diss., Boston University, 2005), 140-252. For a good introduction to mysticism see John Macquarrie, *Two Worlds Are Ours: An Introduction to Christian Mysticism* (Minneapolis: Fortress, 2004). For historical treatments of mysticism see Nicholas Arseniev, *Mysticism and the Early Church* (Crestwood, N.Y.: St. Vladimir's Seminary Press, 1979); Andrew Louth, *The Origins of the Christian Mystical Tradition* (Oxford: Oxford University Press, 1981); Bernard McGinn, *The Presence of God: A History of Western Mysticism,* vol. 1, *The Foundations of Mysticism* (New York: Crossroad, 1991); Denys Turner, *The Darkness of God: Negativity in Christian Mysticism* (Cambridge: Cambridge University Press, 1995).

9. Peter J. Paris, *The Spirituality of African Peoples: The Search for a Common Moral Discourse* (Minneapolis: Fortress, 1995), 22.

10. Gen 18:19; Amos 5:21-24; Mic 6:6-8.

11. There is a growing group of theologians who write from a mystical-prophetic horizon, including Gustavo Gutiérrez, Dorothee Sölle, David Tracy, and Simone Weil. Joseph Davis, "The Movement toward Mysticism in Gustavo Gutiérrez's Thought: Is This an Open Door to Pentecostal Dialogue?" *Pneuma* 33 (2011): 5-24; Alexander Nava, *The Mystical and Prophetic Thought of Simone Weil and Gustavo Gutiérrez* (New York: SUNY Press, 2001); Dorothee Sölle, *The Silent Cry: Mysticism and Resistance,* trans. Barbara Rumscheidt and Martin Rumscheidt (Minneapolis: Fortress, 2001); David Tracy, "Dialogue and the Prophetic-Mystical Option," in *Dialogue with the Other: The Inter-Religious Dialogue* (Grand Rapids: Eerdmans, 1991), 95-123.

12. Fluker, *They Looked for a City.* My interpretation of Thurman and King is deeply indebted to Fluker's work, including a conversation I had with him at the Samuel Proctor Conference of the Children's Defense Fund on Haley Farm during the summer of 2008.

13. For some of the key writings on King's notion of beloved community, see Lewis V. Baldwin, *Toward the Beloved Community: Martin Luther King, Jr. and South Africa* (Cleveland: Pilgrim Press, 1995); Hill, *Theology of Martin Luther King,* 77-87; Ralph Luker, "The Kingdom of God and the Beloved Community in the Thought of Martin Luther King, Jr.," in *Ideas and the Civil Rights Movement,* ed. Ted Ownby (Jackson: University Press of Mississippi, 2001), 39-54; Charles Marsh, *The Beloved Community: How Faith Shapes Social Justice, from the Civil Rights Movement to Today* (New York: Basic Books, 2005).

14. Martin Luther King Jr., "The American Dream," in Martin Luther King Jr., *A Testament of Hope: The Essential Writings and Speeches of Martin Luther King, Jr.,* ed. James Melvin Washington (San Francisco: HarperCollins, 1986), 215.

15. Thurman to Johnson, June 18, 1918, *My People Need Me: The Papers of Howard Thurman, 1899-1935,* ed. Walter E. Fluker (Charleston: University of South Carolina Press, 2009), 2.

16. Matthew S. Hedstrom, "Rufus Jones and Mysticism for the Masses," *Cross Currents* 54, no. 2 (Summer 2004): 31-44.

17. Quinton Dixie and Peter Eisenstadt, *Visions of a Better World: Howard Thurman's Pilgrimage to India and the Origins of African American Nonviolence* (Boston: Beacon Press, 2011), 52.

18. Thurman, *Jesus and the Disinherited,* 89.

19. Thurman, *Jesus and the Disinherited,* 108.

20. Thurman, *Jesus and the Disinherited,* 106.

21. Howard Thurman, "He Looked for a City," taped sermon, Marsh Chapel, Boston University, January 2, 1955, Special Collections, Mugar Library, Boston University.

22. Howard Thurman, *Disciplines of the Spirit* (Richmond, Ind.: Friends United Press, 1963), 83.

23. For a thoughtful explanation of Mays's influence on the life and thought of Martin Luther King Jr., see Lawrence Edward Carter Sr., *Walking Integrity: Benjamin Elijah Mays, Mentor to Martin Luther King, Jr.* (Macon, Ga.: Mercer University Press, 1998). Cf. Benjamin E. Mays's important work, *Born to Rebel* (New York: Scribner, 1971); cf. Johnny Bernard Hill, "Benjamin Elijah Mays and the Morehouse Experience," in *Theology of Martin Luther King, Jr. and Desmond Mpilo Tutu,* 63-65.

24. For King's connection to the black social gospel see Clayborne Carson, "Martin Luther King, Jr., and the African-American Social Gospel," in *African-American Christianity,* ed. Paul E. Johnson (Berkeley: University of California Press, 1994), 159-77, reprinted in *African-American Religion: Interpretive Essays in History and Culture,* ed. Timothy E. Fulop and Albert J. Raboteau (New York: Routledge, 1997); Walter Earl Fluker also points to this black social gospel tradition, associated with Morehouse, in *Ethical Leadership: The Quest for Character, Civility, and Community* (Minneapolis: Fortress, 2009), chapter 1. For the historical origins of the black social gospel, see Ralph E. Luker, *The Social Gospel in Black and White: American Racial Reform, 1885-1912* (Chapel Hill and London: University of North Carolina Press, 1991); Anthony Pinn, ed., *Making the Gospel Plain: The Writings of Bishop Reverdy C. Ransom* (Harrisburg, Pa.: Trinity, 1999); on Morehouse College see Edward A. Jones, *A Candle in the Dark: A History of Morehouse College* (Valley Forge, Pa.: Judson, 1967).

On the "southern" character of King's life and theology, my thought has been shaped by Lewis V. Baldwin. See Baldwin, "Understanding Martin Luther King, Jr. within the Context of Southern Black Religious History"; Baldwin, "Martin Luther King, the Black Church and the Black Messianic Vision"; Lewis V. Baldwin, *There Is a Balm in Gilead: The Cultural Roots of Martin Luther King, Jr.* (Minneapolis: Fortress, 1991), especially 159-228.

25. Martin Luther King Jr., "Kick Up Dust," Letter to the Editor, *Atlanta Constitution,* August 6, 1946 (written during the summer after his sophomore year at Morehouse), in *Papers,* 1:121.

26. Martin Luther King Jr., "God (Amos)," in *Papers,* 2:165.

27. Martin Luther King Jr., "Social Ethics (Psalms)," in *Papers,* 2:167.

28. Martin Luther King Jr., "Pilgrimage to Nonviolence," in *A Testament of Hope,* 40.

29. Martin Luther King Jr., *Stride toward Freedom: The Montgomery Story* (New York: Harper, 1958), 134.

30. For discussion of the influence of Gandhi's nonviolent philosophy on the theology and strategies of King, see Ansbro, *Martin Luther King, Jr.,* 1-7; Baldwin, "Martin Luther King," 97-98; Baldwin, *There Is a Balm,* 171-73, 185-87; Dixie and Eisenstadt, *Visions of a Better World;* Greg Moses, *Revolution of Conscience: Martin Luther King, Jr., and the Philosophy of Nonviolence* (New York: Guilford, 1967); J. Deotis Roberts, "Gandhi and King: On Conflict Resolution," *Shalom Papers: A Journal of Theology and Public Policy* 2, no. 1 (Spring 2000): 29-42; J. Deotis Roberts, "The Fellowship of Kindred Minds: Gandhi, Bonhoeffer, and King," in *Bonhoeffer and King: Speaking Truth to Power* (Louisville: Westminster John Knox, 2005), 61-74; Sean Scalmer, *Gandhi in the West: The Mahatma and the Rise of Radical Protest* (Cambridge: Cambridge University Press, 2011).

31. William Stuart Nelson, a philosopher of religion at Howard University, also mediated the Gandhian tradition to the black social gospel tradition.

32. King, "Pilgrimage to Nonviolence," 38.

33. Martin Luther King Jr., "Against Vietnam: A Time to Break Silence," in *A Testament of Hope,* 242.

34. Martin Luther King Jr., "Where Do We Go from Here: Chaos or Community?" in *A Testament of Hope,* 594.

35. Martin Luther King Jr., "My Trip to the Land of Gandhi," in *A Testament of Hope,* 25.

36. Martin Luther King Jr., "Letter from the Birmingham City Jail," in *A Testament of Hope,* 298. All subsequent quotations of this letter are from this edition.

37. King, "Letter," 300.

38. King, "Letter," 300. Cf. Albert J. Raboteau, "'The Blood of the Martyrs Is the Seed of Faith': Suffering in the Christianity of the American Slaves," in *The Courage to Hope: From Black Suffering to Human Redemption,* ed. Quinton Hosford Dixie and Cornel West (Boston: Beacon Press, 1999), 22-39.

39. King, "Letter," 300.

40. Martin Luther King Jr., "A Comparison and Evaluation of the Theology of Luther with That of Calvin," Boston University, May 15, 1953, in *Papers,* 2:185.

41. King, "Letter," 297.

42. Albert Raboteau, *Slave Religion: The "Invisible Institution" in the Antebellum South* (Oxford: Oxford University Press, 1978).

43. Martin Luther King Jr., "To Chart Our Course for the Future" (address to the

Southern Christian Leadership Conference, Penn Center, Frogmore, South Carolina, May 1967, 2-3; King Library and Archives, King Center, Atlanta), as cited in the Poverty Initiative, Union Theological Seminary, "Introduction," in *A New and Unsettling Force: Reigniting Rev. Dr. Martin Luther King, Jr.'s Poor People's Campaign* (New York: Poverty Initiative, 2009), 9.

44. For a thoughtful discussion of King's growing interest in economic human rights in the 1960s, see Thomas F. Jackson, *From Civil Rights to Human Rights: Martin Luther King, Jr., and the Struggle for Economic Justice* (Philadelphia: University of Pennsylvania Press, 2007).

45. "Bertha Burres: 'Queen of the Mule Train,'" in *A New and Unsettling Force,* 37.

46. "Dr. Martin Luther King, Jr. and Community on the Move for Equality Invite You to March for Justice and Jobs, Friday March 22, 1968," flyer for the March, Exhibit 1, *City of Memphis v. Martin Luther King, Jr. [et al.],* 1968. National Archives and Records Administration Records of the United States District Court, Western District of Tennessee, Western (Memphis) Division, Record Group 21, ARC Identifier 279325.

47. On the unfinished legacy of Dr. King and the promise of the Poor People's Campaign for reconstituting a poor-led movement for global justice, see the Poverty Initiative, *A New and Unsettling Force;* cf. Peter Heltzel, "Radical (Evangelical) Democracy: The Dreams and Nightmares of Martin Luther King, Jr. and Antonio Negri," *Political Theology* 10, no. 2 (April 2009): 287-303.

48. Michael K. Honey, *Southern Labor and Black Civil Rights: Organizing Memphis Workers* (Urbana: University of Illinois Press, 1993).

49. Martin Luther King Jr., "I See the Promised Land," in *A Testament of Hope,* 286.

50. For a firsthand account of Resurrection City, see Charles Fager, *Uncertain Resurrection: The Poor People's Washington Campaign* (Grand Rapids: Eerdmans, 1969). I am grateful to William B. Eerdmans Jr. for introducing me to this book and sharing his own experiences at Resurrection City with me.

51. "Bertha Burres," 35-48; Ronald L. Freeman, *The Mule Train: A Journey of Hope Remembered* (Nashville: Rutledge Hill Press, 1998).

52. Septima Poinsette Clark, *Echo in My Soul* (New York: Dutton, 1962), chapter 5. For a thoughtful discussion of patriarchy in King's theology and ministry, as well as a constructive suggestion of how personalist philosophy can be marshaled on behalf of a prophetic, feminist, intercultural theology, see Rufus Burrow Jr., "The Dignity and Being of Sexism," chapter 5 in *God and Human Dignity: The Personalism, Theology, and Ethics of Martin Luther King, Jr.* (Notre Dame, Ind.: University of Notre Dame Press, 2006).

53. Jacquelyn Grant's "Civil Rights Women: A Source for Doing Womanist Theology" is methodologically important for this paradigm shift that is taking place within Christian theology. Jacquelyn Grant, "Civil Rights Women: A Source for Doing Womanist Theology," in *Women in the Civil Rights Movement,* ed. Vicki L. Crawford, Jacquelin Anne Rouse, and Barbara Woods (Indianapolis: Indiana University Press, 1993), 39-50. See Bettye Collier-Thomas and V. P. Franklin, eds., *Sisters in the Struggle: African American Women in the Civil Rights–Black Power Movement* (New York: New York University Press, 1999); Kai Lee, *For Freedom's Sake: The Life of Fannie Lou Hamer* (Urbana: University of Illinois Press, 1999); Barbara Ransby, *Ella Baker and the Black Freedom Movement: A Radical Democratic Vision* (Chapel Hill: University of North Carolina Press, 2003); Barbara Dianne Savage, *Your Spirit Walks beside Us: The Politics of Black Religion* (Cambridge: Harvard University Press, 2008);

Evelyn Higginbotham, *Righteous Discontent: The Women's Movement in the Black Baptist Church, 1880-1920* (Cambridge: Harvard University Press, 1993).

54. Eboni K. Marshall, "Rent in Twain: Beyond the Veil, toward a Womanist Ethic of Incarnation" (Ph.D. diss., Union Theological Seminary, 2010).

55. Marshall, "Rent in Twain," 177.

56. Marshall, "Rent in Twain," 178.

57. Marshall, "Rent in Twain," 185-86.

58. Marshall, "Rent in Twain," 187.

59. Marshall, "Rent in Twain," 189.

60. For a discussion on patriarchy in the evangelical pro-family movement, see Peter Goodwin Heltzel, "Focus on the Family: Nurturing and Defending the Family," in *Jesus and Justice: Evangelicals, Race, and American Politics* (New Haven: Yale University Press, 2009), 91-126, 101-2; cf. Susan Lynn, *Progressive Women in Conservative Times: Racial Justice, Peace, and Feminism, 1945 to the 1960s* (New Brunswick, N.J.: Rutgers University Press, 1992); Ruth Rosen, *The World Split Open: How the Modern Women's Movement Changed America* (New York: Viking Press, 2000). One of the texts that was formative in conservative social thought that continues to undergird evangelical patriarchy is George Gilder's *Men and Marriage* (Gretna, La.: Pelican Publishing Co., 1993).

61. For more on James Dobson and Focus on the Family's struggle with racism, see my *Jesus and Justice*, 91-126. For a thoughtful treatment of the relationship between masculine identity and the Western civilization project, see Gail Bederman, *Manliness and Civilization: A Cultural History of Gender and Race in the United States, 1880-1917* (Chicago: University of Chicago Press, 1995). J. Kameron Carter argues that the struggle for black masculinity is a response to white racial supremacy and the resilient power of the white masculine. Carter illustrates this in his discussion of Frederick Douglass in "The Death of Christ: A Theological Reading of Fredrick Douglass' 1845 *Narrative*," in *Race: A Theological Account*, 285-312. Carter focuses his theological interpretation of Douglass's 1845 *Narrative* on the episode where Douglass rises up against his white master Covey, illustrating the ways in which the struggle for black identity is intricately related to the struggle for masculine identity. Douglass's 1845 *Narrative* unveils whiteness as fundamentally a problem of the white masculine. On the notion of a false "God-man," which echoes what in classical Christian theology has been called the christological problem, see more recently by J. Kameron Carter, "An Unlikely Convergence: W. E. B. Du Bois, Karl Barth, and the Problem of the Imperial God-Man," *CR: The New Centennial Review* 11, no. 3 (2012): 167-224.

62. Renee Christine Romano, *Race Mixing: Black-White Marriage in Postwar America* (Cambridge: Harvard University Press, 2003).

63. The term "womanist" was first used by Alice Walker in "Womanist," in *In Search of Our Mothers' Gardens: Womanist Prose* (San Diego: Harcourt Brace Jovanovich, 1983), xi; some womanist works include Katie Geneva Cannon, *Black Womanist Ethics* (Atlanta: Scholars, 1988); Katie Geneva Cannon, *Katie's Canon: Womanism and the Soul of the Black Community* (New York: Continuum, 2003); and Delores S. Williams, *Sisters in the Wilderness: The Challenge of Womanist God-Talk* (Maryknoll, N.Y.: Orbis, 1993). For womanist Christology that takes the suffering of black women seriously, see Kelly Brown Douglas, *The Black Christ* (Maryknoll, N.Y.: Orbis, 1994), and Jacquelyn Grant, *White Women's Christ and Black Women's Jesus: Feminist Christology and Womanist Response* (Atlanta: Scholars, 1989);

cf. James H. Cone's recent response to womanist theology: James H. Cone, "Oh Mary: Don't You Weep," in *The Cross and the Lynching Tree* (Maryknoll, N.Y.: Orbis, 2011), 120-251.

64. Williams, *Sisters in the Wilderness,* xiv.

65. See Laura E. Donaldson and Kwok Pui-Lan, eds., *Postcolonialism, Feminism, and Religious Discourse* (New York and London: Routledge, 2002); Serene Jones, *Feminist Theory and Christian Theology: Cartographies of Grace* (Minneapolis: Fortress, 2000).

66. Martin Luther King Jr., "Peace on Earth," in *The Trumpet of Conscience* (New York: Harper and Row, 1968), 69.

Notes to Chapter 6

1. See Augusto Boal, *Theatre of the Oppressed,* trans. Charles A. Maria-Odilia Leal McBride (New York: Theatre Communications Group, 1985). From here on I will put page number references to this book in the text. This work was originally published in Spanish as *Teatro de Oprimido* in 1974, copyright by Augusto Boal. I was first introduced to Augusto Boal's work by my friend Karin Coonrod, the director of Compagnia de' Colombari Theater Company. My theological engagement with Boal has been deepened through many conversations with Shannon Craigo-Snell on theology, theater, and the church. See Shannon Craigo-Snell, *The Empty Church: Theatre, Theology, and Bodily Hope* (Oxford: Oxford University Press, forthcoming); Shannon Craigo-Snell and Shawnthea Monroe, "The Empty Church," in Shannon Craigo-Snell and Shawnthea Monroe, *Living Christianity: A Pastoral Theology for Today* (Minneapolis: Fortress, 2009), 123-42. I am also grateful to Charles A. Gillespie for his argument that theater of the oppressed can be a project of liberation theology. Charles A. Gillespie, "Can Theatre Be a Project of Liberation Theology? Explorations in the Case of a Theological and Dramatic Collaboration in Tanzania," *Union Seminary Quarterly Review* (forthcoming). My attempt to reimagine the urban church as political street theater is indebted to Stanley P. Saunders and Charles L. Campbell, *The Word on the Street: Performing the Scriptures in the Urban Context* (Grand Rapids: Eerdmans, 2000).

2. Karl Marx, "Theses on Feuerbach," in *The Marx-Engels Reader,* ed. Robert C. Tucker (New York: Norton, 1978), 145. Boal was influenced by the German playwright Bertolt Brecht (1898-1956) in appropriating Marx's ideas for his dramaturgy. For Boal's discussion of Brecht, see "Hegel and Brecht: The Character as Subject or the Character as Object?" in *Theatre of the Oppressed,* 83-115.

3. Paulo Freire, *Pedagogy of the Oppressed,* trans. Myra Bergman Ramos (New York: Continuum, 1985), 82. This book was translated from the original Portuguese manuscript in 1968.

4. Freire, *Pedagogy of the Oppressed,* 82.

5. Manfred Halpern, "Choosing between Ways of Life and Death and between Forms of Democracy: An Archetypal Analysis," *In Alternatives: Social Transformation and Humane Governance* 12, no. 1 (1987): 5-35. Manfred Halpern, *Transforming the Personal, Political, Historical, and Sacred in Theory and Practice,* ed. David Abalos (Scranton, Pa.: University of Scranton Press, 2009). I am grateful to Lester Edwin J. Ruiz for introducing me to Halpern's theory of transformation.

6. Bruce Ellis Benson, *The Improvisation of Musical Dialogue* (Cambridge: Cambridge University Press, 2005).

7. Hans-Georg Gadamer, *The Relevance of the Beautiful and Other Essays,* ed. Robert Bernasconi, trans. Nicholas Walker (Cambridge: Cambridge University Press, 1986), 39-65.

8. Gadamer, *Relevance of the Beautiful,* 39.

9. Jürgen Moltmann writes, "The future as God's power in time must then be understood as the source of time." Jürgen Moltmann, *The Coming of God: Christian Eschatology,* trans. Margaret Kohl (Minneapolis: Fortress, 1996), 26; cf. Jürgen Moltmann, *Theology of Hope,* trans. James W. Leitch (New York: Harper and Row, 1967); Jürgen Moltmann, "Theology as Eschatology," in *The Future of Hope: Theology as Eschatology,* ed. Frederick Herzog (New York: Herder and Herder, 1970), 1-50; see Christopher L. Morse, *The Logic of Promise in Moltmann's Theology* (Minneapolis: Fortress, 1979).

10. On the singing self, see David Ford, *Self and Salvation: Being Transformed* (Cambridge: Cambridge University Press, 1999), 109, 120-29, 235.

11. Hans-Georg Gadamer, *Truth and Method,* trans. Joel Weinsheimer and Donald G. Marshall, 2nd rev. ed. (New York: Continuum, 1989), 122.

12. On the movement from place to space see Michel de Certeau, "'Spaces' and 'Places,'" in *The Practice of Everyday Life,* trans. Steven Rendall (Berkeley: University of California Press, 1984), 117-18.

13. David Harvey, *Spaces of Hope* (Berkeley: University of California Press, 2000).

14. David Harvey, *Rebel Cities: From the Right to the City to the Urban Revolution* (London: Verso, 2012).

15. See Alexie M. Torres-Fleming, "Of Things Seen and Unseen," in *What We See: Advancing the Observations of Jane Jacobs,* ed. Stephan A. Goldsmith and Lynne Elizabeth (Oakland: New Village Press, 2010), 78-86; John A. Calhoun, "Alexie Torres-Fleming," in *Hope Matters: The Untold Story of How Faith Works in America* (Washington, D.C.: Bartleby Press, 2007), 43-56.

16. Martin Luther King Jr., "A Time to Break Silence," in *A Testament of Hope: The Essential Writings and Speeches of Martin Luther King, Jr.,* ed. James M. Washington (New York: HarperCollins, 1986), 240.

17. Willis Jenkins, *Ecologies of Grace: Environmental Ethics and Christian Theology* (Oxford: Oxford University Press, 2008), 95.

18. Emilie Townes, *In a Blaze of Glory: Womanist Spirituality as Social Witness* (Nashville: Abingdon, 1995), 55.

19. Dietrich Bonhoeffer, *Life Together,* in *"Life Together" and "Prayerbook of the Bible,"* vol. 5 of *Dietrich Bonhoeffer Works,* trans. Daniel W. Bloesch and James H. Burtness, 16 vols. (Minneapolis: Fortress, 1996), 43.

Index of Subjects and Names

Index of Scripture References